MARTIN JOL
The Inside Story

Harry Harris

KNOW THE SCORE BOOKS PUBLICATIONS

CULT HEROES	Author	ISBN
CARLISLE UNITED	Mark Harrison	978-1-905449-09-7
CHELSEA	Leo Moynihan	1-905449-00-3
MANCHESTER CITY	David Clayton	978-1-905449-05-7
NEWCASTLE	Dylan Younger	1-905449-03-8
NOTTINGHAM FOREST	David McVay	978-1-905449-06-4
RANGERS	Paul Smith	978-1-905449-07-1
SOUTHAMPTON	Jeremy Wilson	1-905449-01-1
WEST BROM	Simon Wright	1-905449-02-X

MATCH OF MY LIFE	Editor	ISBN
DERBY COUNTY	Johnson & Matthews	978-1-905449-68-2
ENGLAND WORLD CUP	Massarella & Moynihan	1-905449-52-6
EUROPEAN CUP FINALS	Ben Lyttleton	1-905449-57-7
FA CUP FINALS 1953-1969	David Saffer	978-1-905449-53-8
FULHAM	Michael Heatley	1-905449-51-8
LEEDS	David Saffer	1-905449-54-2
LIVERPOOL	Leo Moynihan	1-905449-50-X
MANCHESTER UNITED	Ivan Ponting	978-1-905449-59-0
SHEFFIELD UNITED	Nick Johnson	1-905449-62-3
STOKE CITY	Simon Lowe	978-1-905449-55-2
SUNDERLAND	Rob Mason	1-905449-60-7
SPURS	Allen & Massarella	978-1-905449-58-3
WOLVES	Simon Lowe	1-905449-56-9

GENERAL FOOTBALL	Author	ISBN
2006 WORLD CUP DIARY	Harry Harris	1-905449-90-9
2007/08 CHAMPIONS LEAGUE YEARBOOK		978-1-905449-93-4
BURKSEY	Peter Morfoot	1-905449-49-6
The Autobiography of a Football God		
HOLD THE BACK PAGE	Harry Harris	1-905449-91-7
MARTIN JOL: The Inside Story	Harry Harris	978-1-905449-77-4
MY PREMIERSHIP DIARY	Marcus Hahnemann	978-1-905449-33-0
Reading's Season in the Premiership		
OUTCASTS	Steve Menary	978-1-905449-31-6
The Lands FIFA Forgot		

PARISH TO PLANET A History of Football	Eric Midwinter	978-1-905449-30-9
TACKLES LIKE A FERRET (England Cover)	Paul Parker	1-905449-47-X
TACKLES LIKE A FERRET (Manchester United Cover)	Paul Parker	1-905449-46-1

CRICKET	Author	ISBN
MOML: THE ASHES	Pilger & Wightman	1-905449-63-1
GROVEL! The 1976 West IndiesTour of England	David Tossell	978-1-905449-43-9
MY AUTOBIOGRAPHY	Shaun Udal	978-1-905449-42-2
WASTED?	Paul Smith	978-1-905449-45-3
LEAGUE CRICKET YEARBOOK North West edition	Andy Searle	978-1-905449-70-5
LEAGUE CRICKET YEARBOOK Midlands edition	Andy Searle	978-1-905449-72-9

RUGBY LEAGUE	Editor	ISBN
MOML: WIGAN WARRIORS	David Kuzio	978-1-905449-66-8

FORTHCOMING PUBLICATIONS

CULT HEROES	Author	ISBN
CELTIC	David Potter	978-1-905449-08-8

MATCH OF MY LIFE	Editor	ISBN
ASTON VILLA	Neil Moxley	978-1-905449-65-1
BOLTON WANDERERS	David Saffer	978-1-905449-64-4

GENERAL FOOTBALL	Author	ISBN
THE BOOK OF FOOTBALL OBITUARIES	Ivan Ponting	978-1-905449-82-2
THE DOOG	Gordos & Harrison	978-1-905449-02-9
THE RIVALS GAME	Douglas Beattie	978-1-905449-79-8
UNITED THROUGH TRIUMPH AND TRAGEDY	Bill Foulkes	978-1-905449-78-1

MARTIN JOL

The Inside Story

Harry Harris

www.knowthescorebooks.com

First published in the United Kingdom
by Know The Score Books Limited, 2007
Copyright Harry Harris, 2007

Know The Score Books Limited
118 Alcester Road
Studley
Warwickshire
B80 7NT
01527 454482
info@knowthescorebooks.com

www.knowthescorebooks.com

A CIP catalogue record is available for this book from the British Library
ISBN: 978-1-905449-77-4

Jacket design by Lisa David

Printed and bound in Great Britain by William Clowes Ltd, Beccles, Suffolk

Photographs in this book are reproduced by kind permission of:
Action Images, Colorsport & Martin Jol

Front cover:

Happy days: Martin Jol acknowledges the White Hart Lane crowd.

Rear cover:

Top: Jol parades the Dutch Cup after taking the minnows of Roda JC to their first ever major trophy.

Bottom: The pressure mounts as Jol's reign at Tottenham nears its end.

Flap:

Midfield hardman Martin Jol in his West Bromwich Albion days.

Author's Acknowledgements

Any book is the result of a team effort to produce it. First and foremost my thanks to Martin Jol for helping me with this in-depth biography. Martin is one of the few high profile people in football not to either take great offence at such an occurrence or instantly bring out his autobiography to put 'his side of the story'.

This has been a very enjoyable project on which to work simply because when you mention to almost anyone that you want to talk to them about Martin Jol, a smile breaks out across their face and stories begin to pour forth almost before you can switch on the tape recorder. I hope the end result is informative and reveals much of the private man and his background which his fans will not have previously known.

I would also like to thank those closest to Martin Jol for their insights and valuable contributions. The list of people who have contributed to this book illustrates the close bonds that Martin forged in his youth and how those around him remain close friends. Starting from Hans van Eck, his friend from the 1960s with whom Martin grew up and played football in the same street; a street in which Hans still lives. Martin Toet, his best friend in the '70s, who revealed to titters how Martin, when a young lad, wanted to be a singer (no, he cannot sing!). The wner of *Elf*, one of the biggest Dutch football magazines, Jan Hermen, has been Martin's friend for 40 years and has some wonderful personal recollections. Also Arie de Jager, the lovely old boy who brought Martin back to his native fishing town to begin a coaching career which has led him to the very top, and Zelijko Petrovic, who has seen Martin working at first hand and believes he can be the best coach in the world. Ton Verkerk is another to contribute untold insights into the real Martin Jol as does John Blok, captain of Scheveningen, Martin's first club as a coach.

Add to these Dutchmen the host of Spurs legends, industry leaders such as Ken Bates, and close friends and associates of Martin and you have a wonderful cast who each reveal their own insights into this fascinating character. Thank you all for co-operating in putting together a definitive biography of the former Dutch Footballer of the Year, West Bromwich Albion and Coventry City midfielder and Tottenham Hotspur manager.

Harry Harris
October 2007

DEDICATED TO: SIMON HARRIS, FOLLOWING IN THE
HARRIS FAMILY TRADITIONS AS A SPURS FAN.
AND TO BARRY CHAUVEAU, FRIEND AND LOYAL
SPURS SUPPORTER.

Contents

PREFACE

BY MARTIN JOL

I STILL DON'T REALLY KNOW the full truth about all that went on the day Spurs finally decided to sack me. But it is important that everyone realises that I did not know I had been sacked before the game, and that I was only told, officially, after it. Had I been told before the game, I would not have taken the team out, I would not have sat on the bench or been in the right frame of mind to lead out the team that night. I just couldn't have done it.

When the final whistle went, my nephew Robert ran over to me and told me to go left when we went down the tunnel into my own dressing room. He had heard on BBC radio that I had been sacked. He said to me: "They've sacked you". That was the first I knew about it. The club secretary John Alexander came into my dressing room, while I was putting on my suit, changing from my track suit. He said: "the chairman would like you to see him with Chris Hughton". I said "OK" and then went into the players dressing room and told the boys: "I will always follow you. Do your best. Tonight, this was not good enough, I know you can do much better and I will always follow you and it has been great knowing you."

The players applauded me.

I then went up to see Daniel Levy and Sir Keith Mills. The first sentence I said was: "Fellows, let's call it a day."

Daniel told me that it had been a huge embarrassment for him and the club that the news had leaked out during the day. He told me that they had done everything to try to avoid it. They said they tried to stop a certain press man from releasing it before the game. I was even told that they thought the club must be bugged for it to have leaked. They said any information that was being dealt with had been embargoed, that no-one could have leaked that they knew about.

Daniel being embarrassed made me feel better. He said he regretted how it came out. If he'd sat me down eight weeks earlier and said: "We've got someone who can do better", that would have been okay.

There has been much said in the media about how angry I had got, and that there had been a heated row. Not true. Daniel is not like that. I am not like that. I can control myself. There have only been three or four times I couldn't control myself with the players, but I made it a rule that I never shouted at them. Yes, I admit there were a few times I got angry over the seasons. But if you shout all the time as a manger it doesn't work, the players stop listening and take no notice. In any case, I look serious, I look as though I am angry, and that's enough!

I hate the fact that I ended my career with defeat at White Hart Lane in Europe. We had never lost at home. Even in all the pre-season friendlies against some of the biggest names in the world like Inter Milan, Lyon and Boca Juniors, we had never lost. We won tournaments in South Africa, in France and must have played 24 games at this kind of level, which was evidence that we could play against the top European teams. But I could sense that night that something was wrong with the players virtually from the moment the game kicked off. My players were giving the opposition far too much space, they didn't seem to be giving that extra 10 per cent of commitment that they normally would do, and we lost in the last few minutes. I just had this feeling something was wrong.

Something very strange happened just one minute before the kick off that night. Berbatov came over to me and said: "Sorry boss! Come on!"

I thought to myself, whatever can he mean? It felt awkward. But I was unsure what he meant. I thought that perhaps he was regretting what had happened in the previous match at Newcastle, or that he hadn't given me his best before, but it did not cross my mind that he and the rest of the players had already been told by friends who had been texting them that I had been sacked.

At St. James Park, a lot had been made in the media about Berbatov's attitude, that he didn't want to come on because he was sulking at being left on the bench. Well, when it came to the time I wanted to make a change I was out in my technical area and I looked over my shoulder to tell Berbatov to warm up. Normally Chris Hughton would tell the players to warm up, but not this time. However, he didn't seem that keen to do it. I turned my shoulder again and this time I looked him in the eye and told him: "come on, warm up" and he began to warm up. He never said he didn't want to come on, but that's how it has been perceived. But that was Berbatov, he always seemed reluctant to do anything. He was like it last year and it was the same this season. But I didn't take any notice of it. It was because he was an introverted character and the dressing room is made up of all sorts of characters. The point is that he is a gifted individual. He is like Johan Cruyff and I cannot put him any higher than that.Gifted, yes. But he is not a fighter. Perhaps you need others who are fighters to balance out the team.

So when he came up to me a minute before kick off in what turned out to be my last game, I thought he was apologising for what had been said about everything at Newcastle.

Everyone got it wrong. They said I stayed on the bench and didn't go to the touchline, but that was because the German bugger of a fourth official wouldn't let me! Spurs fans were singing my name, but they always sang my name, so I didn't think it was unusual. People say I was crying, but I swear I didn't know – it was probably a windy night. I was stressed because I didn't want to lose. But maybe the players had an idea. Of course there have been rumours about me, there had been rumours every day, so why should I listen to more rumours? I had been waiting so long, I thought it wasn't going to happen.

We all knew the club had been to Seville to see Ramos, but it looked as though he didn't want to take the job, or couldn't take it in the middle of the season and that he wasn't coming until the end of the season. Call me arrogant, but I didn't think the club would find anybody better than me. Not even someone like Jose Mourinho could have done better than me at this club under the circumstances. It was easy to be champions as manager of Chelsea, but when you look at our line up over the last two years, to finish fifth in successive seasons is something I don't believe he, or anyone else for that matter, could have managed at this club. And then when you think that for seven months we were in the top four, and only missed out in the last game of the season, when Arsenal finished fourth, that is one hell of an achievement. For the past four years we have all known who would be in the top four, the only surprise was when Everton finished fourth in 2004/05 to qualify for the Champions League – and even then they finished in the bottom half of the table the following season and were knocked out of the Champions League at the first stage. And we know in the next four years who would be the favourites to be in the top four. Now David Moyes has got strong players, he's got his final sort of article, now he can stay in the top six. But for me, to stay in the top six would have been fantastic. A couple of years ago my target was to be structurally top six every season and we did that. Perhaps with the younger players we could achieve more, but we'll never know.

As for Spurs, and its future and its recent past, I have come to realise that this is the most difficult club in the history of English football to manage, and that would certainly apply in the last 15 years. But I was their manager into a fourth season when the average survival rate for Spurs mangers cannot be much more than 18 months.

I leave the club with a special connection with them. I leave with an unbelievable affection for the best club ever. I realised just how big a club this is last season when I discovered early on how much the club craved the success they had enjoyed in the past. I realised just how passionate their fans are, and how knowledgeable too.

I don't believe many managers, if any, have had such a connection as I have enjoyed with the Spurs fans. Despite all the problems, despite the team not doing so well, in that last game those supporters stood up and chanted my name. I will never forget it.

But God knew I couldn't stay, the results were not good. I knew that. The results were not good enough this season. But I cannot imagine ever being sacked with such a good feeling about the fans, about the club. I cannot believe a manager will ever leave with such a warmth toward the fans who stood up to cheer him off even though they knew it was not a good season. They were good to me, and I know they have not always taken to managers in the past. I have received 7,000 letters and emails, and they are still arriving, from fans and well wishers from all over the country. Why should I leave with any ill feelings after all of that? Yes, it was painful to lose the job I loved, but if anything it has made me even stronger.

Some managers are exhibitionists. I would say I am not really an exhibitionist, but I had to be an exhibitionist this season to put up with all the rubbish, face the media time and time again and keep my cool. Everyone said I had kept my dignity. I thank them for that. I tried. But it wasn't easy to stand in front of the players and explain what was going on when I didn't know it myself. If I had to do that in my early days in management, I would have given up, but I would never have given up on Spurs. I wanted to do better for this club, and I believe I could have done had I stayed.

When the time came and I was sacked, I was upset – yes, of course I was – but I was really disappointed rather than hurt by it. I love it here in England. I love the English people. I get a real sense of justice, but I feel justice wasn't done. I deserved more time.

We lost two points at Liverpool when we should have won there, but despite the defeat at Newcastle we had gone on a run of six games unbeaten, and we scored 26 goals, apart from Portsmouth who scored seven in one cism for. They were the Carling Cup semi-final and the FA Cup quarter-final at Stamford Bridge against Chelsea. We never usually gave away a lead, but these were the two times that everyone seems to remember and point an accusing finger at me. Now I can take it when I am criticised in the media, but I don't like it if not accurate, and you have to live with it at times. The problem is when your Board of Directors start to believe it. Board members don't know about tactics. Why should they? But I felt that Paul Kemsley, the vice-chairman, believed it, and that became a problem. Months after those two games, some people still talked about them. But they forgot...how many times did we lose a game when we were in the lead? Apart from those two they talked about hardly any, because there were none. Two years ago we never gave away a lead, and last year we would always comeback if went a goal down. Of course this year was different, but there were a lot of things different this season. But no-one talked about all the games when we never lost our lead, just those two games from the past, and it was annoying and frustrating.

But I never lost a game at White Hart Lane in the last minute as the team did in the first Premier League game after I left, against Blackburn. The new man sat in the stands next to the chairman, but I know if I had been in that situation I couldn't have sat there, I would have been down on the bench for the second half, but it seemed as if those three points didn't matter, and I don't understand that. I am sure it wouldn't have happened if I had stayed in charge, I was convinced I could repair the damage.

But believe me you cannot finish fifth in the league two years running if you don't know about tactics, you cannot comeback in the last stages of the season as we did without the players being fit. And alright we didn't have a good start in 2007/08 in terms of results at the start of the season, but until the defeat at Newcastle – when the board decided to sack me – we were on a nice unbeaten run.

One of those six games was when I had to make two or three changes during the game against Villa and we stormed back from 4-1 down to draw 4-4. We were drawing 0-0 with Boro and it was not the best of performances, we didn't create, but we won 2-0. In the UEFA Cup we were one down in the away leg to Famagusta, but I made changes and three minutes after the switch around with Keane and Bale we scored. Against Liverpool we were one down and I made a change that I am not proud of if, in fact a change that I hate – we went Route One. But it paid off, a long clearance from the keeper, Berbatov flicked on and Robbie scored. So, in that sequence of six matches I must have made four or five important changes and they paid off.

I never tell lies. Perhaps that's part of the problem. People might like my style as a manager because they can see I tell it as it is. Some people might not like that, but I have always been very honest with the directors at Spurs. I have told them what I think. Also, everybody, the supporters, in particular, could see for themselves what was really happening; the fans, they understood. You cannot kid them.

The trouble is that people who don't understand the game so will start to believe what they are being told or what they read in the newspapers, even though they are not presented with all the facts and a proper explanation. They don't think about the 105 games in which I made substitutions in the second half that changed the game in our favour. They just come up with Chelsea...Arsenal...the two big games in which we blew big leads.

There has been a lot of crap talked about and written about Berbatov. Most of it hinges around games against Chelsea and Arsenal when were within touching distance of famous wins that might have brought a trophy.

Against Chelsea we were 3-1 up and it could easily have been 4-1 with the chances we were getting. Chelsea were shocked after the first half, they didn't have an answer. I played a diamond for the first time in mid-season in the League, but we had practiced it on the training ground a lot, with Aaron Lennon behind the front two strikers. In that game Lennon was carving Chelsea apart, he was on fire. But I had taken a risk with Berbatov. He had a groin strain and was a big doubt for the game. But I decided to play him. This caused a problem because Mido thought the decision had been taken that he would play. I can understand why he thought it, because Berbatov was a little bit injured and it would have been a risk to play him, but when he found out he wasn't in the starting line up Mido was annoyed and for some reason he was convinced that I had been called in to see a member of the club's board who had instructed me to play Berbatov. I swear to God that was never said. And that is why Mido talked later about the politics of the club forcing him out when he signed for Middlesbrough. But it was just not true.

So, in the first half at Stamford Bridge Lennon was on fire and the front three played brilliantly. But there was a problem. Berbatov was telling me at half-time: "gaffer, I have to come off I cannot walk, I have to come off." But I told him we needed someone to hold the ball up and I needed him to carry on, and play at least the next 10 minutes. Eventually, though, I had to take him off. After 20 minutes he kept looking over to me pleading to come off. I couldn't risk him pulling a 'string' [hamstring], which would have been a long term injury and I had to put on Mido. Immediately I made that substitution Chelsea had a corner kick and Lampard scored with the second ball after it was headed clear. Paul Robinson came out for it and didn't make it, it was one of those things that can happen at a corner kick. In England they somehow think that defending corner kicks and dead balls is about tactics, but sometimes there is nothing anyone can do. From that goal from a corner, Chelsea came back. Again, it is nothing to do with tactics if your key player, Berbatov, is injured.

At 3-2, I had Anthony Gardner on the bench. Now wouldn't you use your centre-half as a substitute to shore it up at the back at that stage? But he twisted his ankle in the first action when he came off the bench, and Chelsea eventually came back to equalise when Kalou scored with a couple of minutes to go.

Arsenal is the other game in which I have been criticised about my tactics and substitutions when we were 2-0 up in the semi-final first leg. Berbatov was great for the first 20 minutes, but again I had to take him off as his groin had gone once more. Robbie Keane and Defoe played together, but neither of them could hold the ball up. Then Robinson steps up to try and snuff out an attack and he must have been 30 yards out of his goal and it's 2-1 and Arsenal were right back in it. Again it's not tactics.

I have left Spurs with some people in England believing I had my tactics wrong in those two key games. That is not justice. But here they don't seem to understand tactics so much. Maybe it's a Dutch thing, I don't know. But I don't think it's too harsh to say there is an ignorance about tactics in England. If you put it into somebody's head that someone isn't good at tactics, than they might to start to believe it – even if it isn't true.

The truth is that the previous season we came from behind nine times to win games, yet there is a perception out there that I couldn't manage my team to come back once they got behind. There were about a dozen times we held on to leads under extreme pressure. Yet we gave away a lead against Chelsea and Arsenal and those are the games everyone points to.

There was that one game against Middlesbrough when the fans were booing one of my substitutions because I took Defoe off, but they didn't understand why, and as it turned out the substitution worked. If you make the wrong substitutions, you only know in hindsight. Equally if they work you only know at the final whistle. Substitutions are out there for everybody to see. They know if it works, because you get the result. They are convinced they failed, though, if you don't get the right result. But there are far more subtle tactical changes, for example the tactical changes I made in the Boro game, that nobody realised, and they paid off.

Early in the 2007/08 season against Fulham we were 3-1 up at Craven Cottage and could have scored four or five, Jermaine Jenas was twice one against one with the keeper and missed. Then an outrageous deflected shot by Smertin goes over Robinson and suddenly it"s 3-2 when we were strolling the game. I had Michael Dawson on the bench, so I threw him because Fulham were throwing everybody forward. I took off Robbie Keane. Ok, he had got two assists, but he wasn't actually playing very well at the time I opted to put on Defoe, who had looked sharp in training and was desperate to play. Perhaps if Jermaine had taken those two great chances we would have won 4-1 instead of what happened. But he missed and I had to make another substitution to try to keep our narrow lead. Fulham won a throw on the left and Kaboul got caught out in front of Dempsey. The American flicked it on and Kamara earned the draw with that last minute overhead kick. Tell me what that has got to do with tactics?

I remember last season when Manchester United were one-up against Arsenal at the Emirates Stadium with three minutes left and Ferguson put on a defender and Arsenal scored two late goals, the winner from a Thierry Henry header. But I never saw or heard a word of criticism against Ferguson. No-one suggested he made a tactical error.

At the end of that draw at Fulham, for the first time ever I told a player – it was Robbie Keane – that I regretted the substitution. It was the wrong decision to have taken him off and put on Defoe, but I pointed out to Robbie that it was only an error in hindsight, as I thought I had made the right decision at the time. There were two reasons for that confession to Robbie. One was to boost him up, and secondly it is always easy to assess your substitutions in hindsight. At the time I made the decision I thought it was the right one. In fact I would probably make the same decision again under the same circumstances. But I said to Robbie: "I should have left you on".

A lot was made in my final season about not being able to keep four strikers happy, but for three years I had four strikers and, although it is not easy to keep them happy, I still did it.

I signed Dimitar Berbatov for Spurs, and I believe that will be one of the best signings the club has ever made. Berbatov is an immense talent. But Berbatov is how he is. Perhaps that is why, when he played in Germany, he never went to Bayern Munich. He is a great player, but introverted. I'm still not sure what Berbatov is thinking. He has that look, you know, that look of depression. But I am sure that cannot be the case, he cannot always be depressed!

Everyone has focused on my relationship with Berbatov, as if I didn't have a good relationship with him. I did. I have always had a good relationship with him. He has not been a problem, despite what everyone might think. The trouble is he wanted to go to Manchester United. That was in his mind and I could not do anything about it. I tried. I told him if he wants to be a champion of England, he has to make it happen with this club. I told him: "You have to make the difference, you have to make us great".

I loved Berba. He was my player. He came to me once and said: "Boss, I want to achieve something. I'm not worse than Eto'o or Rooney or Tevez …" And he's right. The only thing I said to him is: "You need to be more consistent. You have to make the difference and win us prizes." Last season he scored 11 goals in the league and with his talent he should score 20. Two days after that last game, when I saw him he had tears in his eyes when I left. He is such a great lad.

I wanted to make it happen at Spurs, and I know, 100 per cent, had I been given the chance I would have done it. We had brought some talented youngsters to the club, we had bought 'ball' players, the next step was to find players who could also make it stick. But of course the 2007/08 season was difficult, especially after starting with two defeats in two games and then the non-stop press speculation about Ramos, and other managers. I felt lonely. It was a bad situation, almost impossible, and the players never gave up, except maybe in the last match. Getafe was an injustice, because if we'd won, we'd have been unbeaten in my last eight games, except for Newcastle. We were still managing to play good football. I had to inspire the players while they knew every day I could be gone the next minute. They were looking at the papers and still, for 10 weeks, I had to motivate them. That was probably my biggest achievement ever. You can throw the ball at the players, but if you might be leaving, they'll throw it back. Human nature. But those boys are special and, as much as they could, they fought for me, they still afforded me respect. I said to them: "I will always watch you, but you have to be strong. Stronger. With our talent, we have to do better".

As for the Board; one reason I like Daniel is he thinks in structures. I think in structures too. I seemed to be special to Spurs fans because I'm authentic, and if I had some problem with Daniel I'd tell him. Sometimes he didn't like that, but I still worked in his structure because he's the best businessman ever and very ambitious. I'm not against the structure, because they work like that in Europe. I've worked in it before. Ramon Monchi, Seville's sporting director, is probably the best. He gets all his players. They were in the top six already and then he appointed Ramos as manager and it worked. Seville have won the UEFA Cup and been successful in La Liga. Frank Arnesen appointed me. But if you're already there as manager and somebody else comes into the Sporting Director role it won't work. Same with Harry Redknapp at Southampton and Sir Clive Woodward.

I never had any problems with Comolli because he never bothered me. But that actually was the problem. Frank would say to me: "Why did you do this in a game?" Frank was more of a right-hand man, Frank was my friend, so we talked about football. I had nothing against Damien, but we just didn't have that kind of relationship. Now it's a better system for Spurs. Ramos is head coach and Damien's his boss.

As for selling players, they did what I wanted. They never got rid of somebody, other than if they were a bit older, and I appreciated that. I loved Michael Brown, he was one of the biggest characters we had, but I knew if we get so much money from Fulham, okay, he would have to go. But if the Board wanted to sell Teemu Tainio, for example, when Teemu is one of the best-liked characters in the dressing room, who can play in all the positions, that would be bad. So they didn't do that. Most of the time I was fine with what they did.

The press don't help because the press in England only throw figures at you. They said: "You spent £40m this summer". They portrayed it as if I spent the money. I didn't fix the fees and I don't know what they earn. Yes, we spent £40m, but it was £40m for the future. You can only develop talent with good experience. Look at Michael Dawson, He's been outstanding alongside Ledley King, but looked inexperienced since Ledley's been injured. [Gareth] Bale, [Younes] Kaboul and [Darren] Bent have that chance to prove themselves, but they really do need experience alongside them. But Spurs chose the poath to follow. We didn't invest like Liverpool in 2007, who bought [Javier] Mascherano or [Fernando] Torres. That's different, they buy finished articles, top stars. I believed in the players we got, but more experience would have made the difference.

In my first full season we finished fifth with 65 points. Do you know why? We weren't that young. We had Edgar Davids, Michael Carrick, Jermaine Jenas, Tainio. At the back I had Ledley. [Noureddine] Naybet was as old as me! Sure players get older and you have to replace them, but the combination for success is development and results. [Arsène] Wenger: fourth the last couple of seasons. Did he win something? Not the league since 2004. Did Arsenal say: "You have to win a prize or finish third?" No, because he's the man. He can say: "I need time". They believed in him.

Arsenal's young players are exceptional, but [Gael] Clichy, [Cesc] Fabregas needed a few seasons. Look at them now. And look at the other players around them: [Kolo] Toure, [William] Gallas, Gilberto, even [Robin] Van Persie, [Emmanuel] Adebayor – they're experienced. If Newcastle, Manchester City, Aston Villa finish fifth, you get a big celebration. If you are in a club like Southend for example and you achieve what you want you get a big celebration. Spurs is different – finish fifth, that's good, but then it's the next target. The attitude is: 'You've finished fifth twice, now we have to be fourth'. Daniel wants to keep you on your toes. That's not a problem. The problem is, if we still had Frank Arnesen, as a football man, he would have said as an intermediary: "We need some time". I wasn't satisfied with fifth, but we did okay.

It wasn't good enough for some. There were conversations about me being more outspoken about having Champions League ambitions, about how I wasn't ambitious enough, but I didn't want to put too much pressure on the younger players. It was a choice I made.

Of course I wanted to be in the top four, but I would also one day want us to be champions. But is that realistic? Ambition needs to be measured by what you're working with. In a way I don't mind because it's a management style and Daniel is a manager. That is not a problem. The problem is that if, for example, we still had Frank Arnesen as Sporting Director, as a football man he would have said to the Board that it doesn't work like that, we need some time.

I leave Tottenham with my head high. With Ramos they think they can buy success, that they'll now be fourth, but that's business thinking. A football man would think: "But can we be fourth? How easy is that?" Ramos was good at Seville, but can he be good at Spurs? Every club is different. For me there was no turning back. That was my final squad. But I'm certain they will now see it's not the final squad in terms of development and they will buy. I managed two fifth-placed finishes. How important was that for the club? Just the beginning or a peak? Okay, ultimately maybe not enough. In the future we'll see.

I like to think I took the club forward. When I arrived we were going out of the cups to the likes of Leicester and Grimsby, but I took them to five quarter-finals and one semi-final and we only went out to big clubs or in difficult ties. In the League we managed 65 points in a season when we had few injuries. I believe I will be remembered as the manager who took Spurs forward, who has helped them on the road to discovering their right place in English football.

I felt a little beaten up when I was sacked. I still feel very tired, but maybe that's normal. I saw myself on television and thought: "bloody hell", but sometimes I would feel just fantastic. If you are at a stadium like Liverpool and you're under so much pressure and you're still doing it, winning 2-1 with a minute left…that makes you stronger, believe me.

I live in Essex. I love the people here because they have a crazy love for their football, but they also have a feeling for justice. Perhaps that's why my name was chanted during the Getafe game.

I'm 51, I'm not too young. You ask me if I want to be in the Champions League? Of course it's an ambition; or to be the champions of England. I still have ambitions in Holland, too, where I have won every title at all levels apart from the League championship. But I live here. I've been in my house in Essex three-and-a-half years. For me it would be easy to go back to Holland, but what more can you want? A year ago I got offered a job in Holland at a club who get 50,000 fans a week. That's more than Spurs, but it's not the same. I love the people in England because they love their football passionately. Marit, my little daughter, and Nicole, my wife, are settled in and around the London area. We would like to stay, but I also played in lived in Birmingham, so I wouldn't be unfamiliar there. We'll see.

Maybe one day I will comeback to Tottenham. I'm a fighter. I still have the feeling that you never know. I was thinking of Ottmar Hitzfeld. He left Bayern Munich, waited two-and-a-half years, then returned. In football it's all about circumstances, opportunities. In a couple of years I'm not sure the same people will be at Tottenham [on the board], 100% convinced they won't. But there are also other clubs, including PSV Eindhoven, although I want a break and right now I'm going to Brazil for a holiday.

* * * * * *

I can only say that I hope the readers of this book concerning my exit from White Hart Lane will cherish my pride and satisfaction of having been part of the history of the great club that is Tottenhamm Hotspur.

Martin Jol
November 2007

game, and Arsenal, no-one scored more than us in that time. But, of course, in defence we conceded at far too many set plays. But there were pundits who said I didn't train the players enough, didn't work on set pieces on the training ground. That was upsetting because no-one could have worked harder on these aspects of the game.

Naturally I leave with mixed feelings. I want the club to achieve. I want the players to be successful. But I wanted that to happen with me in charge of the team. However I suppose if the team win trophies I will pick up the bonuses! Yes, it's in my contract that I pick up the bonuses even if I am not with the club. I left when we were already in the last 16 of the Carling Cup and it was not a tough game at home to Blackpool, so the club are in the last eight with a good chance in a competition where the big clubs don't play their full strength sides.

Look, I will always have Spurs in my heart. I said to the players when I left: "I will always follow you". They are my players. I know an awful lot has been said about how the players are bought, who buys the players, and the methods that are used, but they are my players in the sense that I coach them, and many of them I watched and wanted to buy. But in England you play three times a week, it is not always possible to see all the players, you have to go on recommendations and take peoples' words for it. The only other issue is that I was not involved in the process of buying a player, again in the sense that if I wanted a player and was told he was not available or the price was prohibitive or that the selling club was being unreasonable, I would have to accept it, because I was not on the inside of that deal knowing what was going on.

There have been comments attributed to me suggesting that I was opposed to some signings or didn't get the signings I wanted, but it was taken from a Dutch magazine and lost in translation. The true situation is far more complex.

The truth is that I needed another Ledley King in central defence, and maybe a leader like Ledley in midfield. The club's policy of buying players for the future was a sound one, but there are occasions when you need a bit of experience, when you need a leader in certain areas of the pitch, like we needed Ledley at the back and didn't have him due to injury this season, so we needed an experienced central defender.

I spoke to many people I respected about the special problems at this club, Spurs legends such as Dave Mackay and Cliff Jones. Mackay told me that when they won the Double the average age of the team was 28, not the 22 or 24 of our teams. He made the point that you need old pros to win the big prizes. It was not a criticism of the current policy, it was just an opinion he held. I spoke only once to Jimmy Greaves, two years ago at the memorial for Bill Nicholson, and I told him that myself and my family really felt for him at missing out on the World Cup Final of '66. It wasn't an appropriate time to talk about Spurs or my situation there.

Perhaps my biggest regret is that Ledley King was not there all of the time, and was not there for this season when I needed him the most. Youngsters cannot do it on their own, they need help. We had some big talents, young players, but we needed experience as well. Ledley has both, experience and a huge talent, as well as being the dressing room leader. Michael Dawson looked a stronger and better player alongside Ledley. He is still a good player, but not as good when Ledley is not there.

Although I have said I leave with no regrets, perhaps there are some, well, not regrets, but issues I really do feel strongly about, that need to be told. For example, I was supposed to be shouting and arguing with Jermain Defoe all the time. It just wasn't true. He came into my office when I left and we parted on good terms. But it is true that it wasn't easy to keep him happy when he was not in the team for so long. I would say that before this season, yes we had a good relationship. But when I didn't pick him for such a long time it was very difficult to have the same relationship.

But Robbie Keane was my main man. He was the only leader for the team in the absence of Ledley. Robbie had the respect of the players and that was why he was captain. Ledley was a big, big miss. So, tell me...without Ledley who should be skipper? We didn't have another skipper. But Robbie had the respect of the other players.

Robbie also developed as a player during my time as a manager at the club. He was always a good striker, the best at avoiding offside, and he could finish, chipping, shooting, he had it all. But I played him in different roles, many times I asked him to do a specific job for the team, to play in a link up role or to play wide, and for that reason I felt he developed as a person as well as a player. He was the most consistent player, just as good away from home as at home, which is rare. And good for team bonding, he's also quite a singer ... U2 and so on!

If there is something that surprises me it is that some people had concerns my tactical knowhow. I have enjoyed a wonderful three year experience in English football, but there is an incorrect perception about my coaching tactics and abilities. I would read that I should have and could have sown up a few games, but failed to do so. There were two games last season in particular when we lost a two-goal lead that I took a lot of criti-

INTRODUCTION

MARTIN JOL, WITHOUT QUESTION Tottenham Hotspur football club's most popular manager since Bill Nicholson, had a problem. He had produced Spurs' best back-to-back seasons in 24 years, dragging the club from perennial underachievers to serious trophy contenders. But the Spurs board wanted more; much more in fact; nothing less than a coveted and lucrative place in the Champions League.

The Dutchman had come close, but not close enough. In the profit-fuelled world of modern football, Jol, a man driven to achieve glory for a club, and its supporters, that had been close to his heart for many years, was put under severe pressure to deliver on every front. Ultimately he was unable to do so and paid the price.

There are lies, damned lies and statistics in football, particularly in the modern era where TV seeks simple answers to show viewers why one team is beating another. So it was with Jol. When it came to the final reckoning, a glut of stats made it easy to argue the case for the Dutchman being one of the best managers in Spurs' proud history.

He was in charge of Tottenham for 112 Premier League games, winning 47 times, but, significantly, only once in the traumatic opening ten league games of the 2007/08 season. He had spent a mammoth £77.8 million, the most on Darren Bent from Charlton at £16m, and received £41.75 million, the biggest sale that of Michael Carrick at £18.6m. Spurs drew 30 games and lost 35 times, giving Jol a final win ratio of 42 per cent, the best of any manager in the club's Premier League history; in fact the best since legendary double-winning manager Nicholson achieved a similar percentage during his 800 plus games in charge from 1958 to 1974.

In the best tradition of the fast, flowing football which has become the hallmark of a classic Tottenham side, Spurs found the back of their opponent's net 166 times during his reign, outscoring the likes of Arsenal, Chelsea and Liverpool in 2007. Jol's Spurs accrued 65 points in the 2005/06 season, the best haul by the club in the Premier League era, and despite falling eight points short of that in 2006/07 his side finished in fifth place for the second year in succession, ensuring UEFA Cup football for a second season in a row, a feat not achieved since the glory days of back-to-back FA Cup victories under manager Keith Burkinshaw, and not achieved through league position since Nicholson in the early 1970s.

But, despite all that, just before the third anniversary of his appointment at White Hart Lane, football's latest Dead Man Walking was shown the door. In many ways the act was a relief as it had seemed inevitable from the moment when Spurs were caught out actively courting his potential successor, Sevilla coach Juande Ramos, at the start of the 2007/08 season.

Or at least so it seemed. However, the inside track on the truth behind the scenes is vastly different to the perception that the Spurs board had already made the decision in August to actively curtail Jol's reign as manager. My high level source told me: "There was absolutely no offer made to Ramos at that time, absolutely not. There should be no doubt about that."

Soundings had been taken, yes, that is true enough. In fact prior to the Ramos connection, Spurs had actually sounded out to other potential managerial candidates as well as Ramos, but no decision had been taken for a variety of reasons.

When pictures of Ramos and a Spurs delegation appeared in a Sunday newspaper in late August 2007, there was a showdown meeting between Jol and chairman Daniel Levy. My source told me: "Daniel made it perfectly clear to Martin that his wish was for Martin to be successful and to stay at the club. In fact Daniel said to Martin: 'the best thing for this club is that we don't have to make a change – because that means you will have been successful.' The pair sat down to discuss all the issues and Martin told Daniel: 'I will turn it around'."

Levy kept his word to Jol, and that is why when lawyer and agent Mel Goldberg contacted the Spurs chairman trying to initiate a meeting with Fabio Capello shortly afterwards, Levy refused to see the Italian coach who had already been dismissed by Real Madrid and would be available without compensation or the hassles that the club experienced in dealing with Sevilla. So Jol, contrary to popular belief, had genuinely got his second chance, being given the entire season to prove he could take Spurs into the top four. He was determined to take it. A change around in results and an unbeaten run helped, but with too many draws, and only one Premiership win, Spurs found themselves rooted in the bottom three.

By 25 October 2007 the board felt they had to make a decision. It was to give Ramos a now-or-never ultimatum and sack Martin Jol as manager of Spurs. A wonderful chapter in the club's history was over.

This is the story of that three-year spell and its ignominious end. But it is also the story of Martin Jol's remarkable rise from a tiny north sea fishing village, via Bayern Munich, the Dutch national team, West Bromwich Albion and Coventry City, his incredible success as a coach in Holland and his passions in other areas of his life including art and literature.

THE END

IN THE EARLY summer of 2007 something strange was happening at White Hart Lane. Birds twittered in Tottenham High Road's budding trees as a shroud of positivity surrounded a club renowned for fickle fans and a distinct lack of success. Amid this contented scene Spurs supporters strode to purchase their season tickets for new 2007/08 season confident in the knowledge that their team, after decades of underachievement and disappointment, would finish in the top four places in the Premiership and thus qualify for the Champions League. Not only that, but in doing so they would deny fierce rivals Arsenal, down on their luck after losing the talismanic Thierry Henry to Barcelona, their supposed divine right to a place at football's top table .

How so? Well, the decline in fortunes of the Gunners since the successful era of the much-heralded 'Unbeatables' of 2003/04 had seen them fail to win a trophy in two seasons. Coupled with that, were successive fifth place finishes in the Premiership for Spurs, plus solid cup runs in both domestic competitions and in the UEFA Cup, and a host of talented big money signings over recent months, including Dimitar Berbatov, Darren Bent and Gareth Bale, to add into the club's growing pool of young talent. This was the hard currency in exchange for which Spurs fans handed over their cash.

But then?

A last gasp goal on the opening day at newly-promoted Sunderland followed but a few days later a heavy home defeat at the hands of Everton left Spurs reeling. The club's Board was decidedly unhappy. Talk, being cheap, seemed ridiculous that Martin Jol, the manager who had hauled Spurs up from mid-table mediocrity in under three years, could be replaced after just two matches of the new season.

I had been in the midst of writing a chronicle of the life and times of Martin Jol for almost a year, with help from all the staff at Tottenham Hotspur FC and the full co-operation of the Dutch Master himself, who offered us several exclusive interviews, the run of his photograph collection and insight into how he had achieved the dream of every Spurs supporter – to complete at the very highest level. The book was intended as a tribute and a celebration of the man. As both a Spurs and Jol fan I'd delighted in his achievements in turning the club into potential serious contenders for the real prizes which exist in the modern game of football, one of the cherished top four spots in the newly renamed Premier League, which guarantee the riches of competing in the Champions League, and apparent repeated success on the pitch and in the stock market in the process. It had been a wholly positive and pleasant task to that point, in the middle of August 2007, when the new season began full of hope and expectation.

Then came news of a serious development – from southern Spain. Everything changed.

One of the most controversial incidents in Spurs' recent history occurred with the now infamous clandestine meeting in Seville to sound out a candidates to replace Jol at the helm of Spurs' floundering ship. The issuing the traditional non-denials, counter claims and 100% backing for Jol by the Spurs Board within days of the notorious events caused an air of intrigue and national outrage as phone-ins glowed red hot with support or the amiable, but stoic Dutchman. My sources inside the Lane told me, though, two vital points in my efforts to clarify the entire sordid tale.

Firstly, I have been assured that while the club deeply regret the publicity the meeting attracted, and accept some of the criticism, there was no offer to Juande Ramos irrespective of what he may have said publicly about a supposedly 'dizzying' deal on the table. Yes, there were soundings, there were indications of the level of possible remuneration – but definitely no offer.

Secondly, the decision by the club to adopt a contingency plan was not a knee-jerk reaction to losing the opening two games of a new season as was widely believed. In fact there was already a lack of confidence in Jol's ability to take Tottenham Hotspur onto that next level because of a perceived lack of ambition being effused by Jol. My source informed me from a high level within the White Hart Lane hierarchy: "While they did not go about it in the right way, they had the best interests of the club at heart. That was indicated by there being no anti-Board chanting at Old Trafford. Yes, there were soundings, a due diligence, if you like, but there was no offer, of that they are categoric. Daniel Levy is Chairman of a plc and could not put out statements to the Stock Exchange or otherwise that are inaccurate. This was not about timing, not even about results."

So what did lie behind it?

Tottenham, like several other major British football clubs such as Chelsea, operate a management system which has dual heads. On the one hand Martin Jol is the Head Coach, responsible for first team affairs and what happens on the pitch during games. On the other, Sporting Director Damien Comolli is responsible for the scouting of future players and the continuity of playing and coaching staff at all levels.

The system was instigated by Spurs Chairman Daniel Levy so as to ensure an end to the days when managers would come and go and the incoming man would want wholesale changes to his playing staff, bringing in favourites and ousting the old incumbent's men. Levy sees this system as being capable of ending the seemingly endless flux which Spurs have experienced since their last period of any sustained success in the 1980s.

My source confirmed: "We have a football management group. That group, among other issues, deals with potential transfers. Shortlists are drawn up, contributions are made, then the names come back to the table and targets are then gone for. No player at this club is bought without the manager giving his consent. Daniel Levy would not authorise fees for a player the manager doesn't want to be at Spurs and therefore wouldn't play."

Explaining the system in the club magazine, *Hotspur*, early in 2007, Comolli was clear about who governed the process. "Obviously we [the scouting department] come up with all the names and I tell Martin this is the reason why we think this player is No 1, No 2, No 3 and so on. Of course Martin has a vital say in all of this and he might say he prefers one player to another, so we can swap around, but basically we're always working on a team of players who currently play for other clubs."

'Vital say' is not 'final say', however, which is what Messrs Ferguson and Wenger enjoy at Manchester United and Arsenal. Spurs, however, insist that Jol does have final say on all playing matters and that the supposed differences between the two major figures, Jol and Comolli, are the victims of idle press gossip over which they have no control.

There is no doubt that while Jol had taken so much credit for rebuilding the club, it was also Levy who had put into place the policy of recruiting young talent for a lasting future, rather than a quick fix solution, as he made clear in a comment in February 2007, saying: "I'm the one that has instilled part of the philosophy we are trying to build here, and that is obviously that we want to have a squad that is capable of challenging for regular European competition, but one that has also got inherent value."

Jol admires Levy's acumen and says the deal his chairman struck to bring Aaron Lennon from Leeds United for just £1m was 'the best business ever in this country over the last 30 years'. Even so Jol has been left with a squad of players for the future that is expected to achieve success right now.

Because of this set up the sale of England midfielder Michael Carrick to Manchester United in the summer of 2006 and the subsequent purchase of Didier Zokora as his replacement is often cited as the first real crack in the way the continental system adopted by the Board broke down; Jol didn't want to sell Carrick and didn't want Zokora. The popular conception is that Comolli, newly installed as Sporting Director believed the opposite. That, however, is untrue. The Carrick situation had gone way beyond the control of anyone at Tottenham, simply because the player himself had decided that he wanted to return to the north of England, closer to his roots, well before Comolli came on the scene.

The popular version of the story held that Carrick had been happy at Spurs, having helped them within a whisker of qualifying for the Champions League by finishing in that hallowed fourth place, when he went to talk to Levy about a new contract in April 2006. The former West Ham youth product had two years left on his existing deal and his inclusion in England's World Cup was imminent. He had been Tottenham's best player over the season and was central to Jol's plans. But Levy played hard-ball and, with talks over a new contract protracted, Sir Alex Ferguson made his play for Carrick… and what Fergie wants, Fergie gets.

In actual fact, Carrick had only recently got married and wanted to start family, so had already taken the decision that he wished to join his own family in the north. Whichever version of the story you choose to believe the outcome was the same. Spurs lost their most influential player and the manager was not happy with how matters had turned out.

The handling of Dimitar Berbatov is also cited as another catalyst for the crisis that engulfed the club. The striker was also courted by United and Jol was not happy with the player's contribution in the opening game of the season at the Stadium of Light. But there is no doubt that the Board wanted to keep Berbatov even though the manager questioned whether the club should cash in on a player with his mind elsewhere. Then Jol publicly fell out with the Bulgarian during Spurs' meek capitulation at Newcastle in front of Sky TV's cameras in what would prove to be Jol's penultimate game in charge when Berbatov, in a huff because he was selected only for the substitute's bench, seemingly refused on two occasions instructions from his manager to warm up.

Ironic then that Carrick and Berbatov should be key players in the high pressure fourth match of the 2007/08 season at Old Trafford where Jol's team excelled and arguably were the better side, yet lost, painfully, 1-0, to a wickedly deflected goal, which just summed up Spurs' season so far. The performance, along with their failure to land Ramos, persuaded the Board that they should give Jol more time. The manager, who had remained typically dignified and diplomatic during a fortnight of unrelenting speculation about his future, looked set to hang on, albeit by his fingernails. "We've never seen a week like it," a club source said. "But he's bearing up amazingly well."

Whatever the truth behind the breakdown in relationship between manager and Board, there are, most certainly, wider forces at work.

Joe Lewis, the sixteenth richest man in Britain according to the 2007 Times Rich List, oversees his investment in Tottenham from the comfort of his mansion in Lyford Cay in the Bahamas, leaving Levy to turn his millions into even more millions. Lewis and Levy would only sell the club for an attractive price. The club need a bigger stadium, with at least a 50,000 capacity, and therefore require regular Champions League football to seriously achieve that aim. There is a waiting list of 10,000 for season tickets and a local fan-base of at least 100,000, so the potential is significant. But space is tight at White Hart Lane and Tottenham would have to buy up property around the ground and turn the pitch through 90 degrees to be able to achieve the increase in capacity and revenue-earning capabilities that near neighbours Arsenal have achieved in moving from hemmed-in Highbury to their new Emirates Stadium.

Paul Kemsley, Tottenham's non-executive director, and one of the leading figures at the Seville summit, is an interesting character. He is a self-made property millionaire, a genuine Spurs fan and close friend of both Alan Sugar, on whose TV show *The Apprentice* he has appeared as a hard-hitting troubleshooter who weedles out the flagging candidates towards the end of the process, and Portsmouth manager Harry Redknapp, with whom he once owned a racehorse. Kemsley and Levy together can theoretically make board decisions for the football club, independently of the plc, from which Kemsley resigned last year to give him a free rein on the football side. But Spurs regularly insist that this would never happen in practice. Of course with his links to Sugar and *The Apprentice*, there had been plenty of opportunites for the 'You're Fired' line to be rehearsed before Jol was finally, controversially and publicly given the boot.

Underpinning the football decisions of the Tottenham board is Comolli. He arrived at the club in September 2005 having been a scout for Arsenal in France, but was not, in fact, as influential in uncovering a sucession of young French players for Arsenal as Spurs made out. He was briefly

Director of Football at St-Etienne before joining Spurs when Frank Arnesen controversially left for Chelsea, but some of his player recommendations have been questionable. Benoit Assou-Ekotto, Ricardo Rocha and Didier Zokora have not yet set the Premier League alight.

Again the press were guilty of creating machinations where there were none. The story ran that, as 2006 turned into 2007, results dipped and Kemsley became unhappy with Jol's tactics. There was also great disappointment at Board level when Chelsea won at White Hart Lane in an FA Cup quarter-final replay, after Tottenham let a winning position slip in the first tie at Stamford Bridge. Only a second successive fifth place in the league temporarily soothed Jol's detractors.

Again I am told that no such situation occurred. In fact the problems only began in the summer of 2007 as Spurs planned for a definitive thrust to oust one of the regular big four from their Champions League berth.

It was then it all bubbled up in the summer, with behind-the-scenes tension over signings. Jol had been desperate for a left-winger for two years, but couldn't get Middlesbrough and England star Stewart Downing. He was further frustrated when he turned his attention to a player he considered an important piece in his jigsaw: Berbatov's compatriot and friend, Martin Petrov, from Atletico Madrid. Jol was provided with 20 year-old Kevin-Prince Boateng, an attack-minded midfielder who had yet to prove himself. Petrov joined the Sven-Göran Eriksson revolution at Manchester City and began the season in a whirl of good form, much to Jol's chagrin.

With Jol having experienced a bad start, with huge question marks looming over his future while almost the entire nation leapt to his defence, he received support from within the game from two unlikely sources; rivals Arsène Wenger and Alex Ferguson. Wenger, who has enjoyed virtually unfettered control for more than a decade at Arsenal, accused Tottenham of impatience, while Ferguson commented: "The difference between Martin Jol and me is that I've been here 20 years. When I first came to this club I faced all that expectation too, because we hadn't won the league in umpteen years. Martin is new at the club and Spurs haven't won the league for over 45 years, so that's quite a lot of expectation, and you are not surprised at the criticism. You are only surprised at the way it all started. I was pleased to see Daniel Levy come out in support of him because he [Jol] is a decent guy. His work in Holland was outstanding, and he did a good job for Tottenham last year. Knee-jerk reactions don't necessarily come from the board, the press play a part too, but still you wonder where these things start. In modern football you get in some of these directors' rooms and boardrooms and you see four or five directors and about 35 hangers-on. And they've all got a voice. That's often where the seed is sown.

When I first came to United they had something they called the 'Second Board'. They used to meet every Monday afternoon in the Grill Room at Old Trafford, assess results, get the axe out for Alex Ferguson, that type of thing. That's the kind of rubbish you had even 20 years ago. I think a lot of clubs have a similar problem – it sort of comes with the corporate hospitality packages nowadays – and perhaps Tottenham suffer from it more than most."

The huge groundswell of support which backed Martin Jol to the hilt after the Seville incident among football fans generally, not just Spurs supporters, proved that he is the most popular manager at White Hart Lane since the legendary Bill Nicholson, who brought the famous double to Tottenham in 1961 and amassed the vast majority of Spurs' silverware, even more than Keith Burkinshaw who presided over the successful spell in the 1980s which saw back-to-back FA Cups and a UEFA Cup triumph on penalties over Feyenoord in 1984; both men were more popular as managers even than Glenn Hoddle and Osvaldo Ardiles, neither of whom could translate their status as legendary Spurs players to management.

Fanzines, messageboards and websites were packed with fans' backing for the under-siege Jol, who took on the mantle of the Dead Man Walking last assumed by Claudio Ranieri under Roman Abramovich at Chelsea before the arrival of Jose Mourinho. Like Ranieri at the Bridge after the arrival of Roman Abramovich's millions, perhaps even more so, Jol is hugely popular with the rank and file. Personally I am a big fan of the man who has the potential to be the best Spurs boss since Bill Nicholson, the man who delivered the double, and back-to-back FA Cup victories in the early 1960s. However, it is misleading to suggest that Jol's record is the best since Billy Nick. True, Spurs have not finished higher in the league for 19 years – reason enough to keep faith with Jol. But three managers since Nicholson have pulled Spurs higher up the final league table. Peter Shreeves, David Pleat and Terry Venables each took Spurs to third in 1985, '87, and '90 respectively. Keith Burkinshaw finished fourth in '83 and won the UEFA Cup the following season.

The money game has become so prominent in the modern game and ENIC believe Spurs could be worth a staggering £400m if they can break into the Champions League and become regular participants. Tottenham announced to the stock exchange that Levy's company had bought more than £67m worth of shares in the club. ENIC, the investment vehicle that he co-owns with Joe Lewis, now holds more than 82% of the fully diluted capital of Tottenham including buying out Sir Alan Sugar's remaining 12 per cent during the summer of 2007. They started out with just under 30 per cent, which cost a mere £22m seven years ago.

Mike Ashley was believed to be a possible suitor, but he preferred Newcastle United for £133m. There are others said to be interested. However, for the selling price to be maximised, Spurs need to be in the top four and consistently a Champions League participant. Both club and owners are being advised by Seymour Pierce, City financiers who specialise in Premier League takeovers and who, through Keith Harris, the former chairman of the Football League, brokered the purchase of Manchester City by Thaksin Shinawatra during the summer of 2007. After accounting for its complex structure of ordinary and preference shares, Tottenham's stock market value as of September 2007 is £212m, meaning they can achieve almost double the value if the aim of regular Champions League football is achieved. The stakes couldn't be much higher for Jol.

During the 2006/07 season the word was that ENIC would settle for a 50% mark-up on that figure, but the £470m buyout of Liverpool by American billionaires Tom Hicks and George Gillett and the battle for Arsenal, which also reared into internecine dispute over the wild and wet summer of 2007, have widened their financial expectations. The asking price for Spurs now stands nearer to £450m, although without an appreciable increase in on-field performance in the immediate future that would be difficult to justify. However ENIC is now looking at selling the club's future potential, rather than its existing reality.

Spurs' strategy seems all well and good when the target is a top-seven finish. In that race competitors are Everton, Bolton, Blackburn and Newcastle United, and you have a manager like Jol who can deliver back-to-back fifth-place finishes, Tottenham's best sequence in 24 years. But that is not enough. Key figures in the Tottenham corridor of power – Levy, Kemsley and Comolli – began to doubt that Jol could take them up a level and into the Champions League as the winter of 2006 wore on and Spurs struggled in mid-table. The rally that would take them to a second successive fifth place was then a distant prospect. Ramos came on to the radar with his success and attacking style of play with Sevilla, with whom he had won the UEFA Cup and ridden high in the Premiera Liga, almost winning the 2006/07 title, losing out at the death to a resurgent Real Madrid. Respect for him grew after they ousted Spurs from the UEFA Cup in the spring and he was appointed to the technical coaching team at UEFA headed by former Liverpool boss Gérard Houllier. Ramos is acknowledged as one of the best coaches in Europe among his peers, even though he is not so well known by British supporters

Meanwhile, with eyes firmly set on that top four finish, over the summer of 2007, players arrived at Spurs amid a spending spree worth over £40m. Not only were the stakes high, they were rising, rapidly. But bloated expectations came back to haunt the club in the first week of the new season with those two defeats, and from then on the situation blew apart.

But was Jol the architect of his own hellfire and damnation? My high-level source informed me that it was his lack of ambition, which had been evident for some months which had created the desire among them to seek alternatives. Indeed Jol began August 2007 by confessing that there would be more pressure on him to succeed this season than ever before. He did state that he was confident his side could develop into one of the best in the Premiership, but he still wasn't talking the here and now that the Board so wanted to hear.

Despite having one of the best young squads in English football and ensuring that the club would be playing on the European stage in the UEFA Cup for a second consecutive season for the first time in over 20 years, he was still equivocating. The club's directors had shown their trust in Jol by handing him nearly £40m to spend on new signings – including the purchase of striker Darren Bent from Charlton for £16.5m. Jol knew the expectation which would come with spending so much money and was honest enough to admit he simply had to have another successful year if he was to justify all the hype surrounding the club this summer. He told me: "There will be a bit more pressure because people expect more. With different players, younger players, it's not always easy. We first have to prove that we can be top-four potential. We've never done that before. It's a bigger step for us than for Arsenal [referencing the Gunners' similarly youthful side] because they're already in the top four.

The board is very happy with me. I was the only one in the last 25 years to get the team into the top five two years in a row, so they can't complain."

But the pressure hadn't only been one-sided in this pot-boiler of a situation. While it lay across Jol's broad shoulders in terms of needing to break into that top four of the Premier League, the Dutchman had also increased the pressure on his employers by perpetuating the rumour in the week following the Ramos meetings that he had held informal talks with other clubs by telling the press that he could have joined a club playing in the Champions League over the summer, but had stayed loyal to Spurs. The reality is that he was never likely to quit his £1.75m-a-year job, but it was a reminder for Tottenham's board that this was a manager in demand.

"I could walk out and go to a Champions League club, but I want to stay here because I believe in these boys," said Jol. "Two years ago, if I told the chairman 'I'll give you two top-five finishes' he would have laughed at me, but we did it. If you said five quarter-finals in the cups and one semi-final it would be a good achievement. But now I realise that the ambition is higher. People tell me I have to win the cup. Tell other managers they have to win a bloody cup!"

Despite the humiliation of being caught courting Ramos, the most likely scenario seemed to be that Tottenham would give Jol the season to prove himself and, if he failed to delvier, or possibly even if he did achieve fourth place or better, he would be replaced by Ramos for the 2008/09 season.

Could Martin Jol survive to fulfil his ambition to bring sustained success to Tottenham Hotspur Football Club?

I kept a diary of how the 2007/08 season began for Spurs as I completed work on this book and the developing situation took on deeper importance to the tale of a fisherman's son made good. The book, which had begun as a celebration of the career of Britain's most popular Premier League manager, ended with the biggest football story of the 2007/08 season blowing up out of all proportion.

Tuesday, August 14

Spurs were booed off after the 3-1 home defeat by Everton with Jol's team rock-bottom of the nascent table. Incredible. Even by Tottenham's erratic standards, this was a shocker as they slumped in front of a full house who booed them off at half and full-time. Goals from Joleon Lescott, Leon Osman and Alan Stubbs rocked White Hart Lane. Defeat could have been even more emphatic, but for two brilliant saves by Paul Robinson that denied England hopeful Andy Robinson late-on.

Tottenham briefly shown promise with a flurry of assaults on the Everton goal in the first ten minutes. But the reality was their threat came to absolutely nothing except an equaliser from Anthony Gardner.

Jol dismissed some of the goals as 'lucky', but he did not show the slightest bit of surprise when none of his defenders jumped to challenge Lescott and the cente-back's powerful header cannoned off the turf past keeper Robinson after just 113 seconds. For Osman's goal, which put put Everton in front again, once more Tottenham's back line was all over the place as Mikel Arteta sent over a floated chip to the back post. Ricardo Rocha, on for injured Kaboul, headed off the line under pressure from Anichebe, clattering into the keeper. Osman slammed in the loose ball with not a defender in sight to put the icing on his 100th appearance for Everton.

Then right on the stroke of half-time Toffees centre-half Alan Stubbs rammed in a free-kick. Lee Carsley created the space by peeling off the side of the Spurs wall with Stubbs' shot taking a slight deflection off Didier Zokora – and in it went.

As the rain swept in across the Lane on a miserable night up went the chant from Everton supporters 'We are top of the league, we are top of the league'.

Wednesday, August 15

Jol's odds on being the first Premier League boss to be axed tumbled – as the race to be his successor began. Jol was quoted at just 6-1 with Ladbrokes, from 25-1, to win the sack race. Sevilla boss Juande Ramos, who won the UEFA Cup with the Spanish club two years in a row, was already quoted as the 7-4 favourite to replace the Dutchman. Former Spurs hitman Jurgen Klinsmann was 3-1, La Liga winner Fabio Capello 5-1 and Blackburn boss Mark Hughes 12-1.

Thursday, August 16

Jol's side faced newly-promoted Derby at home at the weekend and he needed a victory despite Levy reassuring his manager Jol he still had the full support of the board, at least publicly. Privately, it was a vastly different matter.

Jol was characteristically honest: "I hate it at the moment, to be honest. It is not only about me because I know we'll do better. I hate it when people come up with all these judgment calls. We have to do better. Last year we had 60 points and scored over 100 goals and that is what we want. Daniel feels he is in the same boat as the rest of us and we have meetings every week. It is an important time for us. The transfer window shuts in two weeks and you didn't see him last week. That was good because people will probably think he is putting pressure on me before the season even starts. We were discussing our whole situation and he is supportive. We gave this club 125 points in two seasons, so that hasn't been forgotten after four days."

Jol would have to revive his side's fortunes without Berbatov. The Bulgarian ace had aggravated a groin problem. The manager had spent £100m in three years, but his back four had looked a shambles in the absence of injured defenders Ledley King, Michael Dawson, Gareth Bale and Younes Kaboul. Added to all that, Tottenham's board had not been immune to early-season twitches in the past, notably when Glenn Hoddle was sacked in September 2003 after collecting four points from the first six games.

Friday, August 17

An incredible day. A vote of confidence in Jol from Levy was followed by the clandestine summit with Ramos in Seville. The secret meeting between Ramos' agent Alvaro Torres, Spurs vice-chairman Paul Kemsley and club secretary John Alexander was held with Levy's full backing. Spurs were sure Ramos would agree to move following hours of detailed discussions at Seville's King Alfonso Hotel.

The approach to Ramos was not made public in England until the Sunday, yet bookmakers Coral suspended betting on Jol as the next Premier League manager to be sacked after they were alarmed by a series of large transactions in quick succession in the early morning. Although they reopened the book later in the day, a spokesman for the betting company said that they were forced to take precautionary measures after becoming concerned at the "unusual timing" of the punts. The FA would be contacting Coral to ask them for any information relating to the suspension of betting. Under the new licensing system which forms part of the 2005 Gambling Act, all bookmakers will have to share details of suspicious betting patterns with sports governing bodies from September 1. But with the FA determined to avoid a major betting scandal, officials were hopeful they will volunteer to hand over any relevant evidence which will help them decide whether to launch a full investigation. An FA spokesman added that they would also be contacting internet betting exchange Betfair, with whom the FA have a memorandum of understanding to share information, to see if they experienced any similar irregularities.

Mido aimed a parting shot at Spurs when he complained about an unhealthy amount of politics at White Hart Lane, but backed Jol to prosper at his former club. Mido spoke out after completing a £6m move to Middlesbrough that brought to an end a two-year association with the London club. "Tottenham is a club with a lot of politics around the team," he said. "It's not healthy to have this amount of politics. In this club there is not a lot of politics around the team. One of the big reasons I came here was because I thought it would be about football rather than about team politics." Mido suggested Tottenham's first XI is not necessarily picked on merit. He was also eager to quash suggestions that he had fallen out with Jol, who, at times, questioned the Egyptian's fitness levels. "I've never had a problem with Martin Jol," he said. "I believe he's a good manager and I think he's done really well in the last two years. But I wanted to be playing, I wanted a big role in the team. I'm very confident Boro can get into Europe," he added. "I don't see Middlesbrough as being at a lower level than Tottenham."

Saturday, August 18

After Spurs' first points of the season, Jol insisted that nobody from the board had spelled out that he had to finish the season in the top four and reach the Champions League qualifying round. But after an emphatic 4-0 win over Derby, Jol became aware that the next morning's headlines would feature his impending demise.

A double inside seven minutes from Steed Malbranque and goals from Jermaine Jenas and Darren Bent saw off the newly promoted hopefuls, Jol said: "That is a relief for everybody. In this business, you need results. It's horrendous that you can be under pressure after just two results but next week, it will be someone else's turn and that is a good thought."

Well, unfortunately for Jol, it wasn't going to be someone else's turn. In fact, it was going to get even worse.

Still oblivious to the extent of the Sunday paper revelations Jol saluted the likes of Malbranque and Jenas, who were both targeted by Spurs fans during the midweek defeat by Everton. The Tottenham manager said: "Those two players had to show they were mentally strong and they were. They were feeling the pressure and they stood up to it and it was great that they did it for the fans. I think the fans also showed that whatever is said, they are right behind the team. It was a great start to the game and we needed that. I think we can develop into a real force again. But you put the pressure on yourself in this business as well. And next week, I will be putting myself under pressure to get a result."

As journalists knew of the next morning's headlines, Jol was quizzed about his position. He said: "I thought there were whispers last year – and there are whispers at any club all the time. I don't know if I'm being undermined. I don't think so, but you never know."

Jol had finished the game waving to the fans – was it to be a fond goodbye to the Lane?

Sunday, August 19

I was in the Sky studios in Isleworth early morning for a sporting slant on the Paper Review on the day which revealed the true extent of Spurs' pursuit of Juande Ramos.

The People carried pictures that had appeared in the Spanish press of Ramos holding talks on a Tottenham move, with a number of other Sunday papers also splashing their back pages with the story.

The game was up – there was no hiding the fact that Spurs had approached Ramos even though it was through an intermediary.

Live on Sky, I stressed the importance of staying loyal to Jol who has the potential to become the best Spurs boss since Bill Nicholson. I also expressed my concern about the credibility of Ramos who has been throwing himself at Premiership clubs likely to agree a massive hike in his Seville salary. He had been linking himself to Chelsea and my point was that, however much Roman Abramovich had fallen out with Jose Mourinho over his beloved striker Andrij Shevchenko, at the end of the season, the Russian owner had opted to stick with the Portuguese coach. Similarly, I suggested, that would be the best course of action for the Spurs board.

Ramos is a very good coach, however. He had guided Sevilla to five trophies in the last two seasons, including back-to-back UEFA Cups. His side crushed Real Madrid 5-3 to complete a 6-3 aggregate win in the Spanish Super Cup and also had one foot in the Champions League group stage after a 2-0 win over AEK Athens in the first leg of their third qualifying round tie.

Tottenham responded to the stories by insisting they had not made an approach despite reports over the weekend claiming a delegation from the club met with Ramos at a Spanish hotel on Friday. A Tottenham spokes-woman said: "Our secretary John Alexander was there for a private meeting and we are not in negotiations with anybody to replace Martin at this current time. We are a club looking to finish in the top four, but when results are as they have been, we would expect speculation."

Ramos, 52, insisted he did not hold talks behind Jol's back. He said: "I totally deny that I met with any Tottenham representative. Is there any evidence that demonstrates the contrary? It's totally false. I was with one friend in two hotels and I'm only shown leaving and in my car. I didn't speak to anyone about Tottenham or any other team. It's true I was in the hotel as I went to see a friend who has nothing to do with football and who happened to be in Seville on a visit. But there was no meeting about Tottenham."

Jol's relationship with Levy was said to be at an all-time low following a series of clashes with sporting director Damien Comolli. Matters came to a head after the opening-day defeat at Sunderland when £16.5m summer signing Darren Bent was left on the bench. The Board hoped to see an expansive performance that would sweep away newly-promoted opponents and send out a signal of intent for the season. Instead, a row developed. Berbatov expressed his anger at being substituted, Jol responded that he had not been playing well and spoke to Levy about the dispute. Levy was upset that the coach and the team's coveted new hero were at loggerheads right from the start of the new season.

The meeting with Ramos' advisors was set up through Paul Kemsley, who made contact with London-based property developer Tony Jimenez, a man with interests in Seville and who had been acting as UK agent for Ramos. Jimenez – the man pictured alongside Ramos in the Seville hotel – was even in touch with Manchester City a few months earlier, but the club were then in the middle of their takeover. Levy and Comolli flew in to southern Spain from London, along with Spurs secretary John Alexander, who has responsibility for contracts. Kemsley arrived from the south of France, where he had been on holiday. Ramos delivered his blueprint for Spurs' future and making them a Champions League team. He agreed that he was happy to work under Comolli as long as he retained responsibility for coaching and team selection and had a big say in the recruiting of players. The Spurs delegation made it plain, however, that they were not yet in a position to offer him the job. The meeting broke up, the Spurs contingent satisfied that Ramos would be a good appointment in the near future. Levy and Comolli left by the back door, while Kemsley and Alexander were caught in the flashlights at the front. And then the next thing anyone knew Ramos was telling the Spanish press of a 'dizzying' offer he had received by Spurs.

Now the Spurs board had a problem. They knew Jol was popular among the fans and was liked by most of the players, even if there were rumblings from within that certain Comolli favourites were not being selected. This was what the Egyptian striker Mido was referring to when he spoke of 'politics' around the team before he joined Middlesbrough. And anyway, they hadn't actually offered Ramos the job.

Ramos was playing a dicy game. After revealing the news, within hours he was retracting the statement, claiming he had been misinterpreted. It was fairly clear that Spurs had contacted Ramos to stress their displeasure and the result was an exercise in damage limitation.

He also claimed he wanted to see Sevilla through qualifying into the Champions League proper and fulfil the club's European Super Cup match against Milan in Monaco, and would later say that he wanted to see out the remaining year of his contract to the summer of 2008.

This was interpreted by many as the canny Spaniard trying to force an enhanced package, either at Sevilla, Tottenham, or any other club that may enter into the race to sign him up.

Monday, August 20

The media stepped up the story of Jol's impending departure with tales of a rift with Berbatov. It was suggested that Jol had stunned Levy a week earlier by wanting to sell his star striker and it was Jol's astonishing outburst which prompted Levy to sound out Ramos.

The back biting reached its height with speculation that a number of Spurs players expressed their dismay over Jol's team selections and tactics, especially away from home. Many believe Jol has certain favourites chosen to the detriment of the team. Matters had come to a head when Jol hauled off last season's 23-goal top scorer Berbatov during the 1-0 opening-day defeat at Sunderland. Berbatov reacted angrily to the decision, prompting Jol to seek a meeting with Levy on the following Monday to demand the Bulgarian hitman's sale.

Jol argued Berbatov was not a team player and had to go. But Levy, who had already rejected a bid from Manchester United for the striker, insisted that Berbatov stayed. Levy was then convinced changes had to be made.

Berbatov, though, denied a rift with Jol. Berbatov's agent Emil Dantchev categorically denied a fall-out between player and coach, saying: "I can tell you for sure is that there is not a problem."

Sevilla rubbished claims of Ramos' departure from the Ramon Sanchez Pizjuan stadium: "From the club's point of view, Ramos has one year left on his contract with Sevilla. There is no doubt that we want him to continue."

Sevilla's stance was understandable as Ramos had become the most successful coach in the club's history, leading them to five trophies in 15 months.

Tuesday, August 22

Jol held showdown talks at the Tottenham training ground.

Levy sat with Comolli and the directors to discuss home truths with Jol and his assistant Chris Hughton. The lines of power are clearly defined. Levy sought to justify his move for Ramos as Spurs publicly acknowledged meeting Ramos. "We want Champions League football at White Hart Lane," he said. "We, the board, owe it to the club and the supporters to constantly assess our position and performance and to ensure that we have the ability to operate and compete. For that we need our management and coaching standards to be of the highest quality, such that players can fulfil their potential and we can compete with the best." Now at least it was clear what Jol must achieve. Top four or out.

Jol responded by saying: "I fully understand the board's ambition. It is realistic and I have assured the board that is what I shall aim for. Yes, it is pressure to deliver – but that is what we managers expect."

Levy and his fellow board members told the manager they wanted him to show more ambition. They had felt for some time that he was failing to be ambitious enough. They also believed that if Champions League football is out of reach with the existing personnel, then it would be right to explore other options. In his structure the first-team coach is more expendable.

At the showdown meeting, Jol was told it was his first priority to strike an immediate truce with Berbatov. Spurs' chiefs were determined to get Berbatov to sign a lengthy new contract as they regard the powerful striker as the jewel in their crown and did not want a repeat of the situation which had seen Michael Carrick depart the previous summer. Jermain Defoe was another problem. The England striker had refused all offers of a new contract and Spurs believed he planned to let his current agreement run down and leave as a free agent in 2009. That would cost them a considerable sum if they could not sell him.

Sevilla chairman Jose Maria Del Nido ordered his own summit with Ramos. The Sevilla supremo demanded to know if Ramos was intending to quit if offered the Spurs hotseat. Del Nido said: "With a view to ending all the rumours – which seem to have come from England – I wish to announce Juande will continue at Sevilla until 30 June 2008 at least. The coach is going to fulfil his contract. All the speculation that he is going to leave Sevilla is false. With this statement I hope to end once and for all the talk of our coach leaving – because he is not. He looked me in the eyes and told me so and shook my hand. His professionalism demands he cannot leave the team in the lurch three days from the start of the season."

Wednesday, August 23

Conspiracy theorists held that Tottenham still believed that they can appoint Ramos later in the season, regardless of his pledge to see out his current contract at Seville until next summer.

Meanwhile, in a contradictory explanation of events, Ramos said that he had met only with a 'mediator' at the Hotel Alfonso XIII on Friday evening who would then speak to Tottenham. Given that he had met at least the Spurs director Paul Kemsley and club secretary John Alexander, it would appear that Ramos was, at the very least, confused as to exactly who from Tottenham he was meeting with.

Spurs posted a brief communiqué on their website just before 10.30am. "To further clarify the situation – the club wished to make it clear and unequivocal that no individual was or has been offered the position of manager-coach at this club while that position has been held by Martin Jol. It is wholly inaccurate and inappropriate to suggest otherwise."

But before midday, UK time, Ramos appeared at Sevilla's training ground to say he was staying despite receiving an offer from Spurs. Although a squirming Ramos initially sought to deny everything, claiming that he could not understand what all the "fuss" was about, he ended by confessing to having had indirect contact with Spurs. He said that he had not met with Alexander and Kemsley at the Alfonso XIII hotel, despite photographic evidence published by the *Estadio Deportivo* newspaper on Saturday. "I wasn't in a meeting with anyone. What happened was that I met with a person and that person went on to meet other people from Tottenham," Ramos said. Asked if that person then communicated an offer to him, Ramos admitted: "Yes, yes, yes. They made an excellent, dizzying offer to me."

One final question mark hung over the translation of the word 'mare-ante', which literally means '[sea] sick-inducing' and is used to refer to an offer so big as to be staggering or mind-blowing – 'dizzying'.

The seeming disarray at Tottenham deepened with Robinson labelling the club 'ridiculous'. There were fears that Berbatov wanted a transfer to Manchester United, whose search for a new forward had become increasingly desperate over the past few days due to the injury picked up by Wayne Rooney. The Bulgarian international was injured, but there was a belief at Spurs that his poor form in the first two games was linked to his disillusionment at not being granted permission to leave. The club were confident of keeping him past the close of the transfer window in eight days' time. However, his state of mind became one more worry.

Jol had to fight to keep control of his own dressing room after being so spectacularly undermined by his bosses. Former White Hart Lane boss Gerry Francis, who managed Tottenham from 1994-97, said: "The players have to know you are the one in power, that you are in control and in authority. Events of the last few days have seen that taken away from Martin Jol. If anything, this statement from Tottenham puts serious doubts over him and asks more questions than it answers. The players will now be wondering 'How long will this bloke be in charge for? Is there going to be a change soon?'. That erodes authority for Jol. Particularly now he is going to have to drop some big-name players given the squad he has got. You need to feel empowered to do that. Players like Jermain Defoe – who don't play much under him but who are England internationals – will be wondering how long Jol has left and it won't do anything to help the boss. If I was a manager and my club had come out with a statement like that I would be extremely disappointed."

Former Spurs captain Graham Roberts reckoned fans may still see Ramos at White Hart Lane. He said: "I don't think they will give up on Ramos. It's whether they can afford him and make him an offer he can't refuse. If they can get Ramos then I think it would be a great forward move. But let's give Martin a chance and hope he will turn it around."

Thursday, August 24

Levy insisted Jol has his "100 per cent support", after turning down the opportunity of appointing ex-Real Madrid coach Fabio Capello, one of the world's leading managers, to replace the incumbent coach in the latest twist in Tottenham's managerial soap opera.

Rumours were rife that Capello had been sounded out about the Tottenham job after he was pictured in London. Leading sports lawyer, Mel Goldberg, who was also pictured and who has strong links with a number of football clubs, contacted Levy about Capello. Goldberg told me: "There has been a lot of press speculation about Spurs and their manager. So I contacted Daniel Levy on Wednesday and asked him if he wanted a meeting with Capello, as he was available in London and could have a meeting. Daniel Levy sai: 'No, I've got a manager, I don't need to meet him.' I did meet Capello today, Spurs did not set up the meeting, it was not at Spurs' request, I was meeting him about something else."

A Spurs insider told me: "There are a number of people allegedly claiming to represent a number of coaches who have contacted us in the last few days. But they have all been politely but firmly told we are not interested, we already have a manager and do not intend to change him."

Levy went public on Spurs official website to declare his full backing for Jol. Levy told the fans: "No-one has been offered a job either now or in the preceding nearly three years that Martin has been manager. Martin has my 100 per cent support and I'd like the fans to understand that they need to take the last few days in the context of what we think has been significant progress over the last six years. It has not been the best few days but you have got to put it into the context of six years of progress and as far as I am concerned the whole matter is behind us now. Martin and I have all the confidence that we can move this club forward again. No change would be made on the basis of two or three results and I have every confidence that no change will be required and Martin will continue to bring us success. We had a very open meeting and I think it was long overdue on a number of issues that we needed to bring out into the open. Following that meeting I think we are stronger and we're both going in the same direction. We both want success and Martin has assured me that I've got his 100 per cent commitment and I've given it to him."

Friday, August 24

Jol mocked the events of the previous week when, in his first full scale press conference commented: "If my missus would go to Spain and I would see pictures of her I'd be gutted," he said. "But I always realised that she would come back because she speaks French, Dutch, English but no Spanish, so she can't talk to the bugger."

Jokes apart, Jol had a serious message for the Tottenham directors: "It's a big gamble to go for somebody else at this time because I felt that I gave the chairman a lot of continuity, stability and he feels that as well. They told me they were very happy with what we achieved and they better be because before me there were not a lot of managers who did the same. You can't deny we've gone in the right direction. If I had said to the chairman: 'OK, I give you two top fives', he would have laughed at me, but we did that. I've got a great job and there are other people with more problems than I have."

Jol insisted that he did not feel betrayed. "They could have done it last year, they could have done it two years ago, three years ago. When I started the chairman said to me after two games that he couldn't sleep any more, he was very worried. I had to talk to him, to relax him."

Jol and his captain, Robbie Keane, had to brave a blizzard of awkward questions during the scheduled media day at the club's training ground in

Chigwell the Friday before Sunday's showdown with Manchester United, who had started the season equally badly and were without a win themselves in the opening three games.

Major question marks persisted regarding Jol's relationship with Comolli, but Jol remarked: "We've got a big scouting system. I'm the only one responsible for the footballers. That doesn't mean I don't have to argue with someone if players are coming in. It's no problem."

Jol accepted his fate will be decided results: "I'll take the stick but they [the players] will have to repair the damage. If we do well everything will be forgotten."

Martin Jol's wife roared down Luxborough Lane, swung her black BMW into the Tottenham training ground car park, pulled out a crisply-ironed white shirt and dashed in to see her husband. Jol admitted the past week had been one of the toughest of his career, but said that the 6,000 e-mails he had received in support from fans had made him want to stay. He added: "It was not the easiest of weeks, but as a manager you know you have good times and bad times. The board never told me I had to quit and my relationship with Damien Comolli is a professional one. I tried to be realistic about the situation during the week. There are a lot of clubs in the same position and we finished in the top five twice. The pressure is a compliment. There are big expectations and before this there were big expectations as well, but it's difficult as everyone wants to do well."

But what of his relationship with the board? "They have high ambitions," said Jol. "If you finish fifth twice, of course you want to finish fourth. I said to the players at the start of the season that if we give 100 per cent and keep fit we can do even better. If you've watched me over the last three years, the directors have been giving me big hugs and wet kisses."

Sir Alex Ferguson and Arsene Wenger came out in support of embattled rival Jol and called on Levy to remain true to his word that the Spurs coach would not be sacked. Ferguson said: "It is no secret that I interviewed Martin Jol for the position as my No2 when Carlos Queiroz left to go to Real Madrid as manager. Martin had an outstanding record in Holland where he worked with very meagre resources. He does not need me to tell him what a good job he has done. It has all been very sad and a knee-jerk reaction to Tottenham's bad start to the season. The chairman has said his full support is behind the manager and I just hope the support is right. There's only Tottenham who scored more than three goals in one game in the first two weeks of the season – and they're the team getting the most criticism. The only difference between me and Martin Jol is that I have been here 20 years and he hasn't.

We hadn't won the League in 20-odd years when we went into the 1992/93 season and Spurs haven't won it in 40-odd years. At most football clubs these days, there are four or five directors and another 35 hangers-on who all claim to have a voice. United had it, a little group we used to call the second board. They would meet in the Grill Room at Old Trafford every Monday and discuss the weekend result. It's not nice for any manager to put up with criticism when it has started in that way and I am afraid Tottenham seem to me to have more of these people than most other clubs."

Wenger accused Spurs of 'impatience' in heaping so much pressure on Jol. The Arsenal boss said: "You cannot decide that after two games. I'm not in the best position to make any comment on Tottenham but we are in a modern impatient world."

Michael Carrick was staggered by what has happened to his old boss: "Nothing should shock you in football these days but this has. It's incredible and unbelievable the week he has had to go through. Before he got the job, Spurs had been up and down, good and bad, but in the past two seasons, they've done as well as anyone could have hoped. I don't know what else they could have asked from him. I had a great relationship with him and so did most of the other players. People have said that the dressing-room is not behind him but you don't get results like the ones we had when I was there if the players are not getting on with the manager."

Sunday, August 26

Jol faced another barrage of Sunday newspaper back page headlines.

The *Sunday Telegraph* carried an interview with director Sir Keith Mills, who said that shareholders had a right to expect their club to finish higher than last season's fifth place. Mills said: "For the club to expect to do only as well as last year is unacceptable. If you run a large plc and you tell your shareholders you will do the same next year, they get pretty disappointed. They like to see improvement. Martin Jol has done an excellent job over the past two or three years and it's perfectly reasonable for any club to want to do even better. If you don't perform in any sporting environment, you get called into question. In that respect Martin is no different to anyone else."

Mills, a non-executive director of Tottenham Hotspur plc and member of the plc board, blamed the press: "The media have done an enormous disservice to the club in mis-reporting what has been going on because 90 per cent of it is garbage."

Mills also helped mastermind the London Olympic bid and is deputy chairman of the 2012 organising team. He added: "I'm a director of the club and I know what happens and what doesn't happen. The media have totally over-reacted. The speculation that the club would consider making changes after two games is rubbish. What I have read is not remotely close to the briefings I have had. Managers, players and chief executives are only as good as their performance. I've been involved in lots of sports. If my America's Cup skipper or chief executive, for instance, doesn't do the business, we change. We set very high goals at Tottenham and we'll see how the season goes. We have probably the best team we've had for a decade and have invested the time, effort and money to get to where we are."

The situation was further complicated by an interview given to the *News of the World* newspaper by Paul Kemsley who, for the first time, explained why he and a Tottenham delegation, now also understood to have included Levy and sporting director Damien Comolli, were in Spain. Kemsley's explanation was that he was in the same hotel as Sevilla Ramos as a contingency against Jol leaving. "I liken it to being married to a beautiful woman – it's wonderful to have a beautiful wife but it can make you feel insecure and worried that you might lose her," said Kemsley. "That's how I feel about Martin."

Kemsley also claimed he was in Spain for another reason; that he wanted to discuss Sevilla's model for success.

The People carried speculation the Jurgen Klinsmann could front an American takeover of the club and return to White Hart Lane as coach. The former German international striker had become a cult hero with the fans during two playing spells at White Hart Lane and had been enjoying a quiet life in California since leaving his post as manager of Germany after the 2006 World Cup.

And then there was the football. Manchester United went into their encounter with Tottenham in 19th position, one point ahead of bottom-placed Derby County. Spurs were only a point better off themselves.

The game was barely five minutes old when Jol strode into the Old Trafford technical area and prompted the first chant of a sustained show of support for him from the Spurs fans shoehorned into the away section. 'In Jol we trust' read one of the many banners backing the manager in the away end. The support for Jol was relentless and Tottenham's impressive and committed display was proof that, while the Board at White Hart Lane have misgivings, they are not shared by their fans and playing staff.

Jol observed: "My players showed they are for me with this display, and they showed they will do anything for this club. Jol's side did not quite do enough for a first Tottenham victory at Old Trafford since December 1989, but his team left the pitch to rapturous applause from their own fans.

Manchester United's latest Portuguese teen sensation rescued their Premier League title defence from the brink of oblivion at Old Trafford. With United looking set for a point at best from their pulsating tussle with their fellow crisis club, Nani repaid the first portion of his £17m fee, belting a sensational winner past Robinson from 30 yards with the ball taking a deflection in mid-flight off the head of Carlos Tevez, enough to take it away from Robinson.

Spurs had good shouts for a couple of penalties too, which were not given, but even so three defeats in four games looked ominous for a manager charged with qualifying for the Champions League, but on the evidence of this performance it was difficult to question his support in the dressing room or in the stands.

Jol pleaded to be allowed to get on with the job, saying: "The close watchers know where we have come from, in terms of last year, the year before and the year before that. Let me get on with the job and we will be fine."

Monday, August 27

Alan Hansen wrote in his *Daily Telegraph* column: 'In Martin Jol's case, defeat brings him another big step towards what would be a completely undeserved sacking. When you consider the job he has done, where he has taken Tottenham, the players he has assembled and the product on the pitch that was evident yesterday, the pressure on him is ludicrous. You will not find any side outside the Big Three who will come to Old Trafford and play as well as Tottenham did yesterday.'

Hanson went on to describe the impact of yet another major referring decision as he thought it was definitely handball. 'Ferguson knows it will be forgotten in six days but for Jol the consequences could be horrendous. For one reason or another, the board at White Hart Lane have decided he is not the man to take them forward, which is utter folly. Tottenham have not made the top four since 1990 and with the players he has assembled Jol must be the one to take them forward.

Tuesday, August 28

Jol warned Levy that he could end up with another Jacques Santini if he replaces him as manager by pointing out that if Spurs replace him with a manager who doesn't speak much English – as Juande Ramos does not – they could have similar difficulties to those they experienced with Santini.

Jol said: "If someone else wants to come to Spurs and can promise the board they can get into the top four then good luck to them, but I think I have done a good job. But if you go for top managers and they don't know the language you can have a big, big problem. Tottenham have experienced this before."

Asked if he was confident he will still be in a job next month he replied: "we'll see".

Tottenham banned the *Evening Standard* from covering home matches and press conferences after a series of articles from Spurs fan and sports columnist Matthew Norman which were highly critical of Levy. A Tottenham spokesperson said: "Evening Standard journalists will not be granted access to press conferences and matches. Please note that this decision has been taken by the club's management board, not in haste and at a time when quite simply enough is enough. The timing of this is in no way related to comments generated as a result of the past few days' events – Matthew Norman's personal attacks continue regardless of what happens at the club."

Thursday, August 30

Tottenham's sporting director Damien Comolli claimed the crisis that enveloped Spurs was over – and that there are no problems between him and Jol. Comolli said: "I have had always a very good relationship with Martin and it has never stopped."

It is accepted that the pair have heated discussion about players and have a professional rather than friendly relationship. Comolli said: "I don't know where this is coming from because from the day I started I have had always a very good relationship with Martin and it has never stopped. I don't think we could have worked the way we have been working, and brought in the players of the quality we have, if we didn't have a relationship. For me it's not even a subject to talk about. What happened last week is behind us. We have said everything we want to say about that and we want to move forward and look towards our Premier League game tomorrow because we need the points. It's in the past, it's all done and dusted."

Friday, August 31
Tottenham drew Cypriot side Anorthosis Famagusta in today's UEFA Cup draw, with the first leg tie at White Hart Lane. Spurs benefited from being seeded and will be firm favourites to qualify for the group stages. On transfer deadline day, Spurs missed out on West Brom defender Curtis Davies, who instead moved to Aston Villa. Meanwhile Danny Murphy's proposed transfer to Sunderland collapsed over his wage demands. The Black Cats agreed a fee with Tottenham of £1m, for the 30-year-old midfielder. But Murphy demanded £20,000 a week to move to the Stadium of Light and Roy Keane faxed Spurs officials to inform them the deal was off. Instead Murphy signed on loan for London rivals Fulham just before the midnight deadline.

Saturday, September 1
After Tottenham blew a two-goal lead at Fulham, Jol described himself as a "strong f***er," and conceded: "I hate it when the manager of the opposing team says we were the best team to play them in the last five or six months but we end up not getting what we deserve. I took a chance again. Bale and Kaboul came in, Dawson was 80 per cent. If it comes off everyone can see we could end up with a wonderful team. But we are not there yet. I think we are fine. You can't expect us to be a 100 per cent team overnight. We ended up in the top five last season and we had fewer points at this stage than we have now. Can we make the top four? You'll have to wait and see. The top four will have a say about that. If they play well it will be difficult. If not, like Liverpool three years ago when Everton were fourth, why not?"

Yet another defining moment for Jol's managerial decision making came after 68 minutes when Spurs were 3-1 ahead and in total control. Skipper Robbie Keane was taken off as Jol sent on Defoe. Keane seemed bemused after a slow walk off the pitch.

Asked why he had hauled off his skipper, Jol said: "In terms of our shape nothing changed. Jermain was very hungry in training so I thought with all the space we had he could do something. Robbie did not have the best of games, although he was involved in two of the goals. I could see Robbie was not happy but he shook my hand. He's my captain and he knows Jermain is an important part of the squad. We should have held the ball better and then we would have killed them off. I wouldn't have changed things otherwise. If you score three goals and play that well you should end up with a win."

But then, after Smertin's freak deflected strike reduced arrears again, Jol shot himself in the foot as he made the sort of negative substitution the board have been beefing about. He sent on Michael Dawson, went five at the back, and encouraged the late home siege rewarded by Kamara's over-head-kick stunner right on the whistle.

Former Spurs midfielder Simon Davies said: "They should have put their chances away and killed us off. Keano is always a clever player and he causes teams problems, so he did us a favour in going off."

Jol said he had given his players a rocket for their awful defending. But there was also much to admire in a topsy-turvy performance. His side had played some sublime football in establishing their lead and also had been guilty of missing some straight-forward chances after some scintillating approach play.

A game that should have been won easily turned into yet another reason to sack him. The fans, who for most of the game were gleefully chanting: "I love Martin Jol" ended up starting to see the board's point of view. Spurs were so much better than Fulham so the supporters and the Board came away feeling as if they had lost.

Levy might have regretted the way he and his board went about trying to replace Jol, but the Spurs chairman left Craven Cottage without talking to the Dutchman, with some of the reasons in favour of making a change resurfacing.

Sunday, September 2
Yet more misery for Jol with the name of Ronald Koeman touted as a potential successor.

Fredi Kanoute didn't waste any time putting the knife in. He criticised Jol's training techniques and claimed he is not as good a coach as his Seville boss Juande Ramos. He said: "Ramos and Jol are two serious coaches but the Spanish man is closer to the players. You can speak to him without problems but Jol is a more complicated character. I've done many training sessions with Jol shouting and I believe this is simply for him to demon-strate he's the boss. But I prefer a type of coach like Ramos. He develops entertaining training sessions, but during my time there with Jol, I was bored. For me the rumours surrounding the two men are no surprise. Ramos would be able to work for Tottenham or any other Premier League club."

Wednesday, September 5
Jol answered questions from fans in a forum in Enfield, and he was opti-mistic about staying at White Hart Lane. "I was very disappointed with

what happened, but I have moved on. I promise I'm not going anywhere. I have two years left on my contract and I would like to think that I will see those years out. I told the chairman that if I'm not sitting in the dug out I will be sitting in the stands as a fan because that's what I am. He won't get rid of me that easily. I used to wave at the fans quite quickly when they sang my name, but now I leave it a while so the board can see and hear it."

He confessed that his defence made him a bag of nerves as they couldn't defend set pieces. "I am shitting myself every time someone has a corner against us. We know it's not right, but we are working on it twice a week so it should get better. Our form does need to be sorted out, it's not good enough. I'm very very miserable because we have only won one of five games and it's not good enough."

Sunday, September 9
Another Sunday, and yet another name linked to the Spurs job in the footie gossip columns. This time it is Marcello Lippi, manager of Italy when they won the 2006 World Cup in Germany.

Wednesday, September 12
A fresh complication as it was revealed that Pascal Chimbonda was questioned by police on Monday. The 28-year-old full-back was interviewed by City of London police on suspicion of conspiracy to defraud and bailed until October. Jol said: "Pascal trained Monday and Tuesday, yesterday he was off so there is no issue. He will train today, so for me there's no problem." The City of London police are carrying out an investigation into corruption in football that is separate to the inquiry by Lord Stevens firm Quest.

Chimbonda was the second person to be arrested by the force's investigation team – a 61-year-old man was arrested in Manchester in March on suspicion of money laundering. In July, officers from the City of London police carried out raids at Newcastle, Portsmouth and Rangers and took away computers and documents. Deals involving Chimbonda's agent Willie McKay are also reported to be under investigation by officers but he has insisted repeatedly that he has done nothing wrong: "I think you will find that it is all a load of rubbish."

Berbatov stated that the Spurs camp were fully behind Jol: "The start to this season has been pretty much like the beginning of last season. That didn't go according to plan but look how we ended up. We finished fifth and I am sure we can push on this time around. No-one is worried. We have some great players and a real belief about us. Nothing will put us off. Everyone is behind the boss and we are ready to do even better.

People ask us if everything is back to normal now. But it has been normal all the time. There has never been any problem from inside the camp. We support each other. With a derby to play, everyone is ready. Did it surprise me what people were saying about Martin? None of us want to talk about that any more. We are all behind him. How many games are gone? Four? That is nothing and there is a long way to go. I am confident it will all work out."

Berbatov was still sick at missing last season's Carling Cup semi-final, second leg with an injury. Watching Spurs crash out to Wenger's kids ranks as one of the biggest disappointments of his career: "There is some unfinished business here," he said.

Thursday, September 13

Jol came out fighting, delivering his verdict on his team's results so far and he was damning. "I would give them five marks out of 10, maybe less," he said. Jol was adamant he was not feeling the pressure of lifting his team up from 14th place. Responding to a comment that his job was now at permanent risk, he replied: "I would say that for me there are no worries. I'm looking forward to the game and it's not up to me, I think it's up to the players. We want to make the supporters happy and for them it's a big game as well. For us it is an important game to get the points. I'm always relaxed. If you were in my position, in a couple of years' time I will tell you why I'm always relaxed."

Part of the reason for Spurs' failure to break into the top four had been Jol's inability to regularly beat Arsenal, Chelsea, Liverpool or Manchester United. In a little under three years in charge, Jol had only overseen one victory against those sides, a home win against Chelsea the previous season. Jol defended his record. "My record is OK – I've had a lot of draws against Man United, twice away. Chelsea, a draw and a win last year – but it would be nice to beat them. You have to beat big teams to do well otherwise we will always be in the top five or six like we were last year and the year before. But that is not enough. We want to do better."

Saturday, September 15

"It's so quiet at the Lane," chortled Arsenal's jubilant support even before the third goal, in added time, in their 3-1 victory, after the Gunners roared back from 1-0 down with 25 minutes to go. There was a stunned silence once Tottenham had lost a lead that, although undeserved, might have revived their season.

Jol was serenaded with "you're getting sacked in the morning" by the travelling Gooners, but later he insisted that results will come. Whether they arrive soon enough to save his job remained in doubt.

"I can only listen to what Daniel Levy is telling me," Jol said. "As long as we play good football and have the results, there's no problem. We'll get it right because I know my players. I will fight and they will fight."

Jol admitted missed chances from Berbatov and Bent cost Spurs dear as they capitulated late in a match for the third time this season, having already conceded crucial late goals at Sunderland and Fulham. "The difference between us and them was their clinical finishing. We had one-on-ones at 1-0, at 1-1 and then when we were 2-1 down but we didn't take them."

A trademark free-kick from Spurs' teenage star Gareth Bale gave the hosts the lead after 15 minutes before Adebayor equalised after 65 minutes. Stunning long-range strikes from Fabregas and Adebayor saw Arsenal comeback from a goal down to continue their unbeaten start and go top of the Premier League.

Asked once more whether Tottenham's bid to lure Ramos made his plight even more perilous, Jol joked: "It's like what I said about having a beautiful woman who might look at someone else. Maybe I need to make myself more pretty and buy a wig!"

Strangely bookmakers not only made Jol favourite to be the next Premiership manager sacked, but still had Tottenham the most likely side to finish fifth in the table.

In the main club shop they were selling 'Martin Jol – The Boss' T-shirts. Originally priced at £17.99, they were going for just £5.

Tuesday, September 18
Juande Ramos, the Sevilla coach, was in London, but with his mind concentrated on north London rivals Arsenal rather than White Hart Lane as Sevilla faced the Gunners in the Champions League. Sevilla were still in mourning over the recent death of the midfielder Antonio Puerta, and Ramos, embarking on his first Champions League season, made it clear he did not want to walk out mid-season.

Thursday, September 20
Incredibly Martin Jol was not the first managerial casualty in the Premier League after all. That distinction fell to Jose Mourinho.

"I felt a bit sad," Jol said. "I don't know the ins and outs, but I thought this fella was the jewel in the crown. He gave everybody a lot of excitement but he gave Chelsea a lot as well."

I appeared on phone-in programmes on BBC Radio 5Live, alongside *MOTD2* presenter Adrian Chiles, and witnessed a number of Spurs fans pledging unflinching loyalty to Jol, but also saying that the only manager they would swap their beloved Dutchman for would be Mourinho.

And, perhaps inevitably, during the next 48 hours the media was filled with stories that Levy had called Mourinho's agent, Jorge Mendes, five times in an effort to offer him a £5.2m annual salary to come to the Lane. Mourinho opted instead to finalise his pay off with Chelsea which included a clause that he couldn't join another Premiership club for a year.

That night saw a great start to the so-called five-game deadline to save Jol's job; a thumping 6-1 UEFA Cup win to raise the spirits at the Lane. Reports held that the board had given Jol the five matches until the next internatinal break, in October, to turn results around.

Younes Kaboul got the ball rolling with a fifth-minute header from a corner, then Dawson, Keane and Bent grabbed goals just before half-time. Defoe, who has been urged by Jol to show his commitment to Spurs by signing a new contract, grabbed his goals after coming on as a 63rd-minute replacement.

Jol hailed Defoe as the finest finisher in England following two goals against Anorthosis Famagusta, but insisted he could not guarantee him a place in his starting XI on Sunday. Defoe has not started a game this season and was not even on the bench against Arsenal at the weekend, but he made an instant impact when brought on in the first leg of the UEFA Cup first-round clash. He chipped home with his first touch before sealing that emphatic 6-1 win at White Hart Lane by finding the top corner in stoppage time. It puts him in contention to face Bolton. "Jermain is the best finisher in the league around the box," said Jol. "But Robbie Keane is probably our top scorer over the last two years and there are another two strikers. I'm very happy that they are all here. There is no guarantee for any player. I will look at each game separately. Bolton is a different game."

Sunday, September 23
Jol was naturally in a prickly mood after his Spurs side yet again surrendered a lead, this time at strugglers Bolton. Talk of Ramos or Mourinho taking his job and a place in the bottom three caused irritation. "There is a joke in London now that he is the Special One, but he's not that special,"

said Jol, discounting Mourinho's ability to give Tottenham the Champions League place demanded of their manager. "It would be a hell of a job and he knows it. Daniel Levy phoned me and said all this talk of him pursuing Mourinho is rubbish and that he hopes I will be here with him next year."

In the 1-1 draw at Bolton, where Sammy Lee was also treading precariously after a difficult start to his tenure as Wanderers boss, there was a stay of execution for Jol and his counterpart, but little convincing evidence of a transformation that would rescue either manager. Wanderers did improve and Spurs impressed in brief spells but Jol continued to make life problematical for himself. Omitting Defoe from his travelling party, the striker reportedly livid having scored twice in the Uefa Cup, Jol also invited scorn from his supporters by leaving in-form Gareth Bale in the stands. "Gareth Bale played a lot of games last week and will have opportunities again, Jermain Defoe is the same," said Jol. "But if I leave Bale out as the 17th man he is still a joy to be around." Not so, Defore, presumably!

Keane was preferred to Defoe and made a telling contribution, putting Spurs ahead. In a flowing move Zokora floated a delivery to Jenas inside the area, the midfielder produced an instinctive shot which Jaaskelainen and Campo turned into the path of Keane. Ivan Campo equalised with a header just minutes later. Keane almost stole victory four minutes from time only to be denied by a fine Jaaskelainen save.

Tuesday, September 25
Levy issued a statement denying that a compensation package had been agreed for Jol to leave White Hart Lane. Levy insisted there has been no crisis meeting since the draw against Bolton. Levy said: "There has been no board meeting, let alone any emergency board meeting, and reports that we have agreed a compensation package with Martin are wholly inaccurate – we have not even discussed the subject and there is no reason to do so. We will not allow ourselves to be side-tracked or undermined by external agendas or media hype. Our focus is on winning games."

Wednesday, September 26
Jol warned that Tottenham could easily go into reverse if he is sacked after he gained some desperately needed breathing space as his side beat Middlesbrough 2-0 to reach the fourth round of the League Cup. "The fans know how difficult it is if they change management again, they know you could easily go back years," he said. "I hope people are realistic – you can

get anyone in the world to come here, but to do better you must finish fourth."

Late goals from Gareth Bale and Tom Huddlestone saw off a Boro team struggling to make an impression on the season, although an otherwise positive evening was marred by Jermain Defoe's angry reaction to being substituted with just over 20 minutes left.

Just 30 seconds had gone before Spurs fans were singing Jol's name. 'Give us a wave,' they demanded. When he did raise his fist in defiance, a bigger cheer reverberated around the rain-drenched Lane. But it turned sour when Defoe ignored his manager as he trudged off in disgust, a decision the fans did not take kindly to as he had seemed Spurs' most threatening player in a washout of a game to that point. But Jol said: "It's not about booing me. I have a decision to make, so I made it. We had stopped creating chances, so I had to make the change. I am in a good position here and that is what I deserve because I gave them a bit of success over the last two years and no-one could have done it better. Fear? No. I'm not one to fear things. In Holland they say 'Have no fear Joly is here!'"

Defoe's replacement, Keane, within a few minutes of his arrival, had set up Bale for the decisive first goal. Jol felt vindicated: "Five minutes after the boos, the fans were cheering. I want to win every game, so if Robbie Keane comes on and gets an assist everybody is happy.

People care about Jermain, I care about him as well, but I took him off to try and change the game and sometimes it comes off, sometimes it doesn't – this time it did. At the end everybody is happy because we won but it's not what you want, because I feel more for the people coming on than Jermain, because he had his chance today. He was sharp and he will be important in the future as Dimitar Berbatov will be and Darren Bent as well – though Darren was kept on the bench and will not be happy. But Robbie Keane is always very good as a substitute as well, he's proved that in the last couple of years that he can change games and he did it again."

The pandemonium in the stands when Spurs took the lead was matched by the pandemonium on the touchline as Jol did a jig of delight.

Friday, September 28

Daniel Levy admitted there is an 'element of truth' behind speculation surrounding Jol's future but insists the Dutchman has the squad and board-room backing for success. Levy said: "Obviously with any speculation sometimes there's an element of truth, but there has been a lot of stuff that's been written in the papers which has just been completely untrue. I think it's inevitable with the quality of players we have in this squad that when we're not performing on the pitch there's bound to be speculation. I've made it very clear that I very much want Martin to succeed, Martin is fully aware of our ambition, he also has got ambition – he just needs to get the results. I think we're all fairly thick-skinned if I'm honest, I just think Martin and the players need to ignore the outside pressure and just win, and that's what it's all about."

Monday, October 1

Sacked at half-time, a hero by the end, no one game could encapsulate more the season which Martin Jol and Spurs had been experiencing than the incredible 4-4 draw with Aston Villa.

The Lane echoed to home fans' jeers at half-time with Villa leading 3-1 as Jol looked set to be finally hounded out of Tottenham with Levy preparing to hand over his P45, but three goals in the last 22 minutes salvaged a point and spared the manager.

Characteristically, despite the tension of the past weeks in which he had perhaps been to forthcoming with his thoughts, Jol had not lost his sense of humour. Villa supporters, mocking the hosts' 125th birthday celebrations, sang "Happy birthday, dear Tottenham" after their third goal and also chanted: "You're getting sacked in the morning".

"When their supporters sang that it was the only time I had a smile on my face," Jol grinned afterwards. "That was a great bit of British humour. I don't want to even think what it would have been like to have lost on a night like this, the club's anniversary and with all the legends here."

Spurs took the lead through Dimitar Berbatov but Laursen's double – both of which were down to errors by Robinson – and Agbonlahor's coolly-taken third put Villa in control. O'Neill's side added a fourth after the break when Gardner beat Robinson with a free-kick. But then the fightback. Chimbonda scored Tottenham's second, Keane stroked home a penalty in the 82nd minute and Kaboul scored a stunning equaliser with seconds left on the clock.

After that goal the Tottenham players raced to the touchline to celebrate with Jol. "It's not about me but it was nice to celebrate with them," he said. "You should have seen him when we scored the goal," Keane said. "He had the support from everyone. He's shown what a good manager he is over the past couple of years. To come back from 4-1 down is unbelievable. You talk about dead and buried, but we showed lots of character. That's what we have in this team."

Jol could barely contain his emotions: "I don't know what to feel. It was awful but on the other hand it was a big celebration at the end. We came back from the death and that was a big positive. We could have won it at the end. That was a night about football. I don't want to talk about negative things. Before the game I told the team it wasn't about the League or results, it was about giving the supporters a celebration. We spoiled that, but I'm happy that in the end the fans had their celebration. I don't think they will ever forget this match. In the second half we said we had to play for the shirt and do everything we possibly could. I think we did that, though at 4-1 down it really felt horrible, to say the least. When we got back to 4-2 I started to believe that we might do something. We came back from the death and that was a big positive positive. I don't think I've ever been involved in a game like this."

The incredible fight-back proved there was nothing wrong with team-spirit in the Tottenham dressing room. A relieved Levy stood clapping in that upper tier.

Despite all that, Tottenham remained in the relegation zone with away games to follow against Liverpool and Newcastle United either side of the international break.

Thursday, October 4

Jol blamed a lack of communication among his young defenders and a lack of leadership on the pitch. "Of the last nine goals we've conceded, six have been from set pieces. We've tried to do something about it. If there's no leadership, that's a problem. But these players will never throw in the towel. My family were all in the Marines, so I know the commander never leaves his troops. If you do that, you lose. I had to keep my cool and they have to do the same. There was a lot of commitment and you could see their heart was in it. I was embarrassed to be 4-1 down, but everyone can see that the players fought for me. I am happy for the supporters because it was our anniversary. There was relief when the fourth goal went in. At 70 minutes I was feeling horrendous, but the flags came back out again. If we had lost on such a big night it would have been terrible in front of all these legends. This is a young team and I need time, but there is no problem."

Thursday, October 4

A late Robbie Keane goal, from yet another Gareth Bale cross, salvaged a draw and further potential embarrassment as Spurs made heavy work of disposing of Famagusta, a team they had hammered 6-1 just a fortnight earlier.

Fabio De Matos Pereira, known as Fabinho, had given the hosts the lead at the Antonis Papadopoulos Stadium. But Keane came off the bench to level on the night after the Premier League side had established a 6-1 lead from the first leg two weeks earlier. Losing the tie was never realistic and Jol looked as relaxed as he has been all season as Spurs created chances for Defoe in the first half. But he was more animated in the second half when Fabinho broke the deadlock – and then brought on Bale and Keane. At least Keane's strike meant Tottenham were unbeaten in five games since Arsenal defeated them.

As for suggestions Jol was feeling the heat, the manager responded: "I'm used to it, I have to cope with it. It's been going on for the last six or seven weeks – but I feel in the last month we have done well." Keane added: "I'm sick of people even talking about it to be honest. We are trying to do a job for the team and to get a result. It was good not getting beaten – we knew it would be tough. 6-1 flattered us a little bit in the first leg, but we did our job. The most important thing is we're through to the next round, so we go home happy enough."

Wednesday, October 17
Who would have thought it? Kemsley departs before Jol!

The board member so closely involved in the club's attempts to bring Ramos to White Hart Lane, resigned from the football club board toward the end of the international break. The club confirmed to the stock exchange that Kemsley, a property developer and close friend of former Spurs chairman Sir Alan Sugar, stepped down with immediate effect.

In 2006 Kemsley had resigned from the board of the Tottenham Plc. His total severing of ties with the club comes just eight weeks after he joined a delegation that travelled to Seville to try and persuade Juande Ramos to succeed Jol. Kemsley was also closely involved in the club's plans for a bigger stadium, and responsible for buying up numerous properties around White Hart Lane in preparation for a potential redevelopment of the ground.

Daniel Levy insisted that Kemsley's departure was amicable and that he wants to concentrate on his business interests in the US. Sources played down the significance of Kemsley's resignation, insisting that Levy and club finance director Matthew Collecott are in day-to-day charge of the club and will oversee plans for stadium expansion.

Tottenham announced record profits of £27.7m thanks to a second successive fifth place in the Premiership, a place in the quarter-finals of the FA Cup and the UEFA Cup, and the semi-final of the Carling Cup. Yet, there wasn't a single mention of Jol. I understand the reason was that Levy felt anything he might say would be misinterpreted. What cannot be denied is that, after all the storm surrounding the club, Jol had emerged with a victory which seemed to give him the rest of the season in which to state his case where it matters, on the pitch, to either remain as manager of Tottenham Hotspur.

Monday, October 22

But was seeing off Kemsley a pyrrhic victory? After a timorous defeat at Newcastle, Jol seemed to be floundering amidst mounting evidence that change was what was needed at White Hart Lane.

Still, though, he continued his campaign of bluster aimed at shouting his own achievements from the rooftops. According to Jol, for example, Tottenham's success over the last two seasons means they are streets ahead of tonight's opponents Newcastle. Jol felt that consecutive top-five finishes meant Spurs have already reached the heights that teams such as Newcastle aspire to. "We had European football for the last two years and they didn't," Jol said. "Why would they be in the same boat? It would be fantastic for them if they were in the first six or seven – playing European football next season would be a good achievement for them. We already did that twice so it's different. We are in the group stages of the UEFA Cup and they would love to do that as well."

When asked about his own tenuous position and the fact that he had survived the two week international break, he added, in a barbed aside: "Everybody was wrong," said Jol. "I'm not someone who doubts. It's confidence, but it's to do with what happened in the past – the results. We are in the last 16 of the Carling Cup, we are in the UEFA Cup and there are a lot of clubs who would like to do the same. There are peaks and troughs, one day you are marvellous the next day look at Robbie Keane [getting criticised] with Ireland, look at Steve McClaren, look at me."

At St James' Park, Spurs were comprehensively outplayed by Newcastle United leaving them with only one win from their ten Premier League fixtures and none in the seven since dispatching hopeless Derby County. Again their defending was wretched. The result made Mike Ashley, the Newcastle owner, £100,000 richer, a consequence of his charity bet with Paul Kemsley, the former Spurs vice-chairman. The two men sat beside each other, wearing their respective colours, in the directors' box.

Spurs fans continued to chant the Dutchman's name on Tyneside, but patience was wearing thin. Worse still Berbatov was visibly miffed on the substitutes' bench, appeared to refuse to warm up when asked to by the manager and he ignored Jol's outstretched hand at the end.

According to Setanta's touch-line reporter, it was only at the third time of asking that Berbatov acceded to Jol's request to warm up in the second half. That claim was rebuffed by the manager. "There is no problem with him," Jol said. "He knows what the schedule is for the next few weeks. I don't know where this sort of rubbish is coming from."

Jol's cause was not helped by Gareth Bale's departure early in the first half with a foot injury that will require a scan. "Even when we play well, we seem to concede goals," Jol said. "You saw the first one – a long ball to a small striker; the second a corner kick. Before the game we tell them who to pick up, but... disastrous."

Before Martins opened the scoring, Faye struck the woodwork and Owen was thwarted by Radek Cerny as Newcastle, supposeldy miles behind Spurs, dominated. With the interval approaching, Enrique thumped a long pass down the right channel that Dawson misjudged, allowing Martins to gain possession and shoot. The ball touched Cerny's trailing leg en route, but a more significant deflection would only have masked Tottenham's imperfections. Dawson's response to another fizzing corner from Emre in the 51st minute was sluggish, with Caçapa rising above him to head with power and conviction.

Finally, Spurs roused themselves. Darren Bent met a deep centre from Chimbonda with a fine header that thudded against the left post, with Keane racing forward to prod the ball home bringing his haul to seven goals. It was now that Berbatov appeared, but it was another replacement who made the decisive intervention. Milner took two attempts, one on either foot, to thump a volley past Cerny.

"If everybody comes back, we have a very good team, but they lack leadership and mental strength," Jol said. "We have had it in the past, but it isn't there." For Newcastle, it was their most accomplished start to a season for 11 years, although they remain eighth in the Premier League. Spurs, by contrast, were impotent. "When things are going badly for the other team, you've got prey on that," Allardyce said. "They've changed their style a bit, but we coped with it. Confidence disappears when you score against the opposition and you could see their confidence draining."

Tim Sherwood ripped into Tottenham's sloppy defence. The former Spurs skipper is now an analyst with Setanta Sports and heavily criticised his old club's back four after the 3-1 defeat at St James' Park. Tottenham had leaked 21 goals in ten Premier League matches and that's more than the combined total conceded by the top four in the division. Sherwood believes Spurs should have bought an experienced defender to cover for the absence of King during the close season and he does not believe France Under-21 prospect Kaboul is ready to shoulder the responsibility of playing alongside Dawson.

He was also openly critical of two players, saying: "Younes Kaboul is a good footballer, but I'm not sure if he is a centre-half. Pascal Chimbonda is a right back who plays mostly for himself and not the team. It's good that he gets forward but they're not keeping clean sheets. I would have these guys back playing forwards versus defenders and getting used to playing with each other if I was Martin Jol. It's not evident if it does happen at the moment in terms of just working with each other. Michael Dawson and Kaboul don't look friendly with each other. Kaboul can score goals, but he's a centre-half."

Tuesday, October 23

Jol focused on turning Tottenham's season around, insisting it would be 'crazy' for him to be distracted by the uncertainty surrounding his future as the UEFA Cup provided a break from their miserable run in domestic football. As he prepared for the tie with Getafe, the bookies were pushing hard in promoting their list of potential successors.

Jol insists he still has the confidence of his squad, but wants to see anger from his players as they fight their way out of trouble. Jol revealed that he was furious with his players after the defeat to Newcastle when defensive lapses cost them again. "I told them: 'I'm angry with you, but you have to be angry with yourself,'" said Jol.

Jol had not spoken to Levy since Newcastle when he appeared to be undermined when Berbatov appeared reluctant to warm up. Jol denied any difference of opinion. "There is no issue," he said. "I always talk to him. If he's not playing well and not scoring goals or if he's playing well and scoring goals. I talked to him yesterday, but it was nothing to do with Newcastle."

Keeping Berbatov, Defoe and Bent happy, though, has proved difficult, especially as Keane's recent form means it is difficult to leave the Republic of Ireland striker out. "It is not easy to have good players and have to tell them they are not playing, but I think I am good at this job otherwise I would not be in this industry. It is more a matter of players having to do better. But I won't blame them if the mentality is good."

The question remained as to whether he could turn things round once again and elicit the kinds of performances which had built his reputation as one of the best coaches in the game from his players.

Thursday, October 25

It was a simple statement when it came: "For me, Martin and Chris's departure is regrettable," said chairman Daniel Levy. "Our greatest wish was to see results turn in our favour and for there to be no need for change."

And with that Martin Jol's tenure as manager of Tottenham Hotspur FC was over. But the turn of events which led to that official statement at 11.30pm, after Spurs had lost just their second ever home game in Europe, 2-1 to a sprightly Getafe side, themselves struggling in La Liga, was far from simple. In fact it was bordering on the incredible.

Viewers watching ITV's coverage of the UEFA Cup group match were treated to the spectacle of a manager sitting in the dugout, realising before the cameras from the reaction of his fans that he had been sacked. Astonishing.

When he spoke, late that night, Jol's statement was equally straightforward: "I want to thank the terrific staff and players. I shall never forget them."

But it was impossible to underplay this tale, which had reached its seemingly inevitable conclusion by the most tortuous route possible.

The credit for the breaking of the story fell to a *Times* journalist, Gary Jacobs, who, to use the Fleet Street vernacular, had stood it up via a couple of sources after learning of Spurs' approach to Gus Poyet to become Ramos's assistant. However spare a thought for the Fleet Street freelance reporter who had actually got the story a couple of hours before the *Times* man. He alerted a major national newspaper to the story who took it as their lead for the back page for the following morning's first editions. Meanwhile, over at the *Times*, a decision was taken not to wait for the newspaper to appear, the story was placed immediately on their website, from where news spread like wildfire just before the delayed kick-off at White Hart Lane. This was the *Times'* website effectively scooping its own newspaper, which would not appear for several hours. The old days of a Fleet Street editor holding their exclusive story back from a first edition so that the opposition would not be able to run with it in their later editions, died in that moment.

Sky Sports were the first to pick up the story and by 7.30pm it was running on their bulletins, while BBC Radio 5Live also had it confirmed by the end of their first half commentary from White Hart Lane. The crowd seemed to be in full knowledge of events. In fact the only people in the stadium who didn't know were Martin Jol, Chris Hughton, Clive Allen (who was installed as caretaker-manager for the interim period) and the players. An incredible set of circumstances that effectively saw the crowd, through their homage to Jol, tell the manager that he had been sacked. At least one could say that the ignominious end fitted perfectly with what had gone before.

There was immediate support for Jol in the shape of Getafe boss, former Danish international forward Michael Laudrup. "Given what he did last season I don't think he will have a problem finding a new job," said Laudrup after his side's win. Perhaps not surprisingly the rumour mill grounnd into instant action and Jol was linked with Dutch giant Ajax who found themselves without a permanent coach following Henk ten Cate's departure to Chelsea just a few days earlier.

The day had began with the *Sun* newspaper carrying a Mickey-taking item headlined 'Jol Gets the Boot', a not-so-amusing story on the morning of such an important UEFA Cup tie. The story revealed how Jol found himself unceremoniously 'booted out' of the new Spurs Monopoly board. The Spurs fans websites went into overdrive, a daily occurence in the last few months, full of inevitable speculation about Jol's precarious position as clearly – according to them – with a lead time of a few months on the production of the board game, the under-pressure manager had been left out many weeks previously by club officials, who clearly didn't expect him to remain in the job much longer. Jol's No. 2, Chris Hughton, though, kept his place in the Monopoly line-up, along with Ledley King, Dimitar Berbatov and Robbie Keane, while legendary double-winning manager Bill Nicholson had a spot.

That was how the papers told it and a source for Monopoly was quoted as saying: "The game has been produced as requested by Spurs. They sent their list of names a few weeks ago. There were a few raised eyebrows when Jol's name was left out."

However, my Spurs source later insisted: "This was typical of the kind of propaganda that was being used to hurt Martin. It just wasn't as the paper were making it out to be. Bill Nicholson was the only manager featured in the board game, not Glenn Hoddle, Gerry Francis, none of the managers since Nicholson."

As with much in this story, that may have been true, but surely the potential for problems being created by producing the game at this delicate time should have been spotted.

Perhaps the manager would gain some relief from a football match? Jol, possibly in an attempt to prove the doubters wrong, selected Jermain Defoe and Dimitar Berbatov in attack for yet another vital game. The pair had been left, sullen-faced, on the bench on Monday evening at St James' Park, but against Getafe they misfired, failing to produce much in front of goal aside from the early strike which saw the Bulgarian set up the Englishman to open the scoring. Was this Jol's final 'I told you so' to all those within the club who had agitated on behalf of the pair? Whatever his motivation in selecting them, after Berbatov set up Defoe for the night's opening goal, everything went wrong for Spurs.

Jol had also taken the decision to drop England goalkeeper Paul Robinson, whose season had descended into a continuing nightmare, with mistakes costing goals on a regular basis for both Tottenham and the national side. Czech keeper Radek Cerny was installed, but could only watch as his defence failed to deal with a free-kick wide on the wing within minutes of the opening goal and the ball sailed into the net for a goal which summed up the state of Spurs' defence. Getafe's winner was similarly shoddy, France Under-21 international centre-half Younes Kaboul stopping in his tracks to allow striker Nóbrega to run onto a cross from the right and perform a classy backflick to send the ball past Cerny from five yards.

Up in the directors' box ITV's cameras spotted Levy and Kemsley sharing a wry smile. The timing was awful and didn't help the feeling that Jol had been dealt the final blow from behind.

But all that was academic as far as the 36,240 supporters in the White Hart Lane stands were concerned. The night was all about saying goodbye to the man they adored as their leader. Songs rang round the stadium in support of Jol for the whole 90 minutes as the fans spontanously stood up to applaud Jol, and give him their personal, extraordinary backing, singing: 'We love Jol, and Jol loves us.' The atmosphere was one of celebration of his achievements rather than sorrow at his impending departure. Its like had never been seen before.

Bizarrely on the same night as Spurs fans stood to a man and woman to cheer their departing manager, Bolton fans, during their team's 1-1 home draw with Braga, were emitting a rousing chorus of boos in the direction of their new manager Gary Megson, mixed with a smattering of 'You don't know what you're doing!' chants in the direction of the Board. Megson had been brought in to replace the recently departed Sammy Lee who had been given only six months, and 14 league games, to prove he was the man to follow the phenomenal success of the reign of Sam Allardyce. Big Sam had been tempted away from the Reebok to attempt to revive the fortunes of Newcastle United and recreate the huge success he had brought to Bolton.

The contrast could not have been more marked. Supporters across the country, and Spurs fans in particular, love Martin Jol. His personality, his dignity, his brand of football and, importantly, his achievements at Spurs, had made a strong and lasting impression.

Monday, October 29

Daniel Levy opted out of an appearance alongside his new manager, thereby avoiding a public inquest over the Jol saga. The chairman left the defence of Spurs' treatment of Jol to Sporting Director Damien Comolli who was "not embarrassed" by the way in which the Dutchman had been undermined.

Comolli maintained that the club had nothing to be embarrassed about in their treatment of Martin Jol. "No, I'm not embarrassed," he said. "Unfortunately, sometimes you have to make decisions like this in football. It was a decision we had to take. We are looking for stability. I'm a great believer in the people who are at the club. They are the people who make a club good or bad. With the appointment of Juande, we are bringing another good person into the club. I'm sure, with Juande here, we will have stability."

Levy watched the press conference on television in another part of the stadium, preferring to choose to speak publicly for the first time about the Jol episode at an EGM at the end of November.

At the press conference the club made it clear that the Juande Ramos, the 53 year-old former Sevilla manager, was "Damien's appointment". Comolli was asked about his role in the painfully slow expiration of Jol's Tottenham tenure. Questioned on how his position came with so much power, but, as it seems, precious little accountability, Comolli said that he "didn't know" what it would take for him to be dismissed. "That's probably something you have to ask Daniel," he said. "I've got things to do for the club. If the chairman and the board are not happy with what I'm doing, they'll probably ask me to leave. But 50 per cent or 60 per cent is about the club in the future, and 40 per cent is about the club now. If they're not happy with what I'm doing, they'll ask me to leave. I'm not interested in this job [being manager himself]. Juande is very competent at what he does, he has a proven record of winning in style."

Comolli denied that the club had told Jol that the minimum requirement for Tottenham, after two fifth-placed finishes, was a Champions League spot this season. "We just said we wanted to do as well as possible and do better, year on year – that's all," Comolli said. "No-one told Martin we had to achieve Champions League football." Yet, on 21 August, the club had released a statement outlining Levy's backing for his manager in which the

Spurs chairman said: "We want Champions League football. We, the board, owe it to the club and the supporters to constantly assess our position and performance." Also, one has to point out that doing "better, year on year", when a club has finished fifth twice in succession by definition means finishing in one of the four Champions League qualification spots, so that argument was full of holes.

Comolli also insisted that the Spurs system of buying players had sat comfortably with Jol and that the new man was already used to the system. Comolli said: "Results matter, and how you get results matters. One of the reasons Juande is here is because he gets results with style. I think that's how you get respect. I'm 100% convinced that the technical director role works – 99% of the clubs around the world use that system, win trophies, win football matches. So it works. Martin always knew the players we bought. I enjoyed working with him and had a good relationship with him."

Back in southern Spain, Sevilla reacted furiously to their manager's defection and announced that they had yet to agree a compensation package with Spurs, with their president José Maria del Nido still threatening to report the Premier League club to FIFA.

Friday, November 2

Jol began his fight back by accusing Damien Comolli of costing him his job.

Jol confirmed that Comolli had ignored his request to buy an experienced midfielder and left winger. Instead Comolli had sanctioned £30m on Darren Bent, Younes Kaboul, Kevin Boateng and Adel Taarabt. Jol said: "I felt the squad would be unbalanced with these signings and it proved to be the case. The funny thing is the new manager will probably come to the same conclusion and the club will go out in January and buy the two players I felt we needed."

He added: "When Frank Arnesen was director of football we spoke together about the players to bring to the club. But I did not have the same relationship with the next man. I think the club wanted to invest in younger players because they wanted to make money on them in the future. The decisions were not being made for footballing reasons. I knew that in the summer and I realised my position was becoming very difficult."

Centre-half Kaboul has been a regular in a poor Spurs defence. Bent struggled, while midfielders Boateng, 20, and Taarabt, 18, barely featured.

Comolli made the point that the current Spurs board has transformed the club in the last six years. What Comolli was unwilling to explain was that the board's confidence in Jol was ebbing last season amid demands from him for wage hikes and a change of title from 'head coach' to 'manager'. Jol was very nearly dismissed before the 4-0 FA Cup victory over Fulham in February and there were elements on the board who wanted to replace him in the summer. The end for Spurs' most popular and successful manager of modern times had been afoot for far longer than many had ever believed.

* * * * * *

After the most traumatic of openings to the 2007/08 season and one of the most contentious episodes in Spurs' recent history, Martin Jol was finally unable to save his career at Tottenham. That the tortuous process of his removal lasted so long, it now appeared, was only because of the club's directors' failure to secure Juande Ramos from Sevilla – and, to a lesser extent, their sudden sensitivity to the reaction of their supporters. Despite the 3-1 home defeat to Arsenal and the astonishing game against Villa, the fans had not turned on their manager.

In early October, when asked if he would still be in the job in a few weeks, Jol had said defiantly: "I was shown a newspaper article recently from back in 2005 which asked how long would I be here. I've been here for another two years, so I think so, yes."

Paul Robinson, Tottenham's England goalkeeper, was equally certain: "The players are fully behind the manager. One result doesn't make him a bad manager. We are hopeful that the manager will be staying and we will dig the results out for the manager in the next few weeks."

To Jol's many supporters across the globe, the frenzy which had accompanied the destabilisation of his managerial position at the Lane in such a short space of time had felt as if it had come right out of the blue after a halcyon period of progress under a man who had become the most popular manager in the country, especially with supporters of other clubs. A man who, it seemed, after two and a half fantastic years, could do little wrong – and yet was shown the door. A man who had spent his life working towards what he believed was his destiny to be in charge at White Hart Lane.

THE TONY SOPRANO OF
FOOTBALL MANAGERS

*'Like any manager, when things aren't going well he's not happy
and he can be quite scary at times.'*
Jermaine Defoe

MARTIN JOL WAS Tottenham Hotspur's twelfth boss in 15 years and phenomenally popular. Spurs fans affectionately sang 'He's Got No Hair, But We Don't Care', and he waved to them in response. 'He loves us and we love him', was another fans' favourite song.

Spurs' status since Jol's arrival had been the 'best of the rest', as he liked to put it. Under his stewardship Tottenham finished fifth in two successive Premiership seasons earning back-to-back European campaigns for the first time in more than 20 years, since the glory era of the team led by Steve Perryman and featuring Glenn Hoddle, Garth Crooks, Steve Archibald, Jol's first team coach Chris Hughton and Graham Roberts, which won consecutive FA Cups and the UEFA Cup in the early 1980s.

But being manager of Tottenham meant so much more to Jol than merely the final league placing. There was the tradition of good football to be upheld, begun by Arthur Rowe's Push and Run side in the 1950s, continued by Bill Nicholson's double-winning team of the early 1960s and perpetuated by that early '80s team. Jol achieved this in spades. His second season in charge, 2006/07, saw his strikers score more than 60 goals between them. They also came close to a first trophy since the 1999 victory in the League Cup, with quarter-final places in the UEFA and FA Cups, as well as that narrow semi-final defeat to neighbours Arsenal in the Carling Cup.

There's another reason why Martin Jol, aside from being the most popular Spurs manager in decades, was by far the most popular Premier League manager in the country. Jol looks tough, acts tough and his no-nonsense approach won him legions of admirers. In fact, Jol became officially the toughest manager in the Premiership after coming out on top of a poll which asked football fans of all hues to nominate which manager they would least want to pick a fight with.

Often portrayed as the petulant victim of Jol's rotation policy with his forwards, and despite endless speculation about his future, striker Jermain Defoe retained the utmost respect for his former, hard-line boss, saying: "I had the same relationship with Martin as I have with the other boys. He's a very funny man and made us laugh a lot in team meetings. Like any manager, when things weren't going well he wasn't happy and he could be quite scary at times."

The pair had their fallings out, with Defoe having stormed off the pitch and out of team meetings when he was unhappy at being taken off during a game or not being selected. Once, when Jol substituted Defoe, yet again, the striker thumped the roof of the dug out in frustration. Jol barely flinched. He understands the passion and the commitment. He just has to make the calls. That also earns respect in a man's world, where supporters adore those they can look up to as men, real men, who are as passionate as they are about their club.

The poll was conducted in the aftermath of the infamous touchline brawl between Arsène Wenger and Alan Pardew in an early afternoon match that preceded Spurs' league encounter with Chelsea before which Jol explained to then manager Jose Mourinho in graphic detail what had occurred between the warring London bosses – to their unified amusement.

The former Chelsea manager was always far more temperamental than Jol. In contrast to the Dutchman's mainly phlegmatic response to petulance, when Mourinho was under pressure, with his relationship with Roman Abramovich put to the test over the £30.8m signing Andrij Schevchenko, the Chelsea boss refused to acknowledge the Ukrainian World Cup captain when he came off the field at the end of a 2-0 defeat at Anfield.

Jol's famed sense of humour is another reason for his sustained popularity. When told of the honour of being 'the most feared manager in the Premiership' he said: "I'm sure that poll was only physical if Steve Coppell was at the bottom. Now he is scary! ... based on physical attributes, that poll would be just about right. At least that is one league I am top of!

You need physical and mental toughness in the team. That is why I encourage players like Didier Zokora, and why I bought Edgar Davids. I feel you need to be a tough team to beat. You can be tough and kick everybody or you can be tough and play a bit, and I think that combination is a good one. If you don't have the ball you can't play, so you need to get it back. I think that is an English philosophy; it is Sir Alex Ferguson's way to get the ball back as soon as possible and then play and pass."

But as Jol rightly said, Tottenham were still nearly men. They have not won anything yet for him and now he has brought them so tantalisingly close the expectation levels have rocketed.

The 2006/07 Carling Cup semi-final defeat by Arsenal, after being two goals to the good at half-time in the first leg at White Hart Lane, exemplified how Spurs had managed to up their game, but not yet join the elite group of winners. That occasion was not the first time Tottenham suffered heartache by missing out to their arch-rivals under Jol. On the final day of 2005/06 season, Tottenham just failed in their attempt to snatch the final qualifying place for the Champions League by losing at West Ham. Who else should benefit but the Gunners.

The 2006/07 season was a defining point in the history of Spurs, and a critical one in the reign of Jol, with Spurs back in Europe for the first time in seven years having qualified for the UEFA Cup by virtue of that fifth-placed finish. Much was expected of Jol and his team in the bid to make up for the heartache of the final day of the previous season. But Spurs started poorly, with only one win in the first five league games and it looked as if the disappointment of failing to qualify for the Champions League had seriously affected the squad. Jol got things back on track during October, and a 2-1 defeat of champions Chelsea sparked a fabulous run both at home and in the UEFA Cup. But a shock 3-1 set back at Reading left the players in no doubt about the southern equivalent of Sir Alex Ferguson's northern hairdryer treatment. Displaying his fearsome side by what was left unsaid outside the inner sanctum, Jol said: "I would never reveal what was said after the Reading defeat in the changing room, but I was not happy. I am always myself and the players can always see when I am happy or angry. I am always the same as a manager. I love them if they win and don't if they lose."

The players responded to the defeat, but there was an even worse setback in the club's first ever game at Arsenal's plush new home, the Emirates Stadium, where it wasn't just a heavy 3-0 defeat that pained Jol, but Spurs' complete capitulation. Prior to that north London derby Jol made some pertinent observations about the team's development during his tenure and how it contrasted with the day he took charge with an unwield-ly large first team squad and the distance between themselves and the 'Unbeatables' of Arsenal seemingly unbreachable. Two years on and Jol had made enormous strides. He observed: "We haven't had one transition in my time, we have had two or three. We have 24 players now, which is just right, but when I started I had 36 players. Can you imagine that? When I started

I didn't know that I would be given the chance to be here five years. I'm not here because I just want to do well over a couple of months. I am wanting to do well now and come up with a philosophy so that the club will be stronger in a few years time. The last five or six Tottenham managers have been here 18 months on average. I've been here now for two years, but it is evidence we have a real vision. What I would like to have a settled squad that can really challenge for the title. It is arrogant, but I feel we can do it because the foundation is there. The likes of Aaron Lennon, Jermaine Jenas, and Tom Huddlestone will all be at the top level in one year's time, but at the moment, we have to suffer sometimes because they are young players. It is not realistic to compare us with Liverpool and Chelsea now because they don't sign the young players we do, but we could challenge them in two years time."

Making a prediction which would come back to haunt him sooner than he thought, Jol continued: "I have got a great contract. The club is good for me and whichever way you look at it I will be here for the next three years. When the chairman asked me if I wanted to commit myself I didn't hesitate. I could go to a big club in Spain or Holland, but this is my choice. It's not a matter of just being in a job, this is where I want to be. I am 50 years of age and it is an important time in my life. I am 100 per cent certain that this is my mission. I could say the moment we win something, get in the Champions League or win the UEFA Cup that I have achieved what I want and it's time to go. That is probably normal because you have to stop at your highest level, but I am different. I want to achieve these things and get the club to stay there, to be consistently successful and established as a top four club."

The Dutch coach had certainly pulled no punches since his arrival in English football and in truth had totally and spectacularly transformed the club, which was, at the point he took over, at something of a crossroads, both on and off the pitch. Brought in as assistant coach to Jacques Santini, Jol inherited the job when the Frenchman unexpectedly quit just 11 games into his tenure after huge problems within the club's hierarchy surrounding his defensive approach which saw the team score just six goals in that time.

Jol's subsequent success can be measured in any number of ways – league position, points earned, wins average, you name it – but perhaps the most telling is his popularity with the fans, which is earned by total respect for his management style, rather than a deliberate attempt to curry favour with them.

The popular perception of Jol is of a Dutch bruiser; thick accent, quick with the one-liners in press conferences, but equally swift to protect his players when trouble occurs. Among Spurs fans he is known as 'Tony Soprano', after the head of the eponymous clan of the Channel 4 hit US drama. Despite the jokes and invigorating attitude, there is a seriousness about Jol. He is amused by his image. In person, Jol is entertaining, enthusiastic and charming. In contrast to other Premiership managers, he is refreshingly open about his interests outside football, saying he relaxes by going to the National Gallery. "They have a great selection of Dutch painters there. I like walking around looking at the Rembrandts. It's a nice way to spend my time." An art collector himself, he once selected Kafka's *Metamorphosis* as his personal choice in a television poll of Premiership managers who selected their favourite books: "I could have said *David Beckham: My Life*, but that would have been a bit boring and anyway I studied German literature and I always liked the title," he revealed. That throw away remark would later be used to justify barbs thrown in Jol's direction about him being too high-brow and Jol later scotched rumours that his bedtime reading consists of existentialist and modernist literature

He said: "It's often said I read Hemingway and Kafka all the time, but I don't. Well, I did when I was studying. It was because of my mum that I stayed at school until I was 18, and of course as part of my school work we had to read Hemingway and Kafta."

In fact Jol's true love is modern art as he explains: "Football is my passion, but art is my hobby. I own almost 200 original canvases, from Dutch masters to modern works by Eastern European artists. One, by the Ukrainian Yuri Zurkan, is a semi-fantastical scene of two women, one in white, one red. Arsenal and Spurs. There's a cockerel and the red woman is handing the white woman a ball. I started out 30 years ago with about five or six. I would like to auction them for a little girl who has brain damage and who needs treatment in America.

I believe in God and it's great having so much family around. I want to spend some time with them. I have other interests outside football – paintings, property. In fact I want to buy the lighthouse in my hometown of Scheveningen; it's for sale. It is protected by the government, so I couldn't do anything but rent it out, but it is a symbol of our town."

Hardly the ambitions of The Godfather.

Jol may have been lampooned as the 'Sopranos boss' and he will never have the smouldering good looks of a sophisticated Mourinho or the professorial aura of a Wenger, but he has nevertheless become one of the most charismatic coaches in the modern game. But with success and the high profile always comes the downside, and in Britain that so often means the press. Jol has been riled by the way in which certain papers mocked the fact his two brothers are named Cock and Dick. "My poor brother. He has to go around and introduce himself as Cornelius to everyone now. It's stupid. Cock is just a nickname in Holland, a short version of his name. I mean, what's so funny about that? It's his name and my other brother's name is Dick. This is normal in Holland."

In fact Dick Jol is one of Europe's foremost referees, having taken charge of the 2001 UEFA Champions League final.

How did he feel about his own nickname? Jol laughs: "I asked my wife about that. I said: 'Do you think I look like Tony Soprano?' and she said she didn't think so. And I was glad because he's not really a good-looking man... Then again, I suppose that all women say nice things to you if you ask them a question like that."

In pure football terms Jol was a Tottenham traditionalist, who wanted the past to be an inspiration for the present and future generations – not a burden. On his office wall, adjacent to the tactics board, were pictures of legends such as Jimmy Greaves, Cliff Jones and Clive Allen, one of the members of his back room staff. He explains: "I am not frightened by the club's history and I'm not going to fight it. I could have come in and stripped the walls of White Hare Lane, taken down all the pictures, but that would be turning my back on the legend that has grown up around Spurs. It's there in every part of the club. I see all these great players every Saturday, Cliff Jones, Bobby Smith and Dave Mackay and I love the fact they are there to remind me what Spurs means. This is all part of the charisma of this club. It's why it is so special and has a place in so many people's hearts. I remember when we held the tribute to Bill Nicholson on the pitch. Suddenly there were legends everywhere. Cliff and Greavesie arm-in-arm. Dave Mackay out there again and it meant so much to me that I was playing a small part in the history of Spurs."

The fact that this kind of talk is exactly what Spurs fans want to hear is, to all intents and purposes irrelevant. It's the fact that this man really meant what he says that has captivated the Tottenham supporters and also the wider football-loving public.

When Jol first took the reins when Jacques Santini quit in contentious circumstances early in the 2004/05 season, he spoke of emulating Bill Nicholson, of being like Bill Nick. But it wasn't quite what he meant. He explains: "Some people misunderstood me when I said I wanted to experience what Bill had experienced, they said I wanted to be the next Bill Nick. But that wasn't the case. I just wanted to taste one of those great occasions, the kind that Bill tasted throughout his career here. Perhaps people in England don't realise just what the name of Spurs means abroad, especially in Europe. Just the name – Spurs – sounds fantastic and then you conjure up memories of those brilliant white shirts on great nights in European competition. Wonderful"

His love for the club, and what the name of Tottenham Hotspur means to football folk around the globe is apparent, but all the more intriguing is the fact that Jol very nearly wasn't Spurs manager at all. He could have joined Manchester United. He talked with Sir Alex Ferguson about becoming his No. 2, but Jol remains delighted it did not work out: "When Alex Ferguson phoned me to fly over for a chat I first thought it was a joke being played by one of my friends. We talked for three hours, but I'm happy he wasn't convinced or that we did not get round to an agreement because maybe I would have done it. I'm not disappointed, as I went to Spurs after that."

Jol certainly believed in maintaining relations between top flight managers. He was often to be seen swapping theories and thoughts in the dugout with opposing bosses as both sets of players warm up before games. Unlike those who often choose the more adversarial route, such a Wenger, Pardew, Ferguson and Mourinho, Jol aspires to contribute more than bluster and barney. Belying his Sopranos image perhaps, he is a deep thinker on the game, is not afraid to try new ideas, make tough decisions about players and develop long term strategies, not just attempt to hold onto his job in an age which sees the average football manager lasts for around 15 months.

That's the Martin Jol we know; the beaming persona and post-match quips on *Match of the Day*. But is the Jol that British supporters have bought into over the past three years as a manager at White Hart Lane, who was defended so stoutly to the hilt by callers to countless phone-ins after the contentious events of the early part of the 2007/08 season unfolded, and who fans of a certain age recall as a tall top flight midfielder in the mid-1980s, the real man? I have always felt there is much more to him, behind the up front persona, beneath the immensely enjoyable and respected surface.

During my year researching this book I grew close to Martin Jol, through interviews with himself and many of his friends and colleagues from throughout his life. I learnt many things about the man, just one I will share with you right now. He disclosed that he has another ambition, as well as to reach the top as coach with Tottenham. He wants to sell the football shirt collection he has amassed over the past few years to raise money for a sick child he has been sponsoring in Holland. He initially gave the jerseys to his 15 year-old son, but the boy prefers rugby and so Jol says, "I have shirts worn by players like Dennis Bergkamp and I want a big bid. There is a little girl in Holland who has brain damage and needs oxygen treatment."

Now there is a man, I thought, that I need to find out more about.

THE BOSS

MARTIN JOL WAS 'The Boss' from the age of five. His best friend from their formative years together in the late 60s, Hans van Eck, remembers playing street football with the slim, fast, and good-looking kid on the block of Wassenaare Strate, the street where Jol grew up in the small Dutch town of Scheveningnen, a suburb of The Hague, the country's administrative capital on the North Sea coast of the Netherlands. Hans recalls: "I have known Martin all my life, we grew up together, went to the same school and played street football. From the age of five, Martin was 'The Boss'. He was the boy in control. He was the best player. He had all the tricks and we would try to copy him but couldn't. He hasn't changed from the age of five. With Martin it's all about football, football, football. That's his character.

We started off at the same Primary School, but it was a Christian school and I then was sent to an open faith school. We were reunited at Secondary School. By then Martin was by far the best player around, scoring nine or ten goals every time he played, and had joined his first club JAC.

He was definitely in charge even then. He once asked me before a game: 'do you want to play?' I was nine at the time and Martin was ten. Without referring to the leader at the football club, I played, simply because Martin said so. And no-one could say anything as he scored ten goals in that game."

But despite his infatuation with the game and early signs of management potential, Jol's ambition as an 11 year-old did not lie in football, or indeed sport at all. He wanted to be the best rock singer in the world. The problem was he couldn't actually sing, according to best friend van Eck: "Martin couldn't sing, and he fell short in an ambition that came later to do with football – becoming the best footballer on the planet too. One can safely say that Pelé still retains that title. Fortunately the young Martin gave up his quest for singing stardom and took the road to the football game, where his other close friends and those who know him best believe he will attain the title of the best coach in the world."

Martin Toet, now a company director in Holland and still very much a close friend and confidante of the man he grew up with in the Hague in the 60s and early 70s, recalls: "He must have been just over 13 when he told me that he wanted to be a singer, and the best singer in the world, and if he couldn't achieve that he wanted to be a footballer and the best footballer in the world. And, no, he couldn't sing, but he loved the Rolling Stones."

Jol confirms his early intentions were far more musically based than sporting, although he insists van Eck has his choice of instrument wrong, telling me: "If I'd had to make a choice in my younger days it would have been to be a guitarist. I don't think I had a brilliant a voice, but I wanted to be a performer. I'd love to have been a lead guitarist, but I never really sang, so my friends must have been mistaken about that. My brother and I loved music. We loved the Small Faces, Status Quo, The Kinks, especially Ray Davies. In fact I wanted to be the lead guitar player with the Rolling Stones. You may not think of me much as a lead guitarist when you look at me now! Nowadays people now call me 'Tony Soprano', but when I was 18 or 19 I had a face like an angel, so they called me 'Angel Face'."

His clear tendencies for leadership and ability with the ball at his feet in those street games, however, meant that by his mid-teens Jol's ambitions were becoming more realistic.

"I had a real talent, not for singing or playing the guitar – it was for playing football," Jol says. "When I was young I was a centre-forward and I would score 13 or 14 goals in every match I played. I was the only one in my village to play for the Haag representative team, even though I played for a small club JAC."

That talent saw Jol identified. At the age of 14 he was selected for the Dutch national age group team alongside players from Holland's major clubs, Ajax, PSV and Feyenoord, being one of only two players among the squad to hail from a small club. Jol remembers this time fondly: "I played at Wembley with the national team and played for every one of the national Dutch sides after I was 14 and I am only one of eight who has achieved that."

Although at this point in Jol's development he was top dog in his little fiefdom, in fact he went on to win 10 Dutch schoolboy caps, 20 'B' caps, 12 Under-21 caps and 12 Under-23 caps as his talent was recognised as quickly as it blossomed.

Martin Toet recalls: "I have known Martin since he was 11. We played for different teams around that age until we got together with the same Hague team after being selected for the district. That's where we first really met each other and became friends. We then also played for one year at the same club team JAC. From the ages of 13 to 23 we played together for The Super Club, Hague. We both represented Dutch teams at the ages of 14 and

16 and played together for the Holland Youth team. We saw each other every day and lived about two kilometres apart."

So, what was the teenage Martin Jol like? "Well," says Toet, "he was a fighter... in the sense that he was always willing to work hard and for his goal in life 100 per cent."

His boyhood friend Hans van Eck confirms: "There are two sides to Martin Jol. The professional, who is fiercely determined and says what he thinks that you all know. But he is also someone who is always there for you. He doesn't forget his friends and he has a big family and he is very much a family man." This fondness is something hard to miss in all the recollections given to me by those who were more thsan happy to talk about the early years of the Martin Jol story.

That fighting spirit and determination had been imbued in Jol from a very early age by his father, a Scheveningen fisherman grafting to earn a living and feed his growing brood. Jol recalls: "My father and mother were the big influences, perhaps my mother more so. My father worked very hard; everyone in our small fishing village worked hard. He had been a fisherman since the age of 15, but had been going to sea since the age nine. When they'd told him in the late 1930s he had to go to sea he hid himself in the toilet. The toilet was outside and that's where he hid. He didn't want to go to sea, as you can imagine. And in those days people didn't own their own boats, they rented them and they were not as perfect as they might be today. They were so old and battered that a lot of men from our village never came back after being caught in storms. They built a monument in Scheveningnen which shows village women looking out to sea, waiting for their men to come back. The fishermen all worked for boat owners and the boats were crap.

Because of this I was 'born' on the beach, I lived just 50 yards from the sea and in my early years in the summer I actually built myself somewhere to live on the beach and played football there too."

The beach has been the cente of life in Scheveningen ever since its Anglo-Saxon roots were laid. It has always been a working fishing village, which has seen many years of devastating storms. In both 1470 and 1570 over half the village's wooden shacks were destroyed by the tempests whipped up by North Sea winds. The sandy beach, later to become a haven of bathing for the cognescenti of The Hague, saw a particular type of boat developed with shallow bottoms on the vessels in order for them to be able to be pulled up far enough from the sea to avoid the squally sea. These boats were known as *bomschuiten* and it wasn't until the villagers built a harbour in 1904 that more modern boats, with deeper drafts, that could withstand the storms could be utilised.

Even then a fisherman's lot was a difficult one. Fishing was well past its heyday as a vocation when Jol's father was forced to go to sea. Despite the customs of the festival to celebrate the capture of the first herring each Spring, money was tight and there was always that risk of one of the regular storms catching the fleet out to sea. It was a hard, working class existence; in stark contrast with one of the many beatiful panoramas of the sandy dunes of Scheveningen beach painted by Dutch masters such as Adriaen van de Velde, Simon de Vlieger and Hendrik Willem Mesdag, whose enormous panorama, 14 m high and 120 m around its almost circular width, preserves the view of the village in 1881.

Jol told me: "My father was a very strong character. He had tremendous will power. I would imagine you would have to be like that if you went to sea at the age of nine. In contrast I was sensitive when I was a kid, but I developed my father's toughness and football was the mechanism that helped to make me tough. I was the best in my town from the age of 10 or 11. Everybody knew it. By the time I was 15 I was playing with seniors in our local club side JAC and when I played my first game I scored two goals. At 18 I played for Den Haag against West Ham in the quarter-finals of the Cup Winners' Cup [in 1976]. I played against Billy Bonds and Frank Lampard's father, Frank senior. We were 4-0 up at one point in the first leg, but they scored two in the second half. Then we went to West Ham and they beat us 3-1 and we went out on away goals.

That's how I started in major club football. People in England don't know anything about me and how I started, but in Holland they know everything and have even made documentaries about me on TV."

Jol had joined his first professional side, ADO Den Haag, at the age of 15, his prodigious talent costing the full-timers 1.2 million guilder. Full of the cockiness of youth he attempted to negotiate a rather different signing on fee – a motorbike. Jan Hermen owns *Elf*, one of the biggest Dutch football magazines with a circulation of 100,000. A former player himself, he first met Jol when the talented youngster signed his first contract as a player. Jol was in his teens and Jan was two years older. He recalls: "We first met the year Martin signed the contract for which, instead of money, I think he received his first small motorised bike, the kind you see often in Holland. He signed for a club called ADO Den Haag of the Hague. The club was run by one or two professionals and by a group of enthusiastic amateurs. I was one of those workers, a fan of football and of the club and I helped out by writing the programme.

I was very good friends with the manager who signed Martin. I was 19 and Martin 17. Yes, he had a lot more hair in those days and he was very slim, and very powerful, part of the best youth team the Hague has had in his history. Four members of that group went on to become full Dutch internationals, one of them, named Tscheu La Ling, tore Manchester United's youth team apart in one game can recall. The side had only one older player and the rest were 18, so it was a funny mixture at the time. The one player in his 30s was Aab Mansveld, so the fans called the team 'Uncle Aab and His Nephews!'"

Jol remembers this incident slightly differently: "I asked for the bike, but I didn't get it. They gave me a card for the tram instead. I never got that bike. I was only a young player, but because I was going to training so often they gave me a card for the tram. My best friend was Martin Toet. And we used to go training at 5am and we would be sitting on his bike and he would let me drive. He'd be behind me keeping me warm, bellowing in my ear to slow down."

Even then the tall and rangy Jol cut a dominant figure as he strode across the pitch, dictating most games. Then there was the flowing hair, which contrasts markedly with the image we hold of him today. Jol's cultured, attacking midfield performances with Den Haag soon attracted the attention of one of European football's giants. Although many had felt that it was only a matter of time before pre-eminent Dutch club Ajax made their move, before anything came of any potential interest, German club Bayern Munich, who, like Ajax, had won three successive European Cups in the 1970s, the last as recently as 1976, swooped to pluck Jol from small town Holland and thrust him into the bright lights of Munich.

Jan Hermen remembers: "Martin was not sure of his best position, he very often played central midfield, but he also played as a defensive central player or as a right full-back. It wasn't long before he became the team's most successful player and they sold him to Bayern Munich. The secretary of the club and myself went over to Munich to conclude the deal having sold him to Bayern for 500,000 German marks. If we went over personally, we could avoid paying so much tax, and the club needed the extra money. So it was quite funny going to the bank with the manager of Bayern Munich, who went into its cellars to take out the 500,000 in cash, and then we flew back to the Hague with the cash in a large bag."

Despite this cross-border smuggling, Jol, however, was joining a club in decline.Despite boasting the likes of German legends Gerd 'Der Bomber' Müller and Franz Beckenbauer amongst their ranks, and having won three consecutive European Cups from 1974 to 1976, Bayern would not win the German league again until 1979/80, having last won it in 1974, and failed to even qualify for Europe for the season 1978/79. As much as it was a period of transition for the club, it became so for Jol, who did not make the adjustment well after being the big fish in the small pond of Den Haag.

Jol says: "When I was 21 I went to Germany, but, as much as I loved the opportunity, it didn't work out for me. I kept having to say to myself, 'This is my job. I have to do this'. Every week I drove home – ten, twelve hours. I did really enjoy myself for the first few months. I was playing well until I encountered a few personal problems – and decided I had to get home at all costs. The manager Uli Hoeness offered me another two-year contract but I turned him down. I regret that now because after I left the club they went on to win the Championship."

Jol's time at Bayern saw him play with some of the legends of the game, still left at the club after their dominance of the European Cup in the mid-1970s such as Paul Brietner, a rangy full-back who was an important member of the West German World Cup-winning team in the 1974 tournament held in their homeland, and legendary goalscorer . Jol has special mem ories of the shaggy-haired defender.

Jol says: "Paul Breitner. This guy was a real legend, who played for Bayern and also Real Madrid. In our playing days at Bayern I was a bit taken aback by Paul. He was a socialist, almost a communist! He was always wearing T-shirts with the images of Che Guevara or Mau Tse-tung, so you would have thought he was a communist. Yet he was the first footballer I had ever seen to drive around Germany in a big Opel sports car – so he was really a socialist!

Breitner was an incredible athlete, who took his training seriously. He would also run from his house to the school every morning. He invited me to his house at Christmas 1978, and we had one of those big German dinners, full of meats. I don't think I could possibly eat as much ever again.

It was nice that I saw him when he came to White Hart Lane during my time there. It turned out that we had a mutual friend of his daughter's living in England, so he popped in to see me. We talked about the old days and he told me how he had fallen out with Uli Hoeness in the last ten years."

But despite enjoying himself off the pitch, Jol discovered that he wasn't ready for his big adventure in Bavaria. Jan Hermen recalls: "Martin didn't enjoy his experience in Munich. It was the end of an era there with some of the club's biggest names stars coming to the climax of their careers, such as Franz Beckenbauer, and they didn't seem all that interested in taking care of a young Dutch lad. Martin was in his early 20s and became very lonely. His sister went out there and did his laundry and the cooking. Immediately after playing a game, Martin would be off to catch a flight home, or drive back to the Hague. He only stayed in Munich for one year."

But who'd have thought where he would pitch up next?

ENGLAND CALLING

MARTIN JOL ONLY came to England by accident. In the kind of twist of fate that shapes destinies, newly installed West Bromwich Albion manager Ronnie Allen revealed later that Jol's capture was, well, fortunate to say the least. Allen, himself an England centre-forward who had begun his career among an avalanche of goals at Port Vale and gone on to star for a West Brom side which won the FA Cup in 1954 scoring twice in the final in a career which also saw him win five international caps, scoring two goals, had travelled to Holland to see Romeo Zondervan play for Twente Enschede. Both Zondervan and midfielder Jol impressed the Albion manager, who upon discovering that Zondervan was not available at the time (though he did eventually sign six months later), switched his attentions to Jol after a tip off from a source that will not surprise many people.

Jol says: "Bobby Robson is properly responsible for me coming to England. Bobby was famous in Holland for taking Arnold Muhren and Frank Thijssen from FC Twente, and it was Robson who told Ronnie Allen that there was another player at that club that he should look at, and that player was me."

Allen, himself, was a well-travelled man in a game which was still very parochial in those days. He had managed Athletic Bilbao in Spain (where his team missed out on winning the league title on goal difference from Atletico Madrid), Sporting Lisbon in Portugal, the Saudi national side and, most recently, Panathinaikos in Greece. Mixed in with these exotic and enlightening spells abroad were stints at Wolves, Walsall and a few months in charge of West Brom in 1977. Allen, therefore, was a man well versed in the virtues of foreign footballers, and the right man to take a risk on a young Dutch footballer such as Martin Jol.

It was certainly the case that it was never Jol's intention that life would work out that way. Jol recalls: "After playing for Bayern Munich, I returned to Holland to sign for Twente Enschede [in summer 1979] and I swore I'd never play abroad again. I didn't enjoy being away form my friends and family and didn't want to go through that feeling of being home sick again. Arsenal tried to sign me and I said 'no'. Albion tried and I said 'no'. Six months later Albion phoned again and asked me over for a week to see what it was like.

Ronnie was very persuasive. He said: 'Come over for five days just to have a look around.' When I got to West Brom, I was shown into the manager's office, and suddenly Ronnie Allen told me we had to go out onto the pitch and kick the ball around. But I told him I hadn't brought any boots because I thought I had just come over to have a look around. He said: 'I'm just in the mood to have a kick around' And out we went in our ordinary shoes for a kick about.

Again, out of the blue, he just kicked the ball about 50 yards in the air and shouted: 'ok, yours'

I stuck out my bottom and controlled it with my backside.

He said: "Ok, we can go back in now and agree terms."

I suppose if I had miscontrolled the ball that would have been that, I would have been straight back to Holland. He offered me an £80,000 signing on fee which was unbelievable money at that time. Despite the fact that signing for West Brom meant I had to go abroad again, I thought it might work out better in England than staying in Holland where there had been a drain of players to other leagues. So I stayed. Then, when [manager] Ronnie Allen asked if I knew any good right-sided midfield players I recommended my friend, Romeo Zondervan. He played on the right for Albion, and then Ipswich, for the next ten years."

It was a huge risk for Jol, possibly even more so than for Albion. They were acquiring a fully-fledged Dutch international midfielder, who as a 24 year-old had won three caps during the Netherlands' participation in the Confederation Cup in South Africa over the summer of 1980. Jol was placing his chances of making a spot in the Dutch national side his own in jeopardy.

Jol recalls the decision he faced: "I played three times for the national team about a month before I went to England. so, it was a big decision to go to play in England because at that time there were only eight or nine foreigners in your league. But worse still the Dutch coach never went abroad to watch any players, so it was a huge risk. For the senior side I had played in the Confederation Cup in South Africa and made my debut against West Germany on 11th October 1980 in a 1-1 draw. I played alongside Jonny Metgod who went on to play for Spurs and Nottingham Forest in the mid-80s, and Jan Peters who once scored twice at Wembley. But once I went to England I never played for the national side again. I never got a look in."

Jol's loss was West Brom's game. The departure of midfielders Bryan Robson and Remi Moses weeks into the 1981/82 season had left Albion in much disarray. The pair had been tempted to join former Baggies manager Ron Atkinson as he began his mission to end Manchester United's 15 year wait for a league championship title for a combined fee of £1.5 million.

Robson is symbolic of a golden era for West Brom when, with other stars such as Cyrille Regis, Brendan Batson and Laurie Cunningham, they were a major force in the old First Division rather than being the yo-yo club we know today. He was a talisman and Ronnie Allen needed to provide his expectant fans with a suitable replacement. Yes, that transfer meant the new Baggies manager had money to spend – more than ever before in their club's history – but spending it wisely wasn't easy. It never has been in football, as Jol, himself, has found out to his cost. Neither was replacing Robson, arguably the most complete midfielder in England, and a man who had attained legendary status among Baggies fans and would go on to star for England and United, becoming known as Captain Marvel or Captain Fantastic, over the next decade.

The solution to this problem, according to the ageing Allen, was to plump for the Baggies' first ever foreign signing and go Dutch, in the shape of Maarten Jol (as his name was originally written but quickly the more anglicised version 'Martin' became commonplace). The fee to Twente Enschede was £250,000, for what was then described as a 'utility player'. Said Allen of his new charge: "We have lost two ball winners in our midfield. But now we have got one back. He will provide the steel we have been lacking."

Yes here we discover the true depth of the steely nerve, the imposing presence which give Jol his well-known demeanour in the modern game. His philosophy as a manager and coach may now be to pass and move in the traditional Tottenham style, the passing game, as players such as George Best and Johan Cruyff were his heroes. Yet, he has reinvented himself. Because his style as a manager is in stark contrast to that when he was a player in English football with West Brom and then Coventry. Maybe this is what fans perceive when likening him to Tony Soprano. It is a side of his character which reveals itself only chinks as he talks about his early career as a player.

The departures of key men Atkinson, Robson and Moses had thrown Albion into turmoil. They needed a steadying hand and that job fell to Jol. He hadn't played for a fortnight but was hurled straight into the first team against Southampton in October 1981. Allen and Albion supporters were becoming desperate. Results were poor [Albion were fourth from bottom] and a number of senior players wanted out, but Jol's introduction was to make an appreciable difference.

He lined up in a defensive midfield role. Understandably his contribution was low-key though local reporter Ray Matts commented on "signs of class." Ian Barratt of the *Daily Express* suggested Jol "paced himself well but faced a difficult task filling the gap left by Bryan Robson."

Albion went nine games with just one defeat [a 2-1 home reverse to Stoke City] as Jol, playing in his new role as midfield enforcer, something he had not been used to in his career until now, provided the kind of stability that the likes of Claude Makalele give modern day Chelsea.

But in 1981 Jol had become one of the very few foreign players in England at the time. Proof of his impact in the game comes with the bald statistic that he was booked six times in his first seven games. That was a contrast to his Total Football upbringing in Holland, but it was a role Jol was happy to play as he asserted himself in England's top flight. "I was a playmaker with Den Haag, Bayern Munich and Twente, but at West Brom they asked me to mark the opposing playmaker," he recalls. "So I was always playing against the attacking midfielder or the second striker – Keegan, Dalglish, Hoddle, Brooking, players like that. Actually I had a terrific time in England."

The other foreign imports plying their trade in the English top flight included the impressive Dutch duo Arnold Muhren and Franz Thijssen at Ipswich. Both came from the same ball-playing school as Jol and had helped propel parochial little Ipswich to becoming the only serious challengers to perennial Champions Liverpool now that Brian Clough's League and European Champions Nottingham Forest were in the midst of a rebuilding process.

The new boy said: "I have seen English teams only on television and the pace looks very quick. But I will play as I can play in the position the manager requires."

Later he revealed: "When I heard a top English club had made a bid for me I expected it to be someone like Arsenal. At the time, I didn't place West Brom in that bracket and that's why I insisted on spending four days over here to see if I liked the place. Once I'd been to The Hawthorns, it wasn't a difficult decision to make. My contract at Twente was due to expire at the end of the season and Dutch football was in the doldrums."

Jol's role just in front of the Baggies back four was pivotal in their revival that season. David Harrison of the *Birmingham Evening Mail* commented

"Jol tackled like a rat trap, sprays passes around with machine gun effective-ness and can score goals too." Beamed Ronnie Allen: "This lad is a real ball winner. He has played five times and is yet to be on the losing side. It's early days but I hope that in time people will say he will have proved one of the best signings of the season."

Founder of West Brom fanzine *Grorty Dick*, now sadly defunct, Simon Wright recalls: "Martin was tall, thin and muscular. He could play and was tall enough to dominate in aerial encounters, but quickly his ability to make an accurate pass was subsumed by his hardman reputa-tion. In his early days, I believe he was genuinely unlucky to pick up bookings. Albion needed three matches to overcome West Ham in the League Cup and Jol ended up in the ref's notebook in each game for fouls on either Devonshire or Brooking. As the latter admitted: 'he has come into their side and done an excellent job. It's not very pretty but highly effective.'"

Early in his playing career, on 7 November 1981, came a seminal moment in Jol's life – his first visit to White Hart Lane. Of course he had no idea what an important part the ground and Tottenham Hotspur would play in his life twenty years hence, but it certainly made an immediate impact on the 25 year-old midfielder.

"I remember my first visit to White Hart Lane very well. It came at the start of my West Brom career and I scored the winner in a league game," he recalls with enormous pride, "It's one of my proudest memories; scoring a winning goal against them – even if not too many others remember it! To play against Ardiles, Villa and Hoddle was something amazing for me."

That goal came in his third league game as Jol swivelled onto a loose ball following a 34th minute Albion corner. Spurs manager Burkinshaw was impressed "I have never seen them (Albion) run or try so hard." An early sign of the influence Jol had brought to the team perhaps.

This was in fact a pivotal moment for Jol, who still keeps the clipping from this match to remind him of the importance of White Hart Lane in his pre-Spurs life. To a certain extent he believed his arrival at the club as manager was pre-ordained.

He told me early on during the year of researching this book: "When I was Coach of the Year in Holland, two years before I even came back, I was asked what my dream was. I said to go back to England and be a manager. When I was asked who I wanted to manage, I automatically said Spurs. It was like fate. Now I'm here, I want to embrace what the club's history means, but also make my own piece of history."

Scottish-based Baggie Paul Collins recalls: "Martin came to the Albion at a very difficult time. Big Fat Ron had ripped the heart out of the 'England' midfield of Robson, Moses and Owen by taking Bryan and Remi to Manchester and we were left with Gary Owen, Andy King plus a very out of position Ally Robertson (leaving John Wile and Martyn Bennett at the back). Jol arrived about six games later – most of which we lost and didn't score – and immediately stopped the rot. I missed his debut, but I remember the game against Tottenham at White Hart Lane. We won 2-1 and MJ scored that winner!

Now energetic, aggressive, physically imposing, hard tackling ball winner he was, but a goalscorer he certainly wasn't. He was the kind of player whose normal senses left him whenever he got near to the opposition goalmouth. I only remember perhaps one more goal during his three seasons. This was a really good Tottenham team, in addition to Hoddle, Perryman, Villa and Archibald there were several who ended up at the Albion, Ardiles, Crooks, Roberts and their manager was one Keith Burkinshaw (he was quite good then), anyway MJ spent most of that game kicking them and then scored the winner!"

Is all this 'hardman' stuff the truth, though?

Baggies fan John Clegg recalls: "Given the football we regularly watched the Dutch national side play in international tournaments on our tellies, when he signed we were expecting a graceful master of tippy tappy football and triangles with team mates. WRONG!!!! Martin could pass a ball and no doubt would have done all the total football stuff if his new team mates had been up to it (not that we had a bad side) but the abiding memory from the first time I saw him was that somebody had dug up Rocky Marciano and given him a pair of football boots. I wondered if the rest of our lot would turn up for training on Monday and cry off the five-a-side?

My old away travelling companion John Jones and I had a conversation recently when we were both bemoaning the lack of an uncompromising hard man in midfield and both agreed that Jol was the last 'proper' one we had seen in the Blue and White stripes. Our view was and remains that he was a vastly underrated player by both the Albion and the English game in general and I never did quite understand why we got rid of him at all, or indeed why Coventry did even more quickly. I think it speaks volumes that he was voted Footballer of the Year when he went back to Holland.

I suppose he was our replacement for Bryan Robson, but he wasn't the same player at all in box to box terms. But his marshalling role in the middle of the park was just what the side needed and unlike Robson, who the press lauded in this country while the 'replacement' went unnoticed by and large, he was rather better at breaking other people's legs than his own, metaphorically speaking. Martin was not brave in the tackle as Robson was often described. More totally unemotional and fearless. And no doubt fearsome to his opponents as a consequence.

John's theory is that match officials had a downer on him big time over here – he recalls Jol leaving the pitch when sent off against Spurs with a look on his face that said: 'What is the matter with people over here? What was wrong with that?'"

Paul Collins says: "A couple of months later it was Albion versus Spurs again a two legged League Cup semi final, Spurs set him up and sure enough he fell for it and got injured and then sent off during the first game at the Hawthorns and we inevitably went out. He then didn't play again until a token effort in the last game of the season and Albion sorely missed him, that was the ten losses in 11 run which put then in severe relegation trouble until a Cyrille Regis inspired win over Leeds, who went down with Wolves (the start of their spiralling descent), in the Jol-less penultimate game saw the Albion safe.

Amazing that my memories of him involve Spurs and look where he is now but I suppose these things happen in football."

An indication of just how strong Albion were in the early 1980s was the Dutchman's involvement in two semi-finals within three months of signing. The second of these was an FA Cup defeat to QPR at Highbury, whose then striker Clive Allen, scorer of the only goal that day, was later to become a coach for Jol at Spurs and eventually take over from him as caretaker-manager on that fateful night against Getafe.

The first semi-final defeat – in February 1982 – was a two-legged League Cup reverse against Tottenham. "That was a great era for Spurs," reminisces Jol. "They had players like Clemence, Hoddle, Ardiles, Villa, Hughton, Archibald and Crooks. They beat us 1-0 over the two legs, but lost to Liverpool in the final."

It was just a single goal by miidfielder Micky Hazard in the second leg at White Hart Lane that prevented the Baggies making a Wembley appearance. Was it a significant factor that Jol's steely determination in the centre of the Albion midfield that night was constricted by what had happened at the Hawthorns in the first leg? In keeping with his hardman image he was sent off.

The incident was unfortunate for Jol. He and Spurs' Irish international winger Tony Galvin had clashed – with the Irishman beginning the running battle with a cold-blooded assault on Jol's leg, which later required four stitches. A booking for each of them wasn't a sufficient deterrent. The battle raged on and in the 86th minute Jol tried to drag back Galvin, who foolishly retaliated. Galvin went for violent conduct, Jol for persistent misconduct. Players from both sides protested to the ref and a young fan raced onto the pitch to meet divine intervention in the form of Glenn Hoddle, who intercepted the interloper before handing him over to the authorities.

Although he did turn out in the second leg defeat at White Hart Lane, Jol's involvement in that League Cup semi-final effectively ended with that kick from the Galvin. "I had to have a cartilage operation," says Jol slightly ruefully. "We had a very good team – Cyrille Regis, Derek Statham, Alistair Brown, Gary Owen and Steve Mackenzie, Andy King – a good cup team – and we came so close to reaching a final."

In the eyes of Albion fans, replacing a club legend such as Robson was an unassailable challenge, but Jol's attempt at mission impossible was well-received. Former team-mate Regis, who is still friends with Jol, says: "You have got to remember that Bryan was phenomenal. He was the complete footballer. I've never seen anyone else like him. It was always going to be a tough job for whoever came in, but Martin held his own and the fans were very supportive. He was big for a midfielder and liked to tackle, but he could also pass the ball as well. I was not surprised he later went into coaching because he also used to think about the game a lot."

Regis recalls Jol the player: "I remember him being highly skilled and great technically. Those were his obvious qualities, and you can see from the team he created at Tottenham that he values technique highly. He arrived in 1981, at the same time as Romeo Zondervan, and started off at right-back, but ended up playing in midfield because Robson had left. He was a tackler, he wasn't afraid to put his foot in. He got a few yellow cards so you could see he was aggressive, but you could also see from what he could do in training that he was very skilful and he showed that in the games. I think coming to England opened his eyes a bit because back in the early Eighties it wasn't as professional as it was in Holland or like it is today, in terms of the boys having a few drinks, the alcohol consumption. Martin wasn't a drinker, not like that, but he did socialise. He came from a different upbringing and lifestyle and he was definitely more professional than us."

Albion fan Neil Reynolds, veteran of over four decades of attendance at the Hawthorns, recalls the impression Jol made in his first season: "I probably saw every game he played and every goal Martin scored for Albion yet I don't remember any of the four goals or any specific incident in any of the games, save for the sending off with Tony Galvin in the 1982 League Cup semi-final against Tottenham. My recollection is a composite of all the games he played – that of a big, strong bloke in a Swan shirt (the sponsor, not the bird) with particularly long legs and short shorts which accentuated the long legs even more. At times those legs seemed telescopic – he'd stretch out and push the ball away from the opponent when it looked as if he'd already been passed. More often though it was the crunching tackles that won him possession and unlike many hard men who're there to win the ball and slip a short pass to a more creative team-mate, Martin could play a bit too. He could spray passes all over the field, long and short, to feet and into space for forwards to run on to. For those who never saw him, it's difficult to think of any recent players who compare. Recent players Derek McInnes and Michael Appleton spring to mind, not for any physical similarity – they were both much smaller – but all three had strength, the same will to win and they all battled from the first whistle to the last, every game they played, and were big favourites with the fans.

I don't know whether it was that semi-final sending off or the many cautions, but Martin became a marked man. Referees talk to each other – I know that from personal experience in junior leagues and I'm quite certain it's the same in the professional game. Referees compare notes and tell colleagues to keep an eye out for so-and so. I don't recall Martin Jol ever arguing with a ref, but it soon got to be the case that officials were looking out for him – penalising him for tackles that were hard but fair, that other players got away with, cautioning him when lesser players would just get a ticking off. Maybe this was some nationalistic thing – there weren't many foreigners playing in England at that time. Whatever the reason, it seemed to me that Martin was singled out and neutralised, not by opposition players but by officials. It seemed as if every tackle was penalised and if he couldn't tackle there was no point in him being on the field."

By December 1981, Jol was serving his first suspension for an accumulation of bookings after just half a dozen games. His manager was quick to defend him. Allen said: "He is a great competitor and really loves playing here. He has so much of the ability you expect from good Dutch players and his time in the German League with Bayern Munich has made him a great ball winner too."

Albion fan Bryn Jones has over 50 years of active support behind him. "One word describes Martin as a player – 'presence'. He was physical but without being overtly dangerous. He was a big, tough player who could, as they say, also play a bit. Size might have been an illusion. Perhaps the players around him were on the short-side but he was big in terms of presence. Martin could win tackles through sheer force. It must have been intimidating to play against him.

But the strangest thing is the contrast between the affable and pleasant image that comes across now as manager of Spurs and the Martin Jol who bone-crunched Albion opponents twenty-five years ago. I never saw Martin smile on the pitch while he was at Albion. He seemed a dour, almost surly character. When he took over at Spurs and appeared on TV, my wife – who was a regular attender of Albion games at that time – refused to believe that the figure on the screen was Martin Jol. Perhaps a confusion, she queried : was the new manager somebody called 'Jolly'? Or maybe Martin's old demeanour was just an act to further terrify the opposition?!"

Certainly the Dutchman was not a regular goalscorer [Robson had managed double figures the previous season]. Albion supporters remember and lament the moving on of goalscorers, which occurs with regularity, especially in the modern era. Jol managed just four – against Spurs, Brighton, Watford and Notts County in his 68 appearances but missed many, many more opportunities. In fact "Missed chance" was a horribly frequent comment on Jol's individual match contribution.

But it is difficult to get away from that disciplinary record. Leon Hickman of the *Birmingham Evening Mail* wrote: "The Dutchman, a bulldozer of a man, with an on-the-ball touch of a ballet master, has now amassed 37 disciplinary points in 16 matches. At more than two a match this must be an entry for the *Guinness Book of Records*. Or for Frightening Stories of the Eighties."

Quickly Jol's reputation had built to the point where he was booked seemingly in every game. The old joke about "book him in the dressing room, ref, and save time later" did the rounds. But for Jol, it was no joke because he just could not operate effectively. After serving his second suspension with a third ban to follow, he protested his innocence to John Wragg of the *Daily Express* on 5 February 1982):

"I am not mean. Perhaps it is other players taking advantage of a reputation I have in this country. It is not justified. In three years in Dutch football I had only eight bookings and in one year in Germany there was only one yellow card.

How is this a bad record? It is worrying me because back home in Holland there are headlines saying how I am getting into trouble. I want to get back into the Dutch national side, too, but I fear the manager will be influenced by what he reads. I am asked to tackle by West Bromwich Albion and I try to do it fairly. I estimate I make 30 or 40 tackles a game and when one is not so good I seem to get into trouble."

But despite his growing reputation amongst match officials, his aggression and passing made Jol an important part of the Albion team, although the injury inflicted by Galvin's assault and those disciplinary problems meant he played just 12 games that first season. Without Jol Albion struggled for form and, from February onwards, won just five of their last 23 games, three of them in the final month of the campaign. Albion's slump meant they had to endure a close-run finish with relegation, only avoiding that fate by beating Second Division-bound Leeds United in their last home game of the season. It cost Allen his job and brought Ron Wylie to the helm at the Hawthorns.

Jol was sad to see his mentor go: "Ronnie Allen was the best manager I ever played under. He was a legend. I had wonderful times with Ronnie, but the club sacked him and that was depressing as he was the man who brought me over and we got to know each other and my wife and me were friendly, too, with his wife."

Despite being back to full fitness, and playing 39 of the 42 league games, Jol's first full season [1982/83] didn't run smoothly for the Dutchman or the team. There was no relegation struggle, but Albion finished solidly mid-table, in 11th place, albeit just a point behind Arsenal. There were some notable victories like over Manchester United (3-1 with Martin booked for dissent) and a hugely popular 1-0 triumph over Villa, with the European Champions' midfield completely dominated by Albion's duo from the Netherlands – Jol and Zondervan. Injuries, new manager Ron Wylie's lack of charisma and boring football led to apathy among the dwindling a number of supporters who came through the gates. Personally, Jol didn't have a great season. 'His form gives cause for concern,' penned one local writer. The few highlights included a hard-earned 0-0 draw in the return at Old Trafford where Jol had a marking job to do on former Baggies powerhouse Bryan Robson, the man he had effectively replaced. Jol's answer to the problem posed by Robson was to get his retaliation in early. 'The Dutchman was booked for a sixth minute tackle on Robson and dogged him conscientiously for the remaining 84,' read the match report in the *Birmingham Mail*. Jol's doggedness reduced the England dynamo to bits and pieces: 'Robson was busy but broken up.'

But the bad days tended to outnumber the good. Problems mounted as the season brought numerous bookings plus a painful hairline fracture of his right arm. Jol also scored only one goal, the Baggies' third against in a 5-0 win over Brighton. The South Coast side, bound for relegation via the FA Cup final, conceded five goals in 24 minutes with the Dutchman taking advantage of confusion caused by centre-half Martyn Bennett running straight at the opposition with the ball at his feet to score his goal.

It is the case that injuries were as much a barrier to Jol as referees. For instance, a hairline fracture of the ankle would keep him out for much of the early part of the 1983/84 season and, worse for the Dutchman, he was replaced by an 18 year-old, Mickey Lewis, who performed well in his absence. This was followed by an operation on Jol's sinuses and treatment for a trapped nerve in his back.

During one brief return, discipline once again reared its ugly head as he was dismissed for two bookable offences at Luton. Yet again, he was hard done by. Even Town's manager David Pleat had sympathy: "I felt a bit sorry for Jol because the fouls he committed were not violent," he said. The Dutchman didn't even bother to wait for the red card after a challenge on Brian Horton. He just walked. Sightings of Jol in Baggies shirt were gradually becoming fewer and fewer, though there was a substitute appearance at West Ham in early 1984 (curiously the only one in his Albion career). Within a minute of coming on, old victim Trevor Brooking was on the receiving end of a bone-shuddering tackle once again – and once more the official took Jol's name.

The Dutchman expressed his frustrations to *Match Weekly* in February 1984 in a full page interview under the heading 'I'm a Marked Man.' He believed that referees "look out for me. If they left me alone, I wouldn't pick up so many bookings. The current situation is annoying because there are many players in the First Division with worse records than me and yet they never get singled out. A lot of people are let off the hook for really hard tackles. When I do something minor in comparison, I'm in trouble."

In the subsequent quarter of a century, only a handful of Albion men – arguably no more than three or four, including one Graham Roberts, a hardman if ever there was one – could fairly claim to have such a tough reputation as Jol. And he paid for it.

Neil Reynolds believes: "Ultimately he was hounded out of English football in my view. God knows how Norman Hunter ever finished a game – but he was English wasn't he."

Paul Collins says: "Martin Jol as a manager/coach is in my view quite outstanding. His teams play attractive attacking football and very effective to given last seasons league position. This in a Premiership which is stifling, predictable, ridiculously expensive for fans and absurdly over-hyped. Ultimately, as a player, I have somewhat mixed memories of MJ and this was, I'm sure, a factor with others when he was available and strongly rumoured to be a candidate for the Albion manager post when they ultimately appointed Bryan Robson. What a mistake!

MJ is a changed man these days but his playing style was such that he regularly got injured and also into trouble with referees. He was sent off twice and booked countless times during an Albion career of only approximately 70 games! I could also go on about the performances of the team. He was part of that team which lost by five at Brian Clough's Nottingham Forest in a League game and then went back a few weeks later for the first leg of a League Cup tie and let in six. There was also a less than memorable six-goal humiliation at Bobby Robson's Ipswich, then flying high but let's not go there."

So there were two schools of thought on Jol the Albion player on the field, but what about off it? In fact Jol was not one for regular interaction with fans. A solitary recollection of once being spotted browsing in WH Smiths in West Bromwich – unusual even in those days – is the sum total of a cross-section of supporters' recollections. It is perhaps indicative of his desire to relax away from the game by indulging his passion for literature.

With injury having decimated his 1983/84 season, in an echo of his comments during the summer of 2007 when his position as manager of Spurs seemed in question, the Dutchman denied speculation that he would be returning home when his contract expired. "There are various options open to me. I could go home, stay at Albion or try a fresh challenge abroad again in Belgium or France." Albion's season had faltered and Ron Wylie was sacked after just 19 months and 69 games at the helm at the Hawthorns – who says short term thinking is the product of the modern game? His replacement, Irishman Johnny Giles, was under pressure to reduce the size of the playing squad as the reality of the mid-80s bit.

Jol recalls: "Johnny Giles changed everything and he told me that I could leave as he was bringing in Tony Grealish, one of his fellow countrymen, you might recall him the midfield player with the beard.

After that news I was set on returning back to the Hague and the removal van had actually arrived at my home in Walsall, but then I received a phone call from Coventry City manager Bobby Gould. I told him I was supposed to be on my way back to Holland five minutes age, but he offered me a £25,000 signing on fee and said: 'so come over and talk'. I ended up signing for three years."

So, in June 1984, Jol found himself given a free transfer to what has become known to Baggies fans as 'the Home for Surplus Albion men' – Coventry City. Just three months earlier, Albion had beaten the Sky Blues partly thanks to 'encouraging spasms of inspiration' from Jol and it may well have been that performance which influenced Gould to snap up the Dutchman, now 28 years-old.

After playing more than 70 games for West Brom off the Holland international went to Coventry. His departure met with supporter indifference. Giles, in his second spell as Albion manager, was enjoying an extended honeymoon period, partly living on the memory of his first time in charge when he led the Baggies back to the First Division in 1976 and partly because the football had been quite superlative in some of his early games in his second spell. A midfield hard man with a reputation wasn't seen as any great loss. (Albion had been fined for their poor disciplinary record and the midfielder was seen as part of the problem). But ultimately the Baggies would rue his departure as, without any kind of backbone, they slumped to the inevitable relegation in 1985/86 with a woeful record of just four wins in their 42 matches, finishing 18 points shy of Leicester, who survived a fearful scrap with Ipswich to secure the safety of 19th position.

BACK TO HIS ROOTS

It's A FRIGHTENING thought in retrospect – particularly for opposing players in the mid-1980s – but Martin Jol and Stuart Pearce were team-mates at Coventry during the Dutchman's spell at Highfield Road in the 1984/85 season.

Bobby Gould's team were full of players such as Brian Kilcline, Micky Gynn, Trevor Peake, Terry Gibson and Steve Ogrizovic who had faced rejection from bigger clubs and were more from the battling school of survival than the school of science. There was quality, though, in their midst as this was the basis of a team which would win the FA Cup in 1987 under the managerial duo of John Sillett and George Curtis.

Of course top flight wages weren't then what they are now, so the Dutchman found an unusual way to supplement his income. Jol had a tidy sideline in flogging fake designer clothes. Over 20 years later he was delighted to meet up again with Pearce when he brought his Manchester City side to White Hart Lane in early 2007 on the back of four straight Premiership defeats. Jol was hoping the ex-England hard man would turn up in one of the jumpers he had sold him 20 years previously! Before the match Jol said: "Stuart is probably still wearing the jumpers I sold him. In Europe, you have all the Lacoste and Armani clothes, but the ones I sold him were fake. He didn't know that, that's why I said he's still wearing them!"

Coventry's 1984/85 season ground along with them occupying a spot in the relegation places until the last two games, when home wins, after the rest of the division had completed their programme, saw them survive by the skin of their teeth, with Norwich plummeting into Division Two. But by then Martin Jol's involvement in the struggle against the drop was well and truly over. A certain starter in August, by the time of City's first victory of the season, at Watford in early October, he had been dropped. In and out of the side until Christmas, his campaign was ended by an injry picked up on Boxing Day in a 2-0 defeat by Luton.

It got worse. Two days after the loss at Kenilworth Road Gould was sacked, with his assistant Don Mackay taking over until the end of the season. The manager who had brought Jol to Highfield Road had gone. Jol recalls: "Unfortunately Coventry sacked Bobby Gould, but just before it was to be announced, he took me to one side, in the toilets, and told me: 'Tell everybody I promised you a free transfer, I'm leaving.'

Don MacKay took over and told me he wanted me to stay. I said: 'No Don. I want to go back to Holland and Bobby promised me a free transfer'.

I think Bobby must have said the same to a few of the players. I was soon on my way back to Den Haag and Don didn't last five minutes."

Jol would not make another appearance for the club. He had played just 15 matches for the Sky Blues and did not find the net in their colours.

Stuart Pearce is another man with a fearsome image. Utterly dedicated as a player, his grounding was in the school of hard knocks that is non-league football. Clearly too talented to remain at that level, he gave up his job as an electrician and signed for Coventry from Wealdstone. It was there he met Jol. Just as jol had a side-line, Pearce kept up his occasional trade to earn some spare cash when he first turned professional, but Jol was not one of the players Pearce used to perform odd electrical jobs for. Jol says: "I can't remember him doing electrical jobs at Coventry. Even then we were on quite good wages of £500 or £600 a week. He was from London and everybody said he was a Cockney. I hadn't heard that expression before. They called him 'Psycho' later, after Coventry, but he had the same approach then. The utter dedication. The eyes! He was not outspoken but was a real pro. He was tough and he had such big legs! He was quiet but had a great mentality and brought that will-to-win into his Man City team and then into the England Under-21 side which did so well in the 2007 Euroeann Championships. And it's not an artificial thing with him. Everybody knows he REALLY wants to win."

Now neither Pearce or Jol manage in the Premiership they share something in common, of course. But back in 1985 as the pair left Coventry to go their separate ways, little did anyone know that each man would be moving on to the greatest period in his career. Pearce joined Brian Clough at Nottingham Forest and became a legendary captain and England full-back. Jol opted to flit back to Holland, rejoining ADO Den Haag, a club which boasted European Cup winner Tony Morley, the former Aston Villa left-winger, among its ranks. Jol went on to become the Dutch Footballer of the Year in 1986/87. Remarkably the club were in the Eerste Divisie (second level), making Jol's achivement all the more laudable. He was enjoying his football again and finding the time and space to be able to express himself. he was used more as a play-maker than a crunching tackler and, it has to be said, the Dutch game ws the poorer for having lost almost all of its great stars to foreign climes, while a new generation had not grown up to replace them at the same level. Having come so close to winning the World Cup in both 1974 and 1978, Holland failed to qualify for both the 1980 and 1984 European Championship finals and the 1986 World Cup. It was not until the likes of Ruud Gullit, Marco van Basten and Frank Rijkaard emerged that the Dutch national side burst back onto the world stage, winning the 1988 European Championship in West Germany in style. By the time of that exciting development, Jol's playing career was effectively over, despite him being aged just 32. He had played 135 games and scored six goals in his second spell at the club at which he had burst onto the scene in the mid-1970s.

The desire and passion that Jol and Pearce shared all too briefly at Coventry is something that Jol carried with him throughout his career as player and then as he began his managerial career. Opting not to join the Del-Boys and Rodneys on the morning market stalls, in an era when players of any standard had to work post-playing career, it was obvious what awaited the talented and driven midfielder upon his retirement in 1989. To those who know him best, coaching seemed a natural progression for Jol. Cyrille Regis, who followed Jol in moving from the Hawthorns to Highfield Road in October 1984, says: "It certainly doesn't surprise me at all. I think that Martin comes across as a very honest manager and he has certainly galvanised Tottenham. The players all seem to enjoy his structure which allows them freedom to express themselves."

There has been precious little previously written about Jol's beginnings either as a player, and even less about his early coaching days. To shed light on the early Jol coaching years a succession of familiar faces from his past in Holland give valuable insights.

Jol's first coaching job was in the Dutch non-League, at the club he had retired from playing at, ADO Den Haag; the ADO in the name stands for *Alles Door Oefening*, which means 'Everything Through Practice'. Taking over at the helm of the club in 1991 from Head Coach Co Adriaanse, who had been hand-picked by Ajax to develop their exciting youth squad which would eventually spawn the likes of Patrick Kluivert, Kiki Musampa Nordin Wooter and Martin Reuser, Jol was tasked with dragging the club, still essentially amateurs, from where it languished in the Third Division of the Dutch league, a division that is in essence a regional league. By the time, four years later, he had cajoled the side into shape, they had risen to the Eerste Divisie, the second rung of the Dutch system. Aside from the years of the Second World War, when the club won the hastily-arranged league title in successive seasons, this was as successful as ADO had ever been. Indeed Jol's platform was the springboard for more recent success which has seen the club in the top flight of Dutch football for four years for the first time in their history, before suffering relegation in 2006/07.

After taking Den Haag as far as he felt he could, Jol was ripe for a new challenge. Perhaps one of the big clubs would take a chance on him, or maybe a middling but established Eredivisie club. But instead Jol found himself head-hunted by the fishing town club close to his heart. In fact Jol couldn't resist the lure of the small seaside suburb in which he was born, Scheveningen. And what a move it would prove to be as Jol brought them amateur trophies galore before he moved on to successful spells at unfashionable mainstream professional club Roda JC, with whom he won the Dutch Cup, the equivalent of the FA Cup, and then RKC Waalwijk. That success brought his coaching skills to wider attention, but is an incredible thought that a man who rose to revive one of football's greatest clubs, began his rise to such acclaim in a tiny north sera fishing town at an amateur team. Incredible but true.

Scheveningen won the Hoofdklasse (the top level of national amateur football) in the 1995/96 season, Jol's first in charge. In order to do so they had to win their regional section of the Saturday amateur championship, then play-off to win the Saturday title outright before playing the Sunday winners for the right to be named national amateur champions. It was the first and only time that Scheveningen have won such an accolade.

Captain of that all-conquering Scheveningen side was teacher John Blok, who recalls: "It was just extraordinary that our small amateur team should become champions in Martin's first season, but then again it shouldn't surprise you because Martin was all about football. A great motivator, he also had great skills, so if he wanted to show you something and you were not getting it, just give him the ball and he would put it away for you. He is the only trainer I have come across who could motivate everybody. He is the only trainer I truly learned something from. Off the pitch he is one of the guys and continues to talk football. I saw him at a game in Holland in May 2006 and we had a few beers and talked about our team. Once a year still, even though it is over a decade ago, all the team get together and a play a game with Martin as the coach. Last year Scheveningen opened our new home, and Martin came over to coach the team for a game."

Most of Jol's friends find it tough to find a 'story' they can tell about Martin. He is not that kind of guy. It begins to become clear that if Jol ever had anything to hide, any skeletons in the cupboard, then these guys were never going to spill the beans.

But John says: "I can tell you this story about Martin. He is very superstitious. So, if he hit on a winning run, he wouldn't want anything different; the guy bringing the coffees would have to put the cups down in the exact spot as always. Martin insisted that he would have to wear the same thick jacket when our team kept winning. Fine. But it was more than a touch uncomfortable in the summer. Even when it was 25 degrees, Martin sat in the dugout wearing this thick winter jacket!"

John was delighted that Jol was making such a success at Spurs when I spoke to him in early 2007. He said: "I think he is doing a great job, two years running in Europe is a wonderful achievement for a club that was a bit down before Martin took control. His team are also playing nice football. But knowing Martin, he wants more, much more for the team. One of his strengths is improving the young guys and you can see that happening at Tottenham. He is a great coach on every level."

But no man knows Jol the embryonic coach in Holland better than the lovely old boy Arie de Jager, who was the major player on the Scheveningen committee that persuaded him to move back 'home' to the seaside on the lavish salary of £120 a week.

Arie recalls: "Martin had stopped playing and was the trainer at Den Haag, but although we were an amateur team we felt that Martin could take us to a higher level and we were right. I was Chairman of the committee, and together with others, felt that Martin Jol was the right man to bring to our club. We had noticed that he did good work for Den Haag, and although we are a small fishing town by the coast, everybody knew everybody, so the fact that Martin was born here meant we knew him very well and wanted him as our trainer and I felt that he would come because the club meant so much to him. He was only with us for one-and-a-half years, but in his first season he won our championship and we then played for the Holland amateur championship and he gave us all the championships in that year, 1995/96. We paid him 1,500 guilders a month, and I would say 10 years ago that was about £500 a month. It was perhaps as much as 20,000 guilders for the season, the normal salary for a coach at our level at that time, but he wasn't part-time. He worked the whole day for the club. He took training three days a week, match days on Saturday, but he also worked every hour for the club. He was good value, a hard worker."

Arie has remained a close friend of Martin as he says: "He came back to our club when Tottenham's season had finished. He visited us on 26 May, just after the Premier League season had ended, and we drank a few beers and spoke to each other. I have been three times to London since he has been there. I went there last year and the year before. Martin is a very nice man and never forgets his friends. He has a great deal of respect for those who, like himself, work hard. He brought success to Tottenham. In Holland, Tottenham had a good reputation for being a big club, but in recent years they have lost some special feeling over here, but since Martin joined them it seemed maybe they could become a big club again."

Close friend Jan Hermen has also kept in touch with Martin. "We have known each other for 40 years, and there are few people in football you can call a friend, but Martin is a friend, a real friend," he told me.

Jan is one of the Jol's inner circle of friends and few know his methods better. He observes: "Martin hasn't changed at all from the first day he went into coaching. He is exactly the same as he was 20 years ago when he began coaching with the local amateur team. In Holland Martin is famous for his knowledge of the game and for his man-handling [man-management]. He can start off by calling a player into his office and telling him off, he might tell him straight that he's too fat, too lazy and how he is going to have to change, but by the end of the conversation Martin concentrates on the player's strengths, giving him compliments and encouragement. The player walks out of the office feeling as if he's won the lottery. He feels good, but then Martin has got his point over at the start of the conversation."

Jan knows that Jol would have spent the summer of 2007 sitting on the beach by his newly purchased house in Spain thinking non-stop about the new season. "He bought the house in 2006 after the World Cup," says Jan, "and I can picture him now sitting his bum on a seat on the beach thinking about what he plans to do in the next season. He never stops thinking about football or talking about it."

Perhaps Jol's greatest success in Holland came at Roda JC, from Kerkrade in the south of the country, an unfashionable club nicknamed 'the coal miner's club'. That reference has a hint of snobbishness about it from the Dutch elite as the coal mines actually closed in the early 1960s, but the team has managed to stick around in the Dutch Eredivisie since winning promotion in 1973. After reaching the final of the KNVB Cup on three previous occasions, Roda finally won the Cup for the first time in their history under the charge of a certain Martin Jol. Now hardened after over five years in management, Jol had come into the club after the sacking of Eddy Achterberg on 1 November 1996. His unprecedented success at the amateur levels had earned him a crack at the big time, and he joined Roda with the blessing at all who had experienced the great times at Scheveningen.

Roda rallied throughout the 1996/97 season and became very difficult to beat under Jol, who instilled his discipline and style of attacking play in equal measure. The club progressed through the Cup rounds until they found themselves facing Heerenveen in the final. A 4-2 win brought Roda's first trophy of any kind for 30 years and a first major win in the two Dutch competitions, the League and Cup. It was an achievement which has to merit on a par with Wimbledon or Jol's old club Coventry lifting the FA Cup in the 1980s.

Job done at Roda, Jol moved on to RKC Waalwijk. The club's name is derived from 'Rooms Katholieke Combinatie' [Roman Catholic] and was a fusion of the previous clubs from the town HEC, WVB and Hercules. Its new stadium, the 6,200 seater Mandemakers Stadion was opened in 1996 and featured a match against Roda JC. Two years later and the Roda manager that day, one Martin Jol, would find himself at the helm of a club capable of challenging the holy trinity of Dutch football, Ajax, PSV and Feyenoord for silverware.

But first there was another job to accomplish. Jol was brought into RKC in 1998 to avert disaster as they teetered above the relegation zone. He managed to steer them to the safety of 16th place, as the 18th and bottom placed club is relegated, being replaced by the Champions of the Eerste Divisie, while the 17th placed club plays off against the second placed team in the division below.

Marcel Brands, Waalwijk's director of football, explains how Jol transformed the club: "At the moment Martin Jol became our trainer in 1998 we were bottom of the list, but he built a new team and we've been going up ever since. We finished 13th in his first season and that was the only year we had problems because we were bottom halfway through. Every other year we were one of the top ten clubs in Holland. Our best performance was seventh place in 2002, when we lost out on a UEFA Cup place on goal difference on the last day of the season. For two or three years in a row we were fighting for the European places, but never quite made it. That was the only disappointment of Martin's time, but we're not a club that aims for European football. We've got a very small budget of seven million euros and get crowds of just 6,000. We're one of the smallest clubs in Holland and to be competing with the top eight or nine teams is a great achievement. We're a very small club in a small town, but had the best period in the club's history under Martin."

Indeed Waalwijk qualifying for Europe would have been like a club such as Colchester doing the same in England. Almost impossible.

Brands believed that Jol possesses all the qualities to achieve success wherever he works, boasting a combination of Arsène Wenger's eye for detail and Jose Mourinho's tactical acumen.

Like his London rivals, Jol is a supremely intense individual with few interests away from his job. Brands told me: "Martin's very intense with football, so doesn't have much of a life outside the game. He has friends and a small child, but never plays golf or any other sports. That's not for him, as he's 100 per cent focused on football. His secret is that he is busy 24 hours a day with football. His greatest quality is his tactical understanding and he was the best tactical coach in Holland. What he can do with a team is amazing. Quite frequently we would have a poor first half, but he would change one or two things and we'd go on to win the game. He thinks about football all the time and is very intense. He's not a great humorist, only in his free time. He's very, very professional, which can be difficult because not everyone has his standards. He always gives 100 per cent and expects the same from the people around him, the players, directors, medical staff and everyone at the club."

Brands also reveals a more sensitive side to Jol the man: "Martin has a good personality, which is also important. He's a very sensitive man and is not always what he seems. He often looks quite angry and in a bad mood, but is a very nice person with a big heart. He's not just focused on results and is also interested in the human being inside the football player. Because of his personality it's not often necessary for him to lose his temper, but he likes discipline and will not tolerate crazy things. He doesn't give privileges to special players and the team is the most important thing. He never needs to punish players because they tend to do what he wants anyway. Martin has the potential to work with the biggest clubs in Europe."

During his time with Waalwijk, Jol brought through talents such as Khalid Boulahrouz, now at Chelsea, as his side finished fourth in 2000/01. Despite experiencing that agonising last-day disappointment by missing out on the UEFA Cup, the club did have a European adventure as it meant they qualified for the Intertoto Cup. Jol's side lost out to TSV Munich 5-2 on aggregate, but he had tasted the big time and wanted more. With progress increasingly difficult at one of Holland's smaller sides, Jol announced he would leave the provincial club at the end of the 2003/04 season, making it clear he was looking for the big move that, at the age of 48, he felt his talents and experience deserved.

Jol had worked wonders at RKC on a very tight budget. He earned a reputation of developing the club's younger stars, with several of them regularly featuring for the Dutch Under-21s. He was named Dutch Football Writers Coach of the Year in 2001, when his side finished seventh in the Eredivisie, and Dutch Players and Coaches Coach of the Year the following season as they ended up eighth. In subsequent seasons Waalwijk could only finish in mid-table, but Jol's credentials were assured as a man on the rise in the game.

Former Ipswich Town and Manchester United midfielder Arnold Muhren revealed how Jol managed to achieve this success for a team with a relatively small budget. "I work with the Ajax academy and I used to see him at our second team matches looking for players he could take to RKC to put in his first-team squad and improve his team. He was very shrewd. He would also look for players at the end of their contracts who he could sign for free. He was very good at picking the right players."

Another close friend and former working colleague Zelijko Petrovic was delighted to talk about the man and the coach he knows intimately on both levels. Petrovic discussed his days as assistant and player in the final year of Jol's five year spell at Waalwijk. Petrovic, who has recently been Ruud Gullit's assistant at Feyenoord and managed Portuguese First Division side Boavista, but is now himself in charge of Waalwijk, disclosed his knowledge of the Jol method: "He is one of the most intelligent coaches in the world. He is tactically very strong. He makes players better. I have played football for more than 20 years, in World Cups for Yugoslavia and Champions League and of all the coaches I have come across Martin is one of the best. They say you have to win something to be one of the best, but people forget that sometimes a big achievement is something other than winning when you are at a club that has less resource. I could see that every year at Waalwijk there was progression with the team under Martin. As his assistant I learned everything from him.

I would want to be the second Martin Jol, that is what I hope, that is what I would call success. I have become very good friends with Martin and I know how he thinks about football for 24 hours a day, I am sure he thinks about football in his sleep. This is what I like about him."

Petrovic has strong views about the challenges that faced Jol as he endeavours to metaorphosise Spurs into a trophy-winning club. He said: "He is a good professional, genuine, always busying himself to make his team and his players better. He strives for improvement. He had a very difficult 2006/07 at Tottenham, but in my opinion in the end he actually had a fantastic season. You cannot be No. 3, No. 2, or champion in England with a club like Tottenham, it is impossible in this day and age. Even clubs such as Newcastle have budgets that are much bigger. Yet to finish No.5 for the second year in a row was just fantastic for a club like Tottenham. In my view Martin has a good chance of being a coach one of the very big clubs in England or one of the big clubs in Europe. And Martin Jol at a big club – he will turn them into champions, for sure. He is a coach of the highest, highest level."

On a personal level, Petrovic says of Jol: "He never forgets a friendship. He brings his friends to London to watch games, He calls me every two weeks to see if I'm OK and to see if I need anything. He is a very good person. Of course it is hard for me to talk about Martin as a friend, but for me he is a good man and a top coach, and I just hope that in one or two years' time he is at a very big club in England."

Ton Verkerk was Jol's right-hand man and assistant at RKC Waalwijk for five years prior to Petrovic's arrival, and succeeded him as coach at the Dutch Second Division side, so there are few people who know Jol more deeply. Verkerk cannot speak highly enough of the man and the professional. He says: "From the first few months working with Martin I began to know him very well. He likes to be in charge, and I like the way he handles a group of players. He is always very consistent with them, and also very persuasive. He makes his meaning very clear, he knows exactly what he wants them to do, and they understand and respond to him. Yes, it took just the first three or four months as we battled against relegation, but I already knew that Martin was an excellent coach. I have since worked with several coaches, some top coaches, but Martin has been the best, and I would rate him one of the best coaches around."

The pattern seems to be identical, once a friend and confidante of Jol's always a friend, and Verkerk is no exception. He keeps in touch on a regular basis and closely followed his career at Spurs. He says: "He was doing a fabulous job, getting the club into the UEFA Cup was special for a club like Tottenham, especially in 2007. It was a very difficult start to the season with so many games in Europe, and the fact that they ended up fifth in the league for the second year running cannot be bad. He was competing with the top four clubs, who are very rich and have far greater resources, but the game isn't always just about money and I believed that if anyone could break into that top four Martin could do that.

I last saw Martin a few months before the end of the 2006/07 season when he invited me to their Chigwell training ground. The fact that we worked together as colleagues and friends for five years means an awful lot to a man like Martin. He is always on the phone, he is regularly in contact and I see him as often as I can."

As for Jol the man, Verkerk reveals: "From the outside, perhaps a manager like Martin Jol doesn't look nice at times; there is a dark side, but inside he is a very good person. In Holland we would say he has a 'little heart', but I suppose you would say he has a big heart. But he is a very nice person, a family man, and at all times he worries about his kids and his family. He is someone who has been brought up in a big family, with brothers and a sister and many relatives, and they are always visiting him in London.

As a professional he has a talent for his team talks. I have been in the dressing room for those five years listening to Martin Jol the manager making his players feel taller before they go out to play. He has the power of finding the right words. Maybe it is more difficult in England because it is a foreign language, but he gets his message across. He knows how to motivate players, with simple words, and phrases such as 'We are building a Church and the players are so important to the foundations,' he gives them a clear message. He can make players believe they are invincible."

THE ARRIVAL AT
WHITE HART LANE

MARTIN JOL'S ELEVATION to Spurs boss proved to be a case of hitting on the right decision by pure chance – and by a somewhat round-about route.

The 2003/04 season had seen the Tottenham board dispense with the services of Glenn Hoddle as manager after just a handful of games. Director of Football David Pleat and first team coach Chris Hughton took charge for the remainder of the season while the board scouted the football world for the man with the kind of ideas that would revolutionise the club as thoroughly as the appointment of Arsène Wenger had done for neighbours Arsenal. The plan was to take the remainder of what was now a 'dead' season to prepare the club for taking a huge leap forward. Chairman Daniel Levy's ambitions were to make Tottenham serious challengers.

The targets were selected carefully and pursued diligently. After a discrete dinner date with Celtic manager Martin O'Neill and an almost year-long, frustrating and ultimately abortive wait for the Ulsterman, Levy turned to then Italian national boss Giovanni Trapattoni as he sought a man with international pedigree and experience. Spurs held a secret summit with Trapattoni in his home town of Cusaro Milanino and the Italian shook hands on an offer that wasn't described as dizzying, but was one 'he could not refuse.' The master plan was for Trapattoni to take up his appointment immediately after the 2004 European Championships irrespective of whether Italy won the tournament or not. Spurs had approached Trapattoni after Daniel Levy had lunch with Sven-Göran Eriksson to listen to recommendations. Roberto Mancini, who would later become the highly successful coach of Intger Milan was also among those on Levy's radar.

A slump in results under Pleat, which at one point took Tottenham alarmingly into the relegation zone towards the end of 2003/04 as the players began to feel the intertia which inevitably followed having no man at the helm for such a prolonged period of time, prompted the board to make a decision sooner rather than wait until the end of the season when the Irishman had indicated over dinner he would consider his options.

So Trapattoni was their man. But despite the deal being essentially in place and a contract ctually being drawn up, Spurs officially refused to confirm or deny what would be a spectacular appointment. The official website said: "We have not commented on any speculation regarding the managerial position and we are not about to do so now. At this point in time, no contract has been signed with any potential new manager."

Trapattoni was due to step down as national coach after the tournament in Portugal, which ultimately proved disastrous for the Azzurri as they failed to qualify from their group, bowing out on a torrent of rain in Guimaraes after failing to beat either Denmark or Sweden. But the whole process of recruiting him ahead of the tournament had the kind of consequences that beset the FA when, in seeking a replacement for Eriksson two years later, they offered the job to incumbent Portugal coach Phil Scolari prior to the World Cup in Germany. It emerges now that Trapattoni's wife influenced the experienced coach to opt to take up the reigns at Benfica, rather than manage in Britain. At the time it seemed that Spurs prevaricated, had a change of heart and settled on recruiting French national coach Jacques Santini, whose own team failed to progress beyond the quarter-finals of Euro 2004 in defence of their trophy despite the talents of Vieira, Henry and Zidane within its ranks. News of Santini's appointment was broken on 3 June, three weeks before the tournament kicked off. Certainly it felt like a bold move but there were questions marks over whether Spurs were opting for third or fourth choice.

Amidst all this, the news of Martin Jol's arrival at White Hart Lane as Santini's assistant on 10 June 2004 hardly made much of a ripple. Jol was just pleased to join a club the size of Tottenham: "I'm extremely happy to be joining Tottenham. I know the club well from my time in England as a player. I enjoyed my time at RKC, but I wanted a new and exciting challenge. Joining Tottenham is the right opportunity for me. I regard Jacques Santini as one of the best coaches in Europe and am very excited at the prospect of working with him, (sporting director) Frank Arnesen and all the good players at the club."

Santini believed Jol's knowledge of the English game could prove invaluable. "All successful coaches have excellent assistants and I'm very pleased I will have Martin as mine," he said.

The French coach had not been the only internationally-renowned name to rate Jol's achivements in Holland. Manchester United manager Sir Alex

Ferguson had been in contact with Jol early in the summer of 2003 about becoming his No. 2 at Old Trafford. It was a tremendous offer and one Jol considered deeply, but in the event he opted to remain at the helm of Waalwijk for one final season and former assistant to Ferguson, Carlos Queiroz, who had taken his leave of Manchester for the opportunity to manage in his own right at Real Madrid, was fired at the end of the 2003/04 Spanish season and was reappointed at Old Trafford in June 2004 after a season of Ferguson being in sole control.

But in an astonishing turnaround which confounded that elongated search for the right man to take the Tottenham job, Santini, whose defensive style was not loved by Spurs fans even though his reign began with a couple of 1-0 victories and an unbeaten run of seven games, left the club for 'personal reasons' after just 13 matches in charge. In a statement, the Frenchman said: "My time at Tottenham has been memorable, and it is with deep regret that I take my leave. Private issues in my personal life have arisen which caused my decision. I have therefore requested to return to France. I very much hope that the wonderful fans will respect my decision. I should like to thank Frank Arnesen and Daniel Levy for their understanding. I wish the club and the supporters all the best for the season." Arnesen added: "We are obviously disappointed that Jacques is leaving us. We fully respect his decision. I can assure you that the club will act swiftly to minimise the impact of Jacques' departure. Our priority is to ensure that this season's performance remains unaffected by this move. I shall make a further statement on Monday clarifying our position. We wish Jacques well."

Santini's departure opened the opportunity for Jol to stake his claim. As he took charge of the team for the game against Charlton, former Tottenham manager David Pleat wrote in his *Guardian* column:

> There are bound to be serious criticisms of the structure in place at the club with a head coach and director of football. It may be unusual to have that system in this country, but I would say without hesitation that it can work. Whatever the reasons for Santini's resignation, Tottenham have no need to rip up or doubt their philosophy. The idea that the head coach will always feel compromised by the director of football is wrong. There shouldn't be any tension. It should be a way of bringing stability, maintaining continuity and taking pressure off the person in charge of the first-team squad. That will not work, though, unless two things

happen. First, that the director of football appoints the head coach. And second, that he does not sign players against the head coach's wishes. If those points are respected the system can be a success. On the continent every club uses it. I see it as logical. The director of football can put down a long-term structure and relate it to the chairman and the rest of the board. The directors at Tottenham and most clubs have never kicked a ball in anger and, with respect to them, would not cross the road to watch a lower-league game on a mid-winter night. They are only interested in their own club and that's the only football they see. They cannot make comparisons, be experts or have an empathy with the dressing room and that is where the director of football comes in. In any other company no-one would think twice about that sort of idea.

The lines of responsibility between the director of football and head coach need to be very clear, though. Take signings, for example. When it comes to buying for the first-team squad, the head coach should request players in certain positions and then get together with the director of football. He can make recommendations which the director of football and the board can either agree or disagree with. There might be times when a head coach is not allowed the player he wants because of their price or age or whatever, but that happens at any club. The important thing is that the director of football does not sign players without the coach's knowledge. That at least applies to the current first team. The director of football can have sole responsibility for acquiring future first-team players.

A role I thoroughly enjoyed at Tottenham was bringing in good, young British players for the future. Simon Davies from Peterborough and Anthony Gardner from Port Vale are examples of how well that can turn out. In general the director of football has to look after the long-term structure, involving the scouting network, the academy set-up and so on. I think it helps if he understands the culture of football in the country, even better the culture of the club. Tottenham brought in Frank Arnesen as director of football and three coaches in Santini, Martin Jol and Dominique Cuperly [Santini's assistant at Olympique Lyonnais]. To bring in four foreign personnel like that at any one time was a massive gamble. I thought Santini never seemed comfortable. His presence on the touchline did not look either particularly animated or authoritative. But it seems that Arsène Wenger's magnificent success at Arsenal has led to an almost slavish desire by some chairmen to go the foreign route.

I would probably have gone for an Alan Curbishley-type of figure, someone who has done the hard miles, known success and failure and has an idea of the Premier League and the British game. What Tottenham do next should become clear soon but I do not think they need doubt their structure.

It was a turbulent time for Tottenham. Not only had they lost a high profile manager for no apparent reason, but the legendary Bill Nicholson had also recently passed on. The club was in a very sombre mood.

In fact Jol's mood was no better. He had been ready to walk out on Spurs just weeks before Santini's resignation. Jol had been appointed 'first assistant to Jacques Santini' in the new management structure devised by Levy that summer. At its pinnacle sat Frank Arnesen, the new sporting director. But, after 15 years in management, and being a strong-willed man who, as he puts it "always bites back", Jol wasn't used to not being in charge.

He told me: "I came to the club as a coach, but then Jacques Santini brought his assistant from Olympique Lyonnais [Dominique Cuperly] in. So I was here for two months, but I didn't do a lot and after a couple of months I thought 'it's been a good experience and it's a great club, but this is not for me.' I was not waiting for him to get sacked or for him to say that it wasn't what he wanted. I would have stayed until January, because what I thought would happen – me working on the training pitch and Jacques in his office – wasn't happening. I told him that too. But then in the November, that's what he did, said it wasn't working.

I had been so delighted when I was offered the job by Frank Arnesen, who called me to tell me I would be the coach or trainer. But. I took that to mean I would be the man coaching the team. That was what we called it in Holland, but when I came over to London and met the chairman Daniel Levy he told me: 'no, somebody else is the man who coaches the team and you will be his assistant; the trainer.' He explained to me that the club had a lot of problems and needed a big name manager from France for a number of reasons and they had lined up Santini. He explained they had promised the supporters a big name. I had to think twice about whether I wanted to stay. Then I walked out onto the White Hart Lane pitch and thought to myself it is not best to be a number two, I had never been, but I wanted to be at this football club I had wanted it for some time. For the first time I decided I was prepared to give being a No. 2 a try and that's what I did. But I wasn't happy.

After a couple of weeks of doing the job I knew it wasn't for me. I already wanted to go back home, but I decided I would give it to January and then I would go back. Fortunately enough for me, after three months Santini had gone and they asked me to take his job. That was exactly what I wanted and what I had wanted from the start. In fact in 2000 when I was taking part in this Dutch TV documentary about me while I was coach at Waalwijk, I was standing on the beach in my fishing village talking about football and told them I wanted to 'go there' and pointed across the water. The Producer asked me where I was pointing and I told him: 'the first beach in England is Clacton-on-Sea and from there I would like to go to Tottenham Hotspur and be their coach/trainer. That was the club I played against in my first game away from home for West Brom. At that time there was a prog called *Saint & Greavesie* and both Ian St John and Jimmy Greaves gave me big compliments about my debut.'

I was always asked why I liked Spurs so much. There was nothing really about their shirts, yet they were special to me even though they wore black and white, because in the 1960s I loved Madrid and Spurs and I loved them for their brand of football. Tottenham was my favourite club for some while and I just loved White Hart Lane and the players who played there as I grew up and became a footballer; Hoddle, Ardiles. Spurs are known as a cup team in Holland and the Producer asked me why I favoured a team who were always an embarrassing cup team only and not strong enough to win the championship. I said I still liked them because of the players and the style and the tradition, because of Jimmy Greaves in '66 and even as a 10 year-old I knew he should have been playing for England in the final because he was the best goalscorer in their country. I remember when I first met Greaves I told him how embarrassed I was that he hadn't played in that game and how much I liked Spurs. Actually a lot of players in Holland pick out Spurs as their favourite club. I even remember Dirk Kuyt telling me how he loved Tottenham. Perhaps that was because we were thinking of signing him at the time and it wasn't long before he was saying how much he loved Liverpool!

If you really want to know whether I really said all that in 2000 it's not difficult because it's on that documentary. You can see it."

In one of those curiosities of the game, I'm assured that Jol could have had the West Bromwich Albion manager's job instead of Bryan Robson in

October 2004 after Gary Megson departed from the club. Albion needed a manager and were looking for a talisman to ignite their battle to stay in the Premiership after winning promotion at the end of the previous season. The story goes that the Dutchman had made the decision to come "home" until lightning moves by the London club saw a rapid promotion to the top job for Jol.

Jol says: "I was asked to go and speak to the board and there were seven people there and they all said: 'we want you to do it'. And I thought this was what I wanted. I'd thought a lot about going to England and when I was young about going to Spurs. I had always said I want to go to England, to Spurs. I didn't say to Blackburn or anyone. Spurs. So when I had the chance there was no way I would say I wasn't doing it."

So Albion were rebuffed, their board opting instead for Bryan Robson as their second choice to replace the man who had, as a player, back in 1981, replaced Robson as midfield enforcer at the Hawthorns.

Incredibly, just five months after being hired as the No. 2, Martin Jol was confirmed, on the 8 November 2004, as the new head coach of Tottenham at the start of the club's AGM at White Hart Lane. Clearly he had made an impression in his few months at the club, but was this simply a case of an unexpected managerial change lumbering the directors with no serious options?

Whatever the circumstances, Jol immediately pledged he would work towards the standards set by the great Bill Nicholson. Jol now reflects on how his Spurs managerial career began boldly, mentioning the feats of the late, great, Bill Nick and admitting he was operating under the shadow that has proved well beyond all Spurs bosses for the past 33 years. "I didn't say I want to be the second Bill Nicholson," Jol recalls. "Although I could have said it; I was already the second Bill Nicholson in my heart. I remember in the stadium, when they sang for Bill Nicholson, I thought: 'I want to have the same feeling from the fans Bill Nicholson had.'"

Jol has always pledged to be 'one thing', at least... "authentic"... by which he means honest. He said: "If that doesn't happen, then I hate myself. Whether it's Daniel Levy, the President or the Queen. If there is something on my mind, I say it. I am totally independent from everyone. I will still eat the same sandwich, with the same thing on it, in 40 years' time."

Jol become the club's sixth premanent manager in seven years, in which time David Pleat and assistant coach Chris Hughton had held the reigns for five interregnums. Spurs' then sporting director Frank Arnesen said at the time: "Martin is a highly experienced coach and I am delighted he has accepted what to me is one of the most prestigious positions in the Premiership. He has a reputation for creating well-organised teams capable of playing attractive football. He is very technically minded with a good knowledge of English and European football, in addition to first-class man-management skills. We started something here at Tottenham in July and I am confident we can continue to build on that start and that Martin can shape and motivate the team to achieve what we know they are capable of. I know Martin is ambitious for this club."

There is deep admiration from Jol for the much-maligned Dane, who has since been poached by rivals Chelsea. Jol reflects: "The first time I met Frank was here at Spurs. Everybody thought, including my friends, that we knew each other. But I'd never met him before in my life. He was at PSV. I knew he wanted me at PSV as his coach, but I'm not the sort of person to phone him and say: 'Hey, Frank, it's me'. I don't do that. So when he moved over to London he phoned me and asked me to go to Spurs.

If you meet Frank, you know he's a typical football man. He was a star, a great player. And I feel that really great players are always nice people. The players who are not that good are always little fishes. But Frank was good to me, always motivating. If you've got someone who is [high] in the pecking order and plays your boss, I can't stand that. I hate authority. I can't work like that. But Frank was good to me, always motivating. If someone tries to tell me what to do, I won't do that. But it was easy because Frank was so likable and so good in that way. Even after a defeat he was always positive."

So it emerges that Arnesen had wanted to appoint Jol as PSV Eindhoven's manager when he was technical director there, and had been his champion during the summer recruitment process at Spurs. Though they had never met before their shared time at Tottenham, the pair established a bond which split the club's French and Dutch-Danish managerial factions. Results reflected the club's tangled structure until, on fireworks night, Santini quit, with rumblings from within the club making it clear that he had been caught in a vice between Arnesen, the senior man with the link to the board, and his "first assistant", Jol.

Jol had used his time on the Spurs sidelines seeing what improvements he might make. He was placed in temporary charge for the 3-2 home defeat by Charlton, and was delighted to be then be given the job on a permanent basis, signing a contract to May 2007. He said at the time: "Tottenham are a big club and I feel very privileged to be their coach. It is still early in the season, I know the players and they know me and I feel strongly that there is a lot we can achieve together. Yesterday all the players and I were at the memorial service for Bill Nicholson and we could not help but be inspired by the values and standards that he set and which we must try to regain."

Whatever the so-called private reasons for Santini's departure, Jol appeared unsympathetic, adding to shareholders: "In the last couple of days we have communicated with the players more than in the last couple of years."

As Jol stepped into the first-team Head Coach's role, Chris Hughton, the one-club man, who had been at White Hart Lane as a player during the Cup glories of the early 1980s and then became a coach, was promoted to become his assistant.

Daniel Levy attempted to place a positive spin on Santini's departure, insisting that the continental structure he initialised in the summer ensured greater continuity than the more usual English management method. Levy recalled the £16m expenditure on George Graham's signing of Sergei Rebrov (a figure that includes the £11m striker's wages) only for the Scot's successor Glenn Hoddle to sideline the Ukrainian and allow him to go on loan and then give him a free transfer. "For the board and the management team, there were clearly difficult decisions to be made," Levy said. "Ultimately we knew that unless there was fundamental change in the club we would face a period of continuing mediocrity. The changes that took place amounted to substantial restructuring within the club, with a professional structure of like-minded people. We are exceedingly disappointed [that Santini resigned], but you have got to deal with it. When we talk of continuity we are talking in relation to the team. We know coaches often do not have enough time, and we wanted to avoid that at Tottenham. If whoever we brought in did not work out, we didn't want to have to spend another £30m. How can you get football success like that? We have every confidence it will work with Martin."

Frank Arnesen pointed out the strength of this new departure in the hierarchy of British football clubs: "We are working under exactly the same structure as Martin had in Holland with [his last club] RKC Waalwijk," the Dane said. "There is a lot of communication. It is always important in that structure that you have a very good relationship. I had seen Martin from a distance and I told Daniel he was a good man to get into the coaching squad."

But irrespective of the system within which he was working, a more pressing problem remained. Jol found himself in the unenviable position of trying to arrest Tottenham's latest slump. But such a scenario was at least territory he was not entirely unfamiliar with, as he had made a habit of starting at rock bottom. He had accepted the job with RKC Waalwijk, cut adrift at the bottom of Holland's top division with half the season gone. As a small town with a population of just 45,000, not much more than Spurs' average attendance, Waalwijk had little tradition of footballing success, but within a couple of years Jol had them challenging for a place in the UEFA Cup. Spurs' position demanded a similar swift turnaround. They found themselves in 12th position, just five points off the relegation zone.

Despite their predicament and lack of form, Jol made an immediate statement of intent, suggesting that Tottenham should be competing for top honours within two years. The new head coach was impressed by the quality of players he inherited from Santini, but wanted fans to be patient while he moulded a team together. Although Tottenham found themselves in the last eight of the Carling Cup courtesy of a 3-0 win at Burnley in his first game in proper charge of the team, Jol was keen to play down fans' expectation levels for the season. "I promise the supporters – who I hope are realistic – that, if we get the time, in two years we will have a terrific side. By that I mean we will be going for prizes. Maybe next year the target will be European football and after that it is going for prizes."

Two goals from Keane and a Defoe strike gave Jol the perfect start to his reign and erased memories of Spurs' cup exit at Turf Moor in 2002. Jol's first task was to stamp his own mark on the team and to that end he made changes. Midfielder Michael Carrick started his first game since his £3m move from West Ham, which meant Pedro Mendes moving out onto the right wing. Although the Portuguese midfielder adjusted well, Jol believed the move highlighted a weakness in his squad. He said: "We have terrific midfield players, terrific strikers, but we need width."

Jol's early assessment of his squad was entirely accurate. Reto Ziegler was not a natural winger and youngster Rohan Ricketts found the going tough. He would later have spells at a succession of lower division clubs.

Jol had an immediate impact with his oration; never better exemplified by the story told by striker Jermain Defoe, a £7m signing from West Ham just nine months earlier, of a comparison between Jol and Santini the week of the change over. The players witnessed two short speeches in eight days. First from Santini; a muted and partially-explained farewell after just 13 games. From Jol they heard a statement of ambition; Tottenham would finish in the top half of the table that season. Jol informed the squad, it would be "great".

Starring for ADO Den Haag as a teenager earned Jol a big money move to Bayern Munich, triple Champions of Europe, at the age of 22.

With West Germany maestro Paul Breitner, the Bayern Munich captain, who loved Che Guevara and a good time and took Jol under his wing during his year in Germany.

Playing for Bayern at Borussia Dortmund.

Jol was signed by West Bromwich Albion manager Ronnie Allen to add steel to their midfield and ended up becoming a marked man by referees.

The match report from Martin Jol's first visit to White Hart Lane in which he score the winning goal for West Brom and which he keeps as a reminder of how he was first inspired by the stadium.

(Left) Jol's stay at Coventry City was brief.
(Right) Celebrating winning the Dutch FA Cup with Roda JC, the first major trophy in the club's history.

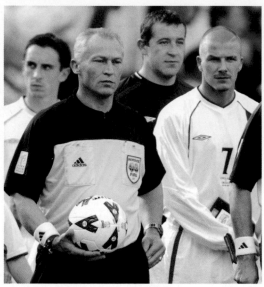

(Left) Coaching RKC Waalwijk, where he turned
perennial strugglers into European contenders.
(Right) Jol's brother Dick, an experienced FIFA referee, leads out the
teams before England's crucial World Cup qualifier against Greece in
November 2001.

Arriving at Spurs as part of the new foreign coaching set up alongside
(left) Dane Frank Arnesen, and (centre) Frenchman Jacques Santini.

Taking control: Jol was handed the reigns after Santini's abrupt departure in early November 2004 and acted as caretaker-manager for the game against Charlton Athletic.

The media scrum that greeted Jol's announcement as the permanent manager of Tottenham Hotspur FC.

Celebrating the opening goal by Noureddine Naybet with the goalscorer during the classic 4-5 home defeat by Arsenal in his first game in charge. Naybet picked up a yellow card from referee Steve Bennett for his exuberant celebration.

With assistant manager Chris Hughton.

Jol joins in the round of applause at the memorial service for legendary Tottenham manager Bill Nicholson. Jol's knowledge and belief in the tradition and heritage of the club stood him in good stead with the fans.

Jol lays down the law in an early training session.

An impressive start both in terms of results and a return to the traditional Spurs way of playing with style and panache led to Jol winning the Manager of the Month award for December 2004.

Making a point to Jermain Defoe in training. The stormy relationship between the two men would eventually come to be a stick with which disenchanted fans beat their manager.

Burying the hatchet with Iain Dowie. An angry Jol had told a newspaper that the Crystal Palace manager was 'not fit to mend my shoelaces', a Dutch phrase that did not translate well.

The reunion with Manchester City manager Stuart Pearce, a former playing colleague at Coventry City, although definitely not wearing one of Jol's dodgy designer jumpers!

Shaking hands with Arsenal's Arsène Wenger in April 2005. The pair almost came to blows on the next occasion they met as Spurs threatened to usurp the Gunners from the fourth Champions League place.

An uneasy partnership: Jol welcomes Sporting Director Damien Comolli to the Lane in the summer of 2005 as replacement for Frank Arnesen, who had controversially moved to Chelsea.

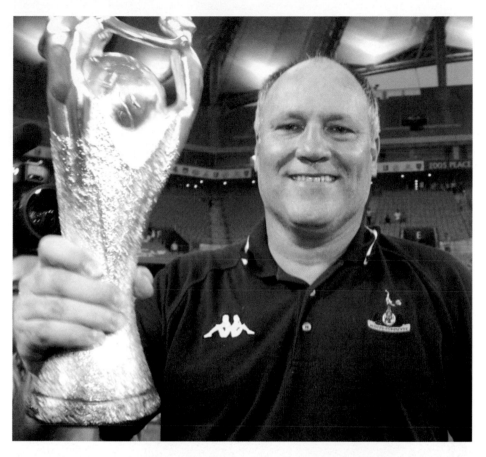

(Above) Celebrating with some silverware: the 2005 Peace Cup.
(Below) The work of a Premiership manager is never done.

Celebrating Martin Jol in pictures.
(Left) Wall art in Holland remembers Jol the player. (Right) Photoshop
helps internet fans christen Jol the 'Tony Soprano of football managers',

Ever popular with supporters across the country, Jol signs programmes
on a visit to Ipswich Town's Portman Road.

Jol cultivated his image as a hardman and a joker and in return earned the respect of millions of fans and the title of 'Most Feared Manager in the Premiership'.

Acknowledging loyal fans at the Lane. Jol became the most popular Tottenham manager in decades.

Jol adopted a wonderfully personable approach to media interviews and believed in answering questions directly and with a smile on his face.

The controversial moment when Roy Carroll fished Pedro Mendes' long range shot out of the Old Trafford net to save a 'goal' when the ball had clearly crossed the line. Jol declared the assistant referee should have 'looked ahead like a fox.'

Jol was not averse to the odd public barb in the direction of his players. 'We have a lot of players who want to play at the club, but they didn't show it here,' was one of his stinging criticisms after a particularly bad defeat.

Nothing scared Jol: not even picking an argument with black belt referee Uriah Rennie after the 1-1 draw at Old Trafford in October 2005.

Sharing a joke with Jose Mourinho.

The glowering Lincolnshire skies match Jol's mood as his team lose to Grimsby in a Carling Cup tie in September 2005.

(Left) Launching the new Tottenham Hotspur club badge alongside club skipper Ledley King.
(Right) Spurs' revival led to Jol's side packing out an expectant White Hart Lane as they strove to finish in the top four of the Premier League for the first time.

The touchline and stands go crazy as the final whistle blows in the last home game of the 2005/06 season. Spurs are just one win away from qualifying for the Champions League after defeating Bolton 1-0.

Defeat at West Ham is painful to take, but especially after the 'Mystery Lasagne' episode which allowed Arsenal to sneak into fourth place.

(Left) The realisation hits that Spurs have been pipped at the post.
(Right) The old magic is still there; pre-season training, August 2006.

Tottenham announce their new signings in July 2006. (From left)
Bulgarian striker Dimitar Berbatov, Cameroonian left-back
Benoit Assou-Ekotto and Ivory Coast midfielder Didier Zokora.

Spurs' slow start to the 2006/07 season began to pick up after Jol's side
went through the UEFA Cup group stage with a 100% record, including
this vital 2-0 victory at Besiktas.

Fireworks on Bonfire Night: Tottenham beat Chelsea for the first time since 1990, coming from behind to win 2-1 at the Lane in November 2006.

Was it or wasn't it a red card for Jol? Hossam Ghaly trudges off after receiving his, but Jol was confused by referee Phil Dowd's instruction at Blackburn and believed he had been dismissed, although Dowd later explained he had only asked Jol to 'stand away'.

The many faces of Martin Jol.

(From left) Michael Dawson, Tom Huddlestone, Robbie Keane and Didier Zokora celebrate after Julio Baptista's own goal has put Spurs 2-0 ahead in the Carling Cup semi-final first leg at White Hart Lane...

...but then two Arsenal goals restored parity and brought the first question marks over Jol's managerial capabilities from fans and board.

Jermaine Jenas celebrates Mido's late equaliser at the Emirates Stadium in the Carling Cup semi-final second leg. Amidst all the criticism over Jol's substitutions in the first leg, no-one spotted that the goal came just five minutes after Jol had introduced the Egyptian as a substitute.

Jol is delighted after a 4-0 thrashing of Fulham in the FA Cup puts Tottenham through to the quarter-final.

Hossam Ghaly has put Spurs 3-1 ahead in the FA Cup quarter-final at Stamford Bridge...

...but the Blues fought back to score a late equaliser and Jol was to be subjected to more criticism after his side lost the replay.

Jol and introspective striker Dimitar Berbatov. The up and down relationship between the pair, and constant speculation about whether the board
forced Jol to play the Bulgarian against his wishes, was another element
which contributed to the manager's eventual downfall.

Meeting his nemesis: Jol encounters then Sevilla manager Juande Ramos before the clubs met in the UEFA Cup quarter-final first leg in Spain.

The game in Seville saw one of the most depressing incidents in recent European football history as Spanish police attacked Tottenham fans without provocation. Jol's stoic reaction backing his supporters won many plaudits.

Jol thanks the White Hart Lane crowd for their support at the end of the 2006/07 season which saw Spurs finish fifth once again.

Spurs' summer 2007 signings: (from left) Jol, Younes Kaboul (£7m from Auxerre), Darren Bent (£16.5m from Charlton), Gareth Bale (up to £10m from Southampton) and Damien Comolli.

The loneliness of the Premiership manager: Jol sees his side concede a last minute goal on the opening day of the 2006/07 season at Sunderland and the machinations to repace him, which have been going on behind the scenes all summer, begin to come to the surface.

A small chink of light in a dreadful opening to the season as Spurs fans celebrate one of the four goals that defeat Derby County.

Robbie Keane and Jol in heated discussion during a break in play of the 3-3 draw at Fulham which Spurs dominated but somehow failed to win. There was heavy criticism of Jol's decision to substitue Keane.

An incredible end to an incredible game as Younes Kaboul celebrates his dramatic injury time equaliser in the 4-4 comeback draw against Aston Villa with his jubilant manager. Was there still hope of survival?

Dimitar Berbatov ends up in the White Hart Lane net, but the ball stays out; just Spurs' and Jol's luck. This time, though, it is in the manager's last game against Getafe... although Jol had no idea it was his swansong.

By the end of the 2-1 defeat, only Spurs' second home loss in Europe, Jol knew something was up.

Jol raises a salute to the fans who had stayed loyal to him right to the end.
The fervent atmosphere at White Hart Lane that night was one of
celebration of the departure of a manager who had brought self-respect
back to the club, rather than doom and gloom at his dismissal.

Happier times. Jol takes the applause after one of his 47 Premier League victories in 112 games; the best record at White Hart Lane since the legendary Bill Nicholson.

Defoe said: "The manager said come the end of the season we should be in the top ten. That would be great. With the players we have, we should be. If we don't do that it'll be devastating for the players, staff and especially the fans."

As for Santini's departure, Defoe said: "At the meeting he apologised that it was the day before a game. I don't think there's much he could have done about it and I don't think there's much we could do. We had the meeting, he said what he wanted to say and that was that, to be honest. It wasn't a long meeting. When you're the manager and you've made your decision, basically that's it. No-one is going to say: 'Mr. Santini, why are you going?' He did say it was for personal reasons and you never know what that means. There's nothing much you can do. But when you're at home you sit down and think: 'pre-season he was here and now he's gone, just like that.' I was warming to Mr Santini, definitely. When someone like him comes to the club, with all his experience, all the players respected him. Obviously it was difficult for him because he didn't speak good English, but he was learning and he was getting better by the day. He was OK. He used to do a lot of the coaching, especially on a Thursday and Friday leading up to games. He would do more then, but Martin did a lot of coaching as well. So it's not like it's someone new again and back to square one. Martin has been here and we have a relationship with him. Hopefully it'll be good for the club."

Defoe pin-pointed the League Cup victory at Burnley as a first sign of Jol's influence. "I think we showed the other night that we got tight to people and he wanted the full-backs to get forward and get crosses in. That showed there was a difference. Martin Jol wants you to play out from the back, full-backs push on, get crosses in. That's what he believes in. As a forward you want that."

Next up a first Premiership victory over Arsenal at the Lane since 1999 would give Jol a much-needed boost, but the game would provide more ways than one of upsetting Jol, Levy and Spurs fans in general. Pre-match, there was little comfort from opposing manager Wenger, who declared he would not have been prepared to operate within the management structure Tottenham persisted with following Santini's resignation. Wenger was unenvious of Jol's position before the north London derby. "Maybe it's because I have too much experience now. There has to be a clear definition of responsibilities," he said. Wenger believed the system could work at Tottenham, though. "The success of that framework depends on complicity and shared vision. Jol and Arnesen look like they share the way they see the job."

The new management team would have little trouble in getting the best out of Carrick as he came up against Arsenal for the first time since they decided not to sign him in the summer. Wenger later apologised to the player for dragging him into the Vieira transfer wrangle as the France midfielder considered his options, but eventually chose to stay at Highbury. Wenger observed: "Tottenham should thank me they got him. I like the boy. He's humble, intelligent and wants to do well. But now I have Flamini and Fabregas."

Santini returned to the Lane in mid-November for the clash with Arsenal as a guest of French television and lost no time in setting the cat amongst the pigeons by denying the official versions of his exit: "I can confirm I have no major family problems and I don't really mind too much what has been said about me. Right from the off there was a problem with who was in charge at Tottenham. I was told I was in charge of first-team matters, but things were not clearly defined. Perhaps we should have spoken more when I signed, but when I arrived it became clear that I was only in charge of coaching the team and not buying players. We never found a way of agreeing how to prepare the season and how to buy new players. It is true that I did not want to sign Michael Carrick. Michael is a good player, and is showing that now, but I didn't need another midfielder. What I really wanted was another centre forward to provide more options and put pressure on other players. Jan Koller was one player I wanted to bring to the club, unfortunately there was not enough money to buy him. I reminded people before the Portsmouth match [18 October] of what I wanted, but they said they weren't that bothered about a new centre-forward. This was frustrating for me, because I was just starting to get my message through and I was not getting any support."

Santini's comments angered Daniel Levy who issued a strongly-worded denial, and pointed out that the role of the head coach was detailed in Santini's contract and the responsibility for securing player signings was made clear from the start. Arnesen, now working in tandem with Jol, denied Santini's claim of a rift: "If he has a problem, then it is his problem. I have no problems with Mr Santini. I stand by what I said previously, absolutely nothing has changed. He is the one in this situation and it is up to him how he handles it. So you will have to ask him why he has said these things. The issues are his. The chairman has made his announcement and that is enough for the club. I want to concentrate on the future and working for the benefit of Tottenham."

Santini saw his successor lose an eventful game, as Arsenal won at White Hart Lane for the first time since May 1999, after four successive draws, in a 5-4 thriller. The televised drama gave other managers pause for comment. "That is not a proper football score; it is an ice hockey result," smouldered Chelsea manager Mourinho. Jol, however, disagreed, pledging himself to romance. "Our crowds saw legends in the past. We want to recreate a bit of our history, and that is all about attacking football." Jol had served up a gripping failure for the White Hart Lane crowd, but it was clear much had to be done before Spurs could go into such games expecting to pick up results.

Jol, who had now supervised two home league defeats and seen his defence leak eight goals in the process, could not find much of a bright side. "One moment I was proud, we were on top and we scored the first goal, then we got sloppy at the back. The equaliser came at a bad moment, just when we needed to kill the game until half-time. We must be doing something right if we can score four against the Arsenal, but although there were some good feelings there were some horrible ones as well." It was Spurs' fifth consecutive Premiership defeat.

After the sixth straight defeat, Jol's third, with another infuriatingly inconsistent performance against Aston Villa, Jol said: "It's difficult if you've had six defeats but we have great team spirit. We're heading for a good spell. We could do with some good results, but are still in the Carling Cup. Every team in the bottom half are worried about their situation. We dominated the first half and it should have been a draw." Jol's main complaint was not with his players, but with referee Chris Foy, who failed to award his side a second-half penalty after Samuel appeared to trip Defoe in the box. Jol said: "I was 80 yards away and thought it was a penalty, but he was ten or 15 yards away and he didn't see it. Samuel clearly stamped on Jermain's feet. I didn't say anything to him because I haven't seen it again on television. Everyone makes a mistake so what can you do? You will probably say my players make a lot of mistakes."

Defoe and strike partner Fredi Kanoute, restored to the starting line-up in place of Robbie Keane, buzzed with life up front, but were starved of service by a woefully ineffective midfield. Michael Brown, a recent acquisition from Championship club Sheffield United, had yet to prove he belonged at this level and Carrick needed to demonstrate the desire to match his undoubted talent. Spurs' defence was even more vulnerable, and it was only the ever reliable Paul Robinson, saving well from Carlton Cole and Solano, who kept them in the game. Swedish left-back Erik Edman was substituted for his own good at half-time after being tormented by Nolberto Solano, although midfielder Thimothee Atouba offered him little protection. It was Solano who grabbed the only goal of the game in the 57th minute. Spurs had no response and their desperation was revealed by the fact that centre-back Callum Davenport made his debut as an auxiliary striker.

Moroccan international Noureddine Naybet added to Spurs' problems by publicly declaring: "This is a moment of crisis but we have a new coach, new system, and new players. It is the worst run of my career and I don't know what to do. I'm very concerned about it, but what can we do?"

Jol's latest setback kept Tottenham only two points off the Premiership relegation zone.

Just 15 days into Jol's resign and the pressure was building up in the media, with an *Evening Standard* headline: 'Jol's in a spot of bother'. The article pointed an accusing finger at Jol suggesting that 'he took control at White Hart Lane pledging to be the next Bill Nicholson, but already he is beginning to resemble a slightly plumper version of Christian Gross'. The *Standard* pointed out that Spurs had not looked like winning any of the three Premiership encounters Jol had supervised and faced Middlesbrough on Sunday fearful of equalling the club's worst ever run of seven successive losses. Could he handle the crisis?

Sunday 28 November 2004 saw a game in which it was possible to envisage Tottenham suffering a club record-equalling seventh successive league defeat, but the match changed decisively with the dismissal of Boro's Franck Queudrue just before the interval, a decision which infuriated then manager Steve McClaren. Jol had little sympathy: "It was a cynical tackle. It was straight on his foot."

Jol at last had a Premiership victory to celebrate and hoped the confidence and flow Spurs showed in the second half could be maintained. Mendes was impressive, setting up Defoe's opener and doing much to link the play and harass Boro. Carrick's distribution was much improved, and King was a mighty presence in defence. Jol made life even harder for ten-men Boro by pushing Atouba forward from left-back. Kanoute scored then clinching second midway through the second half.

There was one cloud that had no silver linging, though, and it marked the beginning of a tense relationship between the manager and one of his most promising players. Defoe ruined his afternoon by picking up a booking for removing his shirt in celebration. That was his fifth caution of the season and ruled him out of the game against Manchester City. A previous yellow card had also come for taking off his jersey. "Amazing," said Jol. "We talk about it and he promises never to do it again. He can't do that." It was pointed out to Jol that Defoe had a birthday message on his T-shirt, suggesting it was planned. "That's even worse if it's true," he replied fearsomely. You had to fear for the tiny striker come training the next day.

The next player to fall foul of Jol's high standards was fellow striker Fredi Kanoute, who cost Tottenham their best chance of silverware in his first season. The Mali international conceded a penalty with an extraordinary handball during extra-time in the Carling Cup quarter-final defeat by Liverpool.

Florent Sinama-Pongolle converted the 117th-minute spot-kick to level the match at 1-1 and force a shoot-out which new Liverpool manager Rafael Benitez's second string won 4-3. To compound Spurs' misery, Liverpool were then handed a plum semi-final draw against Watford. Jol was more conciliatory with this misdemeanour than Defoe's shirt folly, however: "I am disappointed, it was the surest way into Europe. Fredi was too disappointed to say anything. He knows himself he shouldn't have done it because it cost us. The difference between success and failure is so small. I still can't understand it. There was no pressure on him. It was a corner, I mean how could he make a handball? It's one of those things. I don't know why he did it. All you can say is: 'how can you do that?' But he did it and we lost the game because of that. It cost us dearly."

Kanoute also squandered the chance to redeem himself by missing a penalty during the shoot-out. Michael Brown was the other culprit, allowing Pongolle to score from the penalty spot for the second time on the night and seal a dramatic victory for Benitez's side. It was a bad night for more than one reason. Players from both sides wore black armbands as a mark of respect for former Spurs goalkeeper Bill Brown, who had died on the Monday before the cup tie, aged 73. The Scot had made 272 appearances for the club and was part of the 1961 Double-winning team. He had been suffering a long-term illness.

Successive 1-0 away wins in the Premiership at Blackburn and Manchester City got Spurs back on track as Jol's steely influence began the change around which was so vital to the club making progress. The 5-1 victory over Southampton showed that not only could Jol's team grind out away wins, but they could turn on the style at home as well. Recalcitrant strikers Defoe and Kanoute bagged three and one respectively with late substitute Keane the other. This was as good as the Dutchman had promised.

Spurs are never a club far from the headlines, with a mixture of on-the-pitch ups and downs and off-the-pitch political intrigue. It's as traditional as Spurs playing sweet, flowing football and failing to produce consistent enough results to be a serious force in the League. Martin Jol was about to discover how the machiavellian nature of certain elements surrounding the club could create problems from thin air.

On the morning of Spurs' Christmas party, the day after the thumping of Saints, Jol was misquoted in the *News of the World* claiming that the chairman had left the club with an identity crisis because of the large number of managerial changes in recent seasons. Jol swiftly moved to clarify his criticisms and dampen talk of a rift. He said: "It was nice to wake up and read such positive reporting of our game, but one newspaper was still trying to suggest that there are issues at the club. This club has, in the past, had the misfortune of having to change managers due to a lack of success and the chairman altered the management structure in the summer in order to address this. Sporting director Frank Arnesen and I are working hard to get his club back to the top. Daniel Levy is the man who bought us in and we are determined to succeed for him."

His riposte did the trick. Certainly any talk of a rift at that point was way off the mark. There was, instead, a growing belief that Jol was succeeding in turning the club around. King hailed Jol for bringing a winning culture to the Lane that propelled Tottenham out of the doldrums and onto their best run of league form in nearly a decade. The Tottenham squad were brimming with confidence as they headed to Carrow Road on Boxing Day, chasing a fifth consecutive Premiership victory. And that, believed Ledley King, was all down to Jol and the impact he had on the squad since taking over. "He is passionate about his football and wants to be a winner. He is trying to get that across to the players and it is great," said King. "I think it is what we needed, someone to push us on as we've got a lot of young players. We need to get used to being in winning ways and become winners. Over the last few years the club has had to put up with the mediocre, winning a couple of games then losing. We need to get the right mentality to win games regularly and that is what we've started doing."

Tottenham's transformation was remarkable. From losing six straight Premiership games, they embarked on their best run of form since 1995, when managed by Gerry Francis and inspired by Teddy Sheringham up front. "It is great for the club, great for confidence and it has moved us right up the league. We are now looking to work on the back of it," added King. "Everyone is enjoying life at the moment. When you are winning and playing well you enjoy it and are happy about everything – that is how it is now."

Kanoute hit a devastating low when he conceded that penalty late in extra-time against Liverpool, but he had responded with three goals in four games. Was that the influence of Jol at work? Indeed all three of Tottenham's strikers – Kanoute, Keane and especially Defoe – had struck a rich vein of form since Jol had taken over, and he transformed the midfield from its defensive leanings into a creative department. Brown was given the attacking brief, as Carrick shone in the holding role, turning in a sublime performance in the 5-1 win over relegation candidates Southampton.

With the midfield creating chances and the strikers amongst the goals, Tottenham were enjoying the winning habit as Martin Jol's first season in charge really got into the swing.

TOTAL FOOTBALL

'I want Spurs to play like Johan Cruyff.'
Martin Jol

MARTIN JOL ADORES Johan Cruyff's wonderful goals, visionary passes and the kind of dribbling and ball control that set him apart as the maestro of Holland's Total Football in the Seventies. "When I ask people here who was the world's best player, they say Pelé, Maradona or Georgie Best," Jol said early in his tenure. "Ask that question in Holland and they'll all say Johan Cruyff. He was certainly the best dribbler. Look! Look! Who runs with the ball like that? Maybe George Best did, but Cruyff was a better player. He played first-team football from 16 until he was 37. He was a phenomenon.

I told my 13-year-old son 'everybody in my generation tells their children about Johan Cruyff.' Now my son loves rugby. All he talks about is Wilkinson. For me it's a disaster! His education is incomplete if he doesn't know about Cruyff! One Christmas I sat him down and told him all about Cruyff and what he had given to the Dutch people. It was my duty as a father to tell my son as everyone else in Holland must do.

Cruyff brought joy to our football. In the late '60s we were useless. We would lose to Luxembourg. We would never make the big tournaments. No-one gave Dutch football a second glance until Cruyff and coach Rinus Michels came together. Cruyff to anyone in my generation was on a level with Cassius Clay. Cruyff gave us our pride in our country. He played for Ajax and I listened to his exploits on the radio.

I remember the excitement I used to feel as a kid when I watched the great man play. I remember going to watch Ajax putting five past Liverpool in the European Cup in 1966. No-one scored five against Liverpool. In the return at Anfield, Cruyff scored two more. He could dribble, pass, shoot and he used the ball intelligently.

I want to bring the philosophy of Cruyff to Spurs. I want to introduce that kind of quality to Tottenham, starting with the kids in the Academy. Wouldn't you like to see that kind of football in England? Wouldn't you like to see more players like Duff and Robben? I said three years ago that Robben would be a phenomenon. He's as yet a small phenomenon. Cruyff was a big phenomenon. Duff tries to do new things. He's not afraid of failure. It's the Dutch mentality. We like players who take a chance and do unpredictable things, like Robbie Keane. Because I'm Dutch I've always admired players with good technique. I loved Best. He was a legend in Holland. So was Glenn Hoddle. I think he was probably the best two-footed English player of his generation. I want someone at this club who can do things like that again. Sometimes I think we need to go back to basics with the youngsters and teach them all the skills at the very start."

Doing it the Dutch way was a key part of Jol's management style at Tottenham. As much as Cruyff influenced his playing beliefs, Jol was also heavily influenced by another Dutch Master, coach Rinus Michels. "The reason there are so many good Dutch managers at the moment is because of the way we approach football. There are only 15 million people in the Netherlands, but there are one million registered football players. That must be one of the highest ratios in the world. Football is everywhere in my country. Perhaps we are more aware in Holland about the need to support young players not just in the clubs, but throughout the country. When I was a boy we played on the streets all day, every day, and that was how we became good, but you can't do that these days, so now there is the Johan Cruyff Foundation and they are involved in setting up areas for the kids to practise in."

It is for this reason that Jol was keen to work with Premiership sponsors Barclays on helping grassroots football. The Barclays Spaces for Sports scheme, a three-year, £30m partnership between the bank, the Football Foundation and charity Groundwork, aimed to rejuvenate community sport. One of the first sites to benefit is the New River Sports and Recreation Centre, two miles from White Hart Lane, which was renovated by Barclays in partnership with Spurs and Haringey Council.

"There is not as much emphasis on playing the game when you are young here as there is in Holland," Jol said. "Even at Tottenham we do not give our young kids enough training. We see them maybe four or five hours a week. When I was young I played for four or five hours a day. That's why they need somewhere to come to practise and work on their skills. People always think of the Netherlands and Total Football, but that is really only the words of one man, Cruyff, and football is not just about playing a certain way. You have to have organisation as well. And it's not just in Holland that people believe in playing beautifully. People always think that Total Football is about Cruyff, but Bill Nicholson said the same thing years before."

In February 2005 Jol was into only his third month as Tottenham's head coach. From the outset of his Tottenham career, Jol knew that his plans for the future fitted with the club's long-standing traditions of stylish, attacking football. His decision to establish Carrick, ignored and unwanted by Santini, in the heart of Tottenham's midfield gave an indication of his long-term thinking. A creative passer, Carrick enjoyed a vital role in the dramatic reversal of fortunes under Jol which was taking place.

"When I took charge I told the players the three things we needed to succeed – a top mentality, a good team spirit and the intention and desire," the Dutchman said. "That's what I tried to instil in them from day one and I think we've achieved a lot in six or seven weeks. After just a couple of weeks I could see some of the things I was teaching become a reality. But we have to maintain the progress. We have to turn six or seven weeks into months and then years."

Before Spurs' last game of 2004 against struggling Crystal Palace, Jol once again found himself dealing with the fallout of one of his remarks in the press. Palace boss Iain Dowie had been working as a television pundit on the night of Tottenham's defeat to Aston Villa early in Jol's reign and had questioned the selection of Pedro Mendes on the right of midfield.

In return Jol claimed Dowie was "not fit to mend my shoelaces", prompting a response from Dowie challenging the Dutchman to "show some balls" and talk to him face to face.

The row was sparked in an article in the *Daily Mail* by Matt Lawton and it was a harsh but important lesson learnt about how the English press could deal with a foreign manager. blowing things up out of all proportion.

In the article Jol said: "Iain Dowie questions why Martin Jol plays Pedro Mendes on the right. He doesn't know that we had nobody else who could play there. He doesn't know anything about me. I feel like telling him he's not fit to mend my shoelace, but I can't because I have not yet been successful in this country. But Iain Dowie should make a few enquiries about me before he starts criticising me in public. He should also concentrate on the problems he has with his own team at Crystal Palace."

Dowie was infuriated by the comments about the Eagles, who were three points behind Spurs in the Premiership table. Dowie said: "I've had two or three people ring me absolutely flabbergasted by the comments he made. But I'm not worried in the slightest what Martin Jol thinks of me. I'll wait to see him face to face if he's got something to say. What I said was that Pedro Mendes was a central midfield player. Is he a central midfield player? I think he is. Nevertheless he's made very defamatory comments about myself and John Gregory. Mine was never personal. If he's got something personal to say, let him do it face to face and show some balls."

Jol tried to explain that his shoelace comment was not as disparaging in Dutch as it came across in English. "In Holland if you criticise men, you say: 'you can't do my shoelaces', but it is different to say: 'you are not fit to mend my shoelaces.' That is not so bad."

Dowie still wasn't happy. "He took RKC Waalwijk from the verge of bankruptcy in Holland and got them out of it," he said. "I've researched what he's done and I respect it. It's a shame he's not had the decency to do the same."

Jol reiterated his belief that Dowie should not have criticised another team, but insisted he had done his research. "We are good colleagues. He is the same as I was in Holland, he brought a small team to the Premiership. Maybe he didn't know, but I know all about him. I respect him, and he knows that. There is no story. The only thing I said is that it is not done when one manager talks about another manager's team. He shouldn't make comments on my team, but when he is a pundit you have to say something and I appreciate that. I have no problem with him."

Former Aston Villa manager John Gregory had also been critical of Tottenham while working as a pundit alongside Dowie, but his comments did not concern Jol. "John Gregory can say anything he likes because he is not a current manager, so it is not a problem with me," he grizzled. It didn't stop him branding Gregory "useless". Entertainment was coming to London N17.

What the spat did was cement Jol's reputation as a tough-talking, not-to-be-messed-with manager. A call from Jol to Dowie ended the row. Dowie said: "I have spoken to Martin. It's not a problem. He feels he was misquoted and it rumbled and rumbled. We're fine. I have always had respect for him as a coach. That will continue. I look forward to sharing a lager with him."

But then came a different kind of controversy. Jol, along with the entire footballing public, was amazed how his team were robbed at Manchester United when the officials failed to spot that keeper Roy Carroll had dropped the ball over the line from Mendes's shot in the match at Old Trafford in January 2005. The amazing decision, which denied Spurs a 1-0 win sparked debate about the use of electronic assistance for the referee. Jol was firmly in favour: "People are talking about technology, but that is what you use to go into space. This is so easy. Within five seconds, they showed us on the bench that Pedro Mendes had scored. The fourth official knew it was a goal and should have told the ref. They don't do that. Yet I was watching English rugby the other day and you see a big screen which says 'try' after 10 seconds. It seems to work. It's easy."

Jol did not blame referee Mark Clattenburg or linesman Rob Lewis for failing to give the 'goal'. The Dutchman could not be sure either from his vantage point on the Old Trafford touchline, although he did suggest Lewis should have kept his eyes trained on the ball. Jol added: "I always say when you are sprinting, you have to look ahead like a fox. They said he had to be like Linford Christie to catch up. But he was running more like Carl Lewis with his head down. He was quick, though. On TV, they said he was too slow, but he was the quickest linesman I've ever seen. Maybe, in the end, it is not us who will suffer, but Chelsea or Arsenal if United end up champions by one point. You never know."

The goalless draw at Unitedshowed that Spurs' spine was becoming stronger and Jol's success in just a few short months had made him desirable property. Ajax stepped up their efforts to lure Jol in March 2005 to succeed Ronald Koeman, who resigned after they went out of the UEFA Cup to Auxerre. The Dutch champions publicly declared they would speak to their short-listed candidates and, though they did not name the Tottenham head coach, he was known to be their first choice. Jol immediately responded that he was "very happy" and "fully committed" to Tottenham, but Ajax had not given up hope. The Dutch giants were so keen to get Jol that they were willing to abandon their traditional structure of head coach and technical director and give him wide control of affairs, similar to that which he enjoyed during a successful spell at RKC Waalwijk.

The Dutch giants not only tempted the ambitious Jol with regular Champions League football, but also access to Europe's finest breeding ground for young talent. Being a proud Dutchman there was a feeling in his homeland the offer to take charge of Holland's biggest club would be difficult to ignore.

Ajax's interest pushed Tottenham into speeding up the renegotiation of Jol's contract. He got a pay rise after succeeding Santini, but further talks were planned after Jol's positive start. His contract still had two further seasons to run and Spurs would demand significant compensation if he departed. "I'm not in discussions with anyone else at this stage," Jol said. "I don't want to go elsewhere. As I have said before, I want to bring success back to this great club." The negotiations continued.

The talks had been initiated by the club as Spurs had suddenly found themselves in a highly unusual position. Never in the club's recent history had one of their managers been in demand from another high-profile club. In fact the Spurs job had become a poisoned chalice. Francis, Graham and Santini had all vanished into managerial obscurity, while both Ardiles' and

Hoddle's stars had waned. Only Christian Gross, in recent times, had restored his reputation post-White Hart Lane, but he had to return to Switzerland to do so, achieving success with FC Basel, who he has managed since 1999 and taken to a UEFA Cup semi-final.

In Jol, it seemed, Spurs finally had clearly found a coach capable of matching the high expectations of the club's fans and board. Tottenham had won 11 of 20 games under his charge and emerged as realistic contenders for a UEFA Cup place, despite the woeful run in the autumn. For his part, Jol was revelling in his new role: "During my spell in Germany as a young player I had thought that as this was my job I had to keep going, keep trying. Then I went to the east of Holland [Enschede], then I went to [live in] Walsall. Three years. Raining. Always. All that time I found myself thinking: 'OK, I have a job to do'. But this is the first time I've not thought that. This is the best city in the world."

Chairman Daniel Levy was anxious to keep Jol and his best talent. Star players Ledley King and Jermain Defoe were in negotiations over improved deals, even though, like Jol, they had not reached the end of their contracts.

Having beaten Brighton and West Brom in the early rounds, after a 3-0 FA Cup replay win at Nottingham Forest, the quarter-final draw paired Spurs with Newcastle and the bullish Jol spelt out his desire to bring the Cup back to White Hart Lane. "This is a very good opportunity for me and the players. Perhaps it is not the best draw going to Newcastle. However, we beat them in the league and we have to be confident. I know how important the FA Cup is to Tottenham, and our supporters were unbelievable."

In a show of appreciation for his achievements, the 5,000 travelling fans at the City Ground had repeatedly chanted Jol's name and at one stage broke into a chorus of: 'You're Spurs and you know you are.'

Arnesen revealed his part in persuading Jol not to become Koeman's successor at the Amsterdam ArenA. He said at the time: "Whether it is players or coaches or whatever, when they are doing well – and Martin is doing well – they will always be, how I say, attacked from the outside. What I have to do is make them comfortable. Martin has made it very clear for himself that he is very happy with Tottenham and he will continue with Tottenham."

At the time Arnessen seemed content to stay when he said: "Something is happening here and I will not leave the club." But that was a tale to unfold a little way down the line.

Jamie Redknapp hailed the Jol revolution at the Lane. The midfielder, who left Spurs for Southampton two months earlier, played a key role in the

1-0 victory over his former club. But, despite the setback to Tottenham's UEFA Cup ambitions, Redknapp believed there were reasons to be cheerful. He said: "This is the best Spurs team I have seen in an awfully long time. They are always a threat and they have good players. Also they have a bit of backbone to them, which is a criticism which has been levelled at them in the past. It's now a good Spurs team and I'm sure it can only get better because the average age is so young. When Jermain Defoe picks up the ball, it's like it's tied to his foot. Mido looks a threat. There's Fredi Kanoute and I feel Robbie Keane is as good as any player in the country. I am a massive fan of his. When you have got players like that you have always got half a chance."

Redknapp believed their attacking endeavour was testament to the coaching skills of Jol. He said: "I was very impressed with Martin Jol. He's young, he's passionate and he is like of breath of fresh air at Tottenham. I've got a lot of time for him and I think the fans have really taken to him too." Young? Jol would have been delighted at 49 to be described thus!

Not everyone was a fully paid up member of the Martin Jol fan club, though. Jol revealed that keeping Stephen Carr at Tottenham was never an option when he and Arnesen arrived at the club. The Republic of Ireland defender joined Newcastle for £2m in August 2004 after making it clear that he did not want to be part of the new regime at White Hart Lane. Carr's departure – with a year left on his contract – left Pamarot as the club's first-choice right-back with youngsters Stephen Kelly and Phil Ifill also vying for the role. Jol said: "There was nothing we could do because he wanted to go. He wouldn't sign a new contract, so it was straightforward. Even though Noe Pamarot did well defensively and Stephen Kelly is versatile, I think we missed him to start with – he was very experienced. But we have moved on since then and now things are much better."

Carr received a hostile reception from the travelling Spurs fans, many of whom were still unhappy with his determination to leave the club where he spent the first ten years of his career. He further angered them by making a celebratory gesture in their direction after the 1-0 FA Cup victory at St James' Park secured by an early goal by Dutchman Patrick Kluivert. Back-to-back single goal defeats had cost Tottenham dear as they were now all but out of the running for European qualification through the league and had bowed out of the FA Cup. Such are the small margins by which success and failure can be measured, and with the defeat on penalties against Liverpool in the Carling Cup thrown in for good measure it was clear Jol had to add a killer instinct into his burgeoning team.

The end of any football season always throws up some delicious and often ironic twists and turns and Jol's Spurs were presented with an opportunity in a Monday night Sky TV game to take at least a point off neighbours Arsenal at Highbury and clinch the title for Chelsea. It would be a first championship for 50 years for the west London club and a tremendous triumph for another foreign coach, one Jose Mourinho, in his first, incredible season in British football.

Jol was clear about his feelings about football's 'Special One' when he said: "He is a jewel for our profession. There may be other coaches doing really well at smaller clubs, but, of those that are well known, he must be the best in the world at the moment. This season he's going to win the Premiership, he could win the Champions League [Chelsea faced Liverpool in the semi-finals] and he's already won the Carling Cup. Before that, he was a UEFA Cup winner with Porto and then won the Champions League. He started off with a small team – that is impressive – and got everyone's attention. He also didn't know anything about the Premiership when he came here, which is a big disadvantage, but Chelsea now have all the best records. He is an inspiration."

Spurs, however, couldn't dent the Gunners' slim title hopes, in losing 1-0 at Highbury, but that only delayed the inevitable first Chelsea title in fifty years as the Blues won 2-0 at Bolton the following Saturday. With thoughts turning to next season, Jol was convinced Paul Robinson would still be a Tottenham player next season. The England goalkeeper, who was another to be in talks with the club over an improved contract, had been linked with both Manchester United and Barcelona. Jol was determined that he would cling on to the stopper: "Paul likes it here, he is a big player for us and he is much appreciated. There is not a shadow of doubt in my mind that he is even thinking about leaving."

Despite the recovery and positivity which now surrounded the club, Spurs finished ninth in the Premiership and missed out on a guaranteed UEFA Cup place, finishing three points shy of Middlesbrough, the final nail in that particular coffin being a 1-0 defeat at the Riverside in the penultimate game of the season when midfielder George Boateng netted an early goal and Steve McClaren's team held on for a vital victory.

Jol finally signed his new Tottenham contract in the summer of 2005, agreeing an improved deal which included a significant pay-rise, backdated to when he succeeded Santini in November. Spurs also added an option on their side to add the 2007/08 season to his existing two-year deal. The Dutchman declared that he was happy with the agreement and it suited

Spurs not to give him a guaranteed longer contract, as in the past they had paid out large sums to sacked managers with long-term deals. "Martin has demonstrated his commitment and value to us and brought a real sense of optimism to our squad and our fans as well," said chairman Daniel Levy. And boy were the fans happy and looking forward to the new season.

GO CONTINENTAL

'It is hard for the fans because there were times over the past decade when they expected too much of the club. But that's understandable.'
Martin Jol

JUST WHEN TOTTENHAM needed some stability came some seriously damaging news. In the summer of 2005 Sporting Director Frank Arnesen declared his intention to join the Russian Revolution at Chelsea as the Stamford Bridge club's own Sporting Director. Arnesen was suspended by Spurs on 4 June for expressing a desire to move to Chelsea, after the club allegedly made an illegal approach to sign him as manager.

The news that Chelsea were again looking to procure another club's employee, after acquiring Manchester United's Chief Executive Peter Kenyon, emerged after the Premier League chief executive Richard Scudamore was notified of their conduct by Levy. That discussion, however, fell short of an official complaint.

When Arnesen was photographed aboard one of Roman Abramovich's three luxury yachts on 22 June it reinforced Tottenham's compensation case, but at a board meeting at White Hart Lane, Levy canvassed the opinion of his fellow directors as to how to proceed. Holding Arnesen to the remaining 24 months of his £1.2m-a-year contract was discounted and Spurs were resigned to losing their man. But Chelsea did not like to risk having their suspended three-point deduction for the breach of rule K3 over the protracted Ashley Cole tapping-up case being implemented, so Tottenham's decision not to pursue a complaint was appreciated in West London.

Spurs settled instead for cash, and restrictions. In the compensation settlement Tottenham stipulated that Arnesen did not take up his role at Chelsea before the end of the next transfer window and inserted conditions preventing Chelsea from poaching their players. A safety net had been drawn around the famous Chigwell training ground. Two days after Arnesen had been spotted on Abramovich's yacht, both clubs announced that they had reached a financial settlement, later officially disclosed to be £5 million, but widely reported to be closer to £8 million.

Arnesen took up a role as head of scouting and youth development at the Bridge just 12 months after he joined Spurs as sporting director. Jol regretted Arnesen's defection: "I was disappointed because we'd started together on a mission and I felt he'd deserted me. I had the feeling as long as he was there I didn't have to worry even if we lost three games. It took away pressure based on results rather than the quality of football. But I couldn't stay angry with him. He told me it was the most difficult decision in his life and I respect that."

The move drew comparisons to that of Sol Campbell, who had defected to arch-rivals Arsenal under the Bosman ruling in 2001, making the England defender wildly unpopular with Spurs fans. There was no 'Judas' graffitti when Arnesen left, but his decision to take the ruble at Chelski left a void at Tottenham which would eventually, although no-one yet knew it, become a ticking timb bomb for Martin Jol.

Despite all the upheaval, the manager insisted that Spurs would be mad to ditch the continental style management structure simply because of Arnesen's defection. All Jol wanted was the best continuation of what had been a good seven months in his first Premiership job. He understood that people move on in football. After all he himself had racked up five clubs at which he had coached in 13 years. And that is no record of a man who is a serial job-changer in modern day football.

Jol's only concern was about how to take Tottenham forward. Despite paper-talk to the contrary, he made it clear he had no intention of doing both jobs and held talks with chairman Daniel Levy about finding the right man for Arnesen's role. Before Arnesen departed Jol said: "A lot of rubbish has been written about my wanting to do both roles at the club. It is a non-sense. The reason I can make a difference at our club is because I can focus on coaching this squad. If Frank does leave us then the club will have to find a new sporting director. The chairman and I have spoken about this situation and it is something he will take time with, to get the right person, someone who will work well with all of us. The structure works well so we would be mad to change it. Sometimes things like this make you stronger and even more determined. I want to reassure fans that there is a lot to anticipate and we already have our plans in place for this season. We finished last season on an optimistic note and I am determined that we stay that way."

Not everyone had been convinced when Jol was promoted from Santini's assistant to top man at Spurs, but the critics had been silenced by that first part-season in charge. Jol was aware of his doubters: "There is still some cynicism at Spurs, but it's less than it was. That's because the past was the best period for the club. When I first came here and saw all the prizes and great players who had achieved so much, it was really impressive. But history is not the be-all and end-all. The reality is now and what we can achieve with the team. Recently someone wrote that I brought a friendly man-management manner into the club. I don't mind it being written, but it isn't true. Believe me you will never achieve anything by being friendly. But my philosophy is the same as Tottenham's. I'm lucky in that way. It's as if someone from above is guiding me. I don't want to become over-dramatic on this, but I firmly believe in that. I came as Santini's assistant, but if I had been in charge from the beginning it would have been a lot more difficult. I had time to observe the culture and mentality of the players and work out ways of changing things. My first task was the average age. I can also see immediately whether a player has a winner's mentality and it was clear there were a number of players at the end of their career. They weren't performing, so that had to be addressed. I also wanted to change the whole midfield to play more attacking football."

Part of that change was Jol's first summer transfer window, although of course he was without a Sporting Director in charge to consult over such decisions. Initially Tottenham wanted to sign talented young midfielder Scott Parker, but were not prepared to meet his Chelsea wages. Jol prides himself on buying younger, hungry players who are not as costly in wages. He said: "I have to be inventive. We have to find players before they start asking highly-inflated salaries. Players like Jermain Defoe, Michael Carrick, Michael Dawson, Andy Reid and Wayne Routledge are all from the Championship. They are all talented ambitious lads who haven't won anything. Do you think Newcastle or Liverpool would have bought them when we did? I was in Mauritius recently and I was watching an African youth match. There was a striker who was technically a good footballer, but there's no way he can get a work permit unless he marries an English girl or I adopt him! Even for me that was too inventive."

Fredi Kanoute's Spurs career had been less than exceptional, but Jol pre-ferred to play him alongside either Keane or Defoe and was determined to hang on to him unless the club received an offer they couldn't refuse. Then West Ham made an approach to re-sign the Mali striker. It seemed that Spurs would cash in on the hit-and-miss striker, if they could find a replace-ment. Jol was eager to enlist another forward, but was deterred from firming up his interest in the Feyenoord striker Dirk Kuyt, whose club demanded £10m. Aston Villa were believed to be keen on Robbie Keane, but Jol replied firmly that the Republic of Ireland international was not for sale. His search for a striker to allow Kanoute to leave saw Tottenham used in a bidding war in the race to sign Julio Baptista. Jol's interest in the

23-year-old Brazil international was never more than passing, but Sevilla revealed they had received a bid of more than £13.8m for the forward. In fact no such bid was ever made and this was simly a case of Sevilla upping the price to Arsenal. Instead the Gunners lost out to Real Madrid who stumped up the same fee to take The Beast to the Bernabeu, although he would later spend an unhappy season on loan at Arsenal, where he failed to acclimatise.

Jol was not fazed by being used in this way as he was active in other departments, looking to strengthen his squad to make a serious bid for the Champions League places. His first coup came when Tottenham agreed terms with Internazionale to sign the midfielder Edgar Davids. The free transfer move for the 32 year-old fellow Dutchman thrilled Jol. "He is one of the most versatile midfielders, a playmaker, a ball-winner with great stamina and huge charisma and one of the best midfielders to come out of Holland in the last ten years. This is a player who went to Barcelona when they were middle of the league and took them close to winning the title. It's terrific that he is joining us. This is the player we have spoken about who will lift the team's performance. We have a young squad with an average age of 23 and I believe Edgar will come in and lead by example."

The deal was sealed after Spurs scrutinised the knee injury that had plagued Davids, who had won 73 caps for Holland, representing the Dutch in four major finals tournaments. His pedigree also included four Champions League finals, tasting victory with Ajax in 1995. He had spent seven years at Juventus during which he helped them to the final of the Champions League on three occasions – 1997, 1998 and 2003. He also bagged three domestic titles with Juventus in 1998, 2002 and 2003. He moved on loan to Barcelona in the 2003/04 season and was credited with helping turn around the fortunes of the Nou Camp outfit as they finished second that season behind Valencia. He then returned to Italy, joining Inter for the 2004/05 campaign. His capture was a major sign that Jol and Tottenham meant business. Davids also came with a reputation for standing no nonsense. He had had his spats with the likes of Ruud van Nistelrooy and would later fall out spectacularly with national team boss Marco van Basten over his deselection for the World Cup 2006 squad.

Jol was keen for his combative box-to-box play-making to rub off on his young midfield, but Davids didn't come cheap for a player of his age. He may have arrived on a free transfer, but the flip side was that the decision had to break the club's wage structure. Jol offered Davids £47,000 a week plus a £1.5 million signing-on fee. This was significantly less than the

£80,000 a week figure that Spurs had refused to pay the bespectacled Dutchman during previous negotiations in 2003.

The build-up to the new 2005/06 season gained momentum as William Hill released its odds for the Premiership sack race and duly predicted that Newcastle's Graeme Souness would be first to part company with his club. These odds always make uncomfortable reading for those near the top of a list which this particular year featured Souness at 5-1, ahead of Fulham's Chris Coleman, West Ham's Alan Pardew, Charlton's Alan Curbishley and Portsmouth's Alain Perrin, all at 8-1. In contrast odds of 14-1 for Jol did not seem worrying, but Sir Alex Ferguson would not have been overjoyed to see the same applied to him – especially when Chelsea's Jose Mourinho was rated 100-1 and Arsenal's Arsène Wenger 66-1. But for Jol to be on a par with Sir Alex said much for his growing stature. And he hadn't even been in the job a year yet.

There were 36,112 at White Hart Lane to see Jol's new look Spurs beat the Champions League holders Porto in pre-season. The new signings all did well. Paul Stalteri, a Canadian right-back who played in the Champions League with Werder Bremen, burst forward with an energy all the more remarkable for the fact that this was his first game since injuring ankle ligaments at the end of the Bundesliga season. Teemu Tainio, a Finnish international who had spent eight seasons at Auxerre, showed energy and intelligence in midfield.

Davids, appearing for half an hour in his first game for his new club, was greeted with an acclaim he almost justified when he hit a swirling shot from far out and wide on the left that forced keeper Vitor Baia to scramble and stretch. Tottenham supporters were clearly expecting a lot from a 32 year-old with glaucoma and a dodgy knee – they gave him a standing ovation just for getting off the bench. There was tangible excitement in N17. Even Jol betrayed his excitement. "As soon as we can compete with the bigger clubs I would say the sky's the limit."

His first trophy came in pre-season when Spurs won the Peace Cup in South Korea, a competition famously funded by the Moonies. Tottenham won a group featuring Boca Juniors, Real Sociedad and Sundowns of South Africa, qualifying for the final by virtue of having scored more goals than their Argentinian opponents; another example of Jol's attacking philosophy bearing fruit. There they saw off Olympique Lyonnais, highly-rated French champions for the fourth consecutive season under the new stewardship of former Liverpool boss Gérard Houllier, by scoring three goals in a one-sided first half, two from Robbie Keane. The game finished 3-1, but Jol was delighted with the progress against stiff opposition.

Reputations count, not least that of the manager, and Jol's was building; most importantly where it really counts, within his group of players. "He's a really good coach," new signing from Crystal Palace Wayne Routledge observed. "The places he's been, the players he's coached – his resumé is ridiculous. If he can pass on a few things to me and help me improve my game it can only be good for me."

Spurs got off to a winning start in the Premiership. Tainio helped set up the opening goal, an own goal from Portsmouth's Andy Griffin on the stroke of half-time, and gave the sort of all-action display that allowed Tottenham to ultimately take control and wrap up victory with a fine strike from Defoe.

Tottenham were already being widely tipped to make the great leap forward in leaving middling England for high European ground despite closing the previous season without a win in nine away League games, scoring just 11 times on their travels over the campaign. But they had also conceded only 19. "If we give solid performances, then we will do better away," Jol concluded. The Dutchman meant productive performances, since he swiftly pointed out: "Sometimes we played very well away, we had 60%, 65%, 68% possession – and we still didn't win."

Aware of his commitment to entertain as well as improve, Jol promised: "we will score a lot of goals" at home, but also all around the country because, of the "my very good strikers". In this pre-World Cup season it was in Defoe's interest to fulfil all of his exceptional promise for club and country.

Jol persisted in his attempts to land South Korea wing-back Lee Young-Pyo of PSV Eindhoven, whom he considered the ideal foil to Davids as he renovated the left flank of his team. The Dutch champions demanded £5m, but Spurs were confident that, since he had only a year left on his current deal, they could agree a much-reduced fee. Bolton were also interested, but Jol's hand was strengthened by a Premiership season start that brought Spurs maximum points after victory in their second game, at home to Middlesbrough. Jol got his man, touting him as "one of the best left-backs in the world today." One other addition was hoped to be Newcastle's young Englishman Jermaine Jenas, especially as an injury to Routledge left a vacancy in midfield. Newcastle chairman Freddy Shepherd pushed for any deal to include Robbie Keane, but Tottenham wanted a cash-only arrangement. The player stayed – for now.

Jol guided Spurs to second place in the embryonic Premiership table, but Spurs were fortunate to maintain their unbeaten start against a Blackburn side reduced to ten men by the dismissal of Lucas Neill. The Australian had already been booked when he clattered into Davids from behind, giving Dermot Gallagher little option but to brandish a second yellow card.

There was another ugly incident in that game, this one missed by the officials; a headbutt by well-known hothead Andy Todd on new signing from Nottingham Forest Andy Reid. "I think [Todd] was excited a little bit because otherwise I can't understand this," said Jol, who added that Reid had a "bump on his forehead".

At this stage Jol did not appear over eager for anyone to take over all the sporting director's duties. When asked about filling the vacancy Jol replied, "If we bump into the right person we will do that, but it is not a main priority for me. Maybe for the board, but not for me."

Tottenham's position near the summit of the Premiership thanks to their electric start placed them within touching distance of 100% Chelsea and the pair met at the Lane in hte fourth game of the season. But while Mourinho could win with his best players on the sidelines the same did not apply to Spurs. Chelsea won 2-0 after Mido was dismissed before the half-hour mark for an elbow into the back of Asier Del Horno, and goals from Del Horno and Damien Duff sealed the win.

Jol wanted a tall man up front and pushed Michael Dawson into that role late on while leaving Keane on the bench after Mido's dismissal. Chelsea were in control by then, though it had not been so straightforward before Mido's red card. Spurs had claimed a straight red for new Chelsea star Michael Essien for a ferocious challenge on Davids, but referee Styles only waved yellow. He was not so forgiving on the Egyptian. Once Mido went, Chelsea kept the ball and played patiently, avoiding exposure to counter-attacks. Mido denied intent to harm and Jol was right in saying the dismissal was "a bit harsh", but that he could accept it because it was not a clever challenge. Styles felt Mido used excessive force and the ref also ground dirt into the wound by reporting Mido's failure to go off immediately.

Chelsea's hoodoo, which had seen Spurs not win against them in the league since 1987, continued. It would be a major yardstick by which Tottenham's progress could be measured over the coming seasons. Chelsea, were after all, the billionaire playboys who had been moulded into a super-efficient team by Mourinho. They would sweep all before them domestically and any team defeating them placed a metaphoric feather into the cap with pride. Tottenham were clearly not there yet.

Transfer deadline day in August 2005 was a busy one for Spurs. They reached agreement with Newcastle over an £8m transfer for 22 year-old Jenas, while Young-Pyo signed on a four-year contract to become the Tottenham's seventh summer signing at a cost of about £2m. Lee would fill the void left by Erik Edman, the Swedish full-back who joined Rennes on a three-year deal. Reto Ziegler was also on his way out as Jol continued the rebuilding process, joining Hamburg on loan for the season.

Jol was delighted with the signing of Jenas, as he said: "We want young players at this club and if they are already internationals like Jermaine it is always a very good thing for us. I think he will develop into a great player."

Another young Englishman to join the club was 18 year-old Aaron Lennon. The right-winger had been watched by the club for a good while, especially by David Pleat and Frank Arnsen. Now he signed from Leeds United for £1 million as the player to provide him with the width Jol so desperately wanted to get service into a tall central striker. With Routledge suffering a fractured bone in his foot, Jol had been forced to use Jenas on the right wing, an experiment that yielded little return. "Aaron has the potential to be a big player," Jol said. "He's so pacy, the only thing he needs to improve is his service."

Late in the evening Jol landed the 6ft 3in Poland striker Grzegorz Rasiak from Derby County to strengthen the forward line. He had scored 17 goals to help the Rams reach the Championship play-offs and it was that form which prompted Spurs to pay £2 million. But the Raziak deal was only completed after Daniel Levy had failed in an attempt to land Livorno's Cristiano Lucarelli. Levy had flown to Italy to negotiate, but missed out on the the 29 year-old newly-capped Italian international despite increasing an earlier offer to around £3.4 million. Lucarelli opted to stay at his beloved Livorno where he had won Serie A's Golden Boot award the previous season scoring 24 goals in 35 matches in 2004/05. Earlier Jol had sold Kanoute to Sevilla for £4.4m, the West Ham deal having gone south over the fee.

But possibly the most important arrival in the late summer of 2005 was Damien Comolli, who became the club's new sporting director in succession to Arnesen. Arsène Wenger had encouraged Comolli to become a coach when he was his manager at Monaco, and later made him Arsenal's European scout for seven years, but now his protégé became the sporting director of the Highbury club's traditional rivals. Comolli had left Arsenal a year earlier to join St-Etienne, but returned to English football to work for Spurs.

The 33 year-old Frenchman was a multilingual university graduate who played and coached at Monaco under Wenger from 1992-95 and moved on to Japan of his own accord, to Nagasaki, before joining Arsenal in 1996. Comolli said: "I spent long years alongside him so obviously I learned a lot from him, but also from different people, different clubs, different countries and different continents. I've got bits and pieces of everyone."

The self-confessed footballaholic boasted the same obsessive attention to detail as Wenger, whom he helped sign Henry and Pires for Arsenal. Comolli does not take a day off, describing the football world as a village to be explored. "I've got no time" was his reasoning for lack of holiday plans. I have a great family because they are very supportive. When you are in professional football and you are passionate, you don't even know what time it is. Whatever it takes you do it because it's a privilege to live from your passion. I see probably three or four games per week all over Europe including our first-team games. If I'm in the office starting from Monday, travelling during the week, I like to be in the office when I get back. It's 10 or 11 long months but it's fantastic."

Comolli too made it clear that he would speak his mind, which brought the tantalising possibility of fireworks at least behind the scenes between himself and Jol. Comolli said his duties at Tottenham were similar to the ones at St-Etienne, where he was responsible for developing a scouting network, was in charge of negotiations with young players and their families and was involved in player transactions alongside the chairman and managing director. He also acknowledged he had a lot to live up to. "I just want to be judged on what I do and not what people did before," he said. "A great job has been done in the last 24 months by the board, the chairman and recently by Martin. I am just joining to make the club improve more. Where it will take us? See you in three years and we'll see." We did indeed.

Back on the pitch Robbie Keane's pent up frustration was eased with his superb equaliser against Villa; there was no trademark cartwheel, no forward roll and no imaginary pistol. Instead Keane discarded his routine and set off towards the opposite end of the pitch at breakneck speed. The 25 year-old forward had spent more time on the substitutes' bench than any other Tottenham player the previous season and the early signs were that he could expect more of the same, even though Jol's side entered this match having failed to penetrate the opposition goal in more than six hours of football. That record looked like being extended until Keane was summoned from the dug-out with 23 minutes left. The Irishman had already tested Sorensen from distance before he conjured up a wonderful goal to salvage a point for Spurs. "If we're not scoring when Robbie's on the pitch then everyone tells me Jermain Defoe should be playing," Jol reasoned. "Then you try to be stubborn and play them both and teams pressurise you [because] goal-kicks from Robinson keep coming back to you." Jol clearly had plans for the tall Rasiak and was thinking of the team rather than individuals. Could he appease his two diminutive star strikers? It would be a test.

Jol's Spurs' renaissance was halted, like a wet fish in the face, by Grimsby in the League Cup, illustrating how long-suffering Spurs fans needed to lower expectancy booming levels. With the Premiership already as good as won by Chelsea, and competition for European places fierce, the concept of squad rotation was unlikely to find much favour with Jol. The Spurs manager had put out his strongest available team, and a sold-out Blundell Park revelled as their League Two table-toppers took the game to their more illustrious opponents. A late goal from Jean-Paul Kalala compounded a lethargic performance with the ignominy of defeat.

Jol said ominously for his players afterwards: "We didn't show our quality. We have a lot of players who want to play at the club, but they didn't show it here."

After a while the Harry the Haddock jokes wore a bit thin, while Mariners manager Russell Slade, who had been in charge at Notts County, when they knocked Spurs out of the same competition in 1994, revelled in the publicity.

After much rational talk of a revival under Jol, the past five games had made for miserable reading: one goal, no wins and a Carling Cup exit to a League Two side. Yet, Tottenham were still seventh in the Premiership, as Jol stressed that a quick response was imperative as they apologised to fans for the Grimsby debacle. "We aren't scoring goals and we don't look like scoring goals, which is even worse and is not good enough," Jol said in the Blundell Park tunnel.

Grimsby confirmed what Jol knew – Defoe and Keane did not work in tandem. That night Jol had little option with Mido banned and Rasiak cup-tied having played for Derby in the first round, but that could not excuse losing to a team 62 places below them. He later called that 1-0 upset at Grimsby his worst moment in management; it also threatened to change the landscape of Tottenham's season. "Our fans deserve better," added Jol. "That's something we all regret. We have to put things right quickly."

The Grimsby defeat added pressure where expectation had built. Meanwhile screws were being applied from another direction. Record financial results were announced by Tottenham, who posted a club-best turnover of £70.6m, up by £4.3m, and profits of £4.1m in contrast with a loss of £2.7m in 2004. They also announced player trading profits of £5.6m, but spending remained high. £61.8m had been spent on new signings in the two years and two months since 1 July 2003. This constituted an astronomical increase on Spurs' usual outlay. In the six seasons to 2002, Spurs had paid out £53m in transfers. Levy indicated, though, that the board was prepared to underwrite a similar level of expenditure in the future.

More successful exploitation of Spurs' key markets helped fund the expenditure. Merchandising turnover had increased from £1.2m to £5m, while gate revenue increased by £600,000. Tottenham's net debt had only increased by £1.27m to just £1.4m.

"It follows that we now need to deliver success on the pitch if we are to continue to invest at this level," said Levy. "The significant investment that has taken place in the squad to date means that the club has the playing resources to improve performances on the pitch. However, with so many new team members time will be needed to forge a strong playing unit. It is encouraging that we have been able to generate cash at the operating level whilst both aligning good young talent for now and the future and ensuring the club's debt is manageable. All these factors underline the robustness of the business we now have, but also highlight its potential to grow if we can get all elements of the club right both on and off the pitch."

Could Jol respond, or would the club sink back into the spiral of boom and bust that had pock-marked the 1990s and early 2000s?

Perhaps Blundell Park served as a wake up call as Spurs began to re assert themselves in the Premiership with a run of three successive victories. In the middle of these, after trailing Charlton 2-0 early in the second half Spurs clawed back to win 3-2. And there were other big clubs who were in far more dire straits. Everton, who had finished in the fabled fourth place the previous season and qualified for the Champions League only to miss out at the first step, began to take root at the bottom after losing 2-0 at Spurs. Yobo attempted an ill-judged pass from deep in his own half which set up Lennon for a swift counter-attack. Stalteri laid the ball back to Jenas on the right and the midfielder's quick, accurate centre found Mido rising above the defence to beat Martyn with an emphatic header. Six minutes later Defoe crossed from the left and Jenas, timing his jump well, nodded in Tottenham's second. Despite the newboys making their mark, and Jol's side playing with pace and penetration, Tottenham remained something of a paradox. The strength of their start to the season and this win took them to second place, yet Spurs still had the look of a side short of fulfilling its potential.

Jol felt so too. "We will get better and better," he declared. "If we have everyone available we're difficult to beat."

Even so it was hard to suppress expectations with Spurs in second after making their best ever Premiership start. In fact you'd have to go back to 1994/95 to find a table in which Tottenham even made the top seven by season's end. More dewy-eyed Spurs fans argued the Champions League beckoned. Jol didn't yet agree: "The big four all have bigger players than us and are used to playing European football. We only have three players who've ever played European football." Despite Jol playing it all down, there was no denying Spurs were in form as they tackled a Manchester United side stripped of Giggs, Keane, Neville, Brown, Heinze, Saha and Richardson.

United's over-reliance on Wayne Rooney, in his last game as a teenager, was exposed when Spurs deservedly drew level 18 minutes from the end. When Defoe was fouled on the edge of the penalty area, Jenas surprised Edwin van der Sar with a free-kick that whistled through the wall, Smith breaking ranks and clearing a path to goal. The goal equalised Silvestre's early strike that United seemed happy to defend.

Ledley King was outstanding at the back at Old Trafford, with Dawson not far behind, while Defoe never stopped running in attack and Spurs merited a second consecutive draw at the stadium. Jol reminded everyone that only three of his players from the previous season's more controversial draw survived in the line-up. But he still maintained caution about the season's prospects. "It's good that we are high up in the table but there will be some disappointments in the future," said the manager, who would now be without the suspended Davids against Arsenal.

Jol had begun to get into his players' heads, convincing them that they can compete with the big four on the pitch and had spotted that United were no longer a side to be feared. Could they continue it against Arsenal?

Tottenham started the game at White Hart Lane three points ahead of the Gunners in third place. But Jol's spell in charge had not yet included a victory over any of Arsenal, Chelsea, Manchester United or Liverpool, so here was a chance to put down a marker. Jol stressed that four draws against Liverpool demonstrated Spurs were close to mastering a top team and was encouraged by the 1-1 draw at Old Trafford. "If you see our statistics, we have 60% of the possession against Manchester United in the second half. I don't think there are a lot of other teams in the past decade who had that. How many teams will have eight corners at Old Trafford? And we didn't play well, so the signs are there that we can be a good team but we still need another 10%."

He felt a young and much-changed squad needed further time to gel and gain experience, more goals from midfield and a signing to provide greater thrust down the left. But he happily acknowledged the strides made since his first official home match in charge, a 5-4 defeat by Arsenal just 11 months earlier. "The evidence lies in the fact we have only lost against Chelsea at home [since then], so we are doing well," he said, before noting how coveted some of his players had become: "I said when teams like Liverpool and Chelsea or Arsenal or Manchester United would like our players, we do well. That wasn't the case last year, but I think we have four or five now, so everything is going the way I want."

Since Wenger had arrived at Highbury, Tottenham had won one of the clubs' 19 meetings, lifted a solitary League Cup to Arsenal's seven major trophies and never finished better than seven places adrift of their bitter rivals. There were signs Arsenal could no longer take that superiority for granted. Jol, though, sensibly suggested the balance of power had not yet fully shifted. But the gap had clearly shortened as just over a year ago Arsenal had been crowned champions after going 40-odd league games unbeaten, while Spurs were beginning to slide under Santini.

Pre-match Wenger expressed admiration for Jol: "I think he has done extremely well. He has rebuilt an ambition, a hope and a confidence in the club,"

Wenger had so far enjoyed at least a 20-point advantage over a variety of Tottenham managers and his success in bringing Sol Campbell to Highbury was a crushing reminder to Spurs of their relative standings. For all that, Arsenal's pursuit of trophies was now severely hampered by Chelsea's emergence.

The Gunners showed little in a first half dominated comprehensively by Jol's men. Campbell, returning to White Hart Lane, almost scored an own goal and was fortunate to escape punishment for an elbow which required Tainio to have two stitches above an eye. Carrick spent the half demonstrating to Wenger what a useful player he would have been at Highbury. In the 17th minute, he floated the ball into the heart of Arsenal's box and Ledley King tucked his header past Jens Lehmann. The German goalkeeper had an eventful second half, producing another agile stop to deny Defoe with an outstretched leg, before he was struck by a conker thrown from the Park Lane End.

The transformation in Arsenal came with substitute Robert Pires, excluded from the starting line-up, taking control. Until then, the midfield was dominated by Carrick, Jenas, Lennon and Tainio. Arsenal's 13-game undefeated run was preserved when Pires' neat finish became his eighth goal in 10 games. Even then it was not a goal of the beautiful Arsenal creation. Paul Robinson had the biggest impact on the second half, fumbling Bergkamp's free-kick for Pires to equalise. For the second week running Robinson's hesitancy cost Tottenham a crucial goal against the kind of team they expect to be jostling with them in the hunt for Champions League places. Was the England keeper experiencing a crisis of confidence?

By full-time Spurs fans who had come expecting so much were deflated. Reports of Arsenal's demise, and Tottenham's rise, were premature.

Jol revealed how he had nearly got involved a cheeky swoop for Chelsea winger Arjen Robben, who had experienced a public falling out with his manager, Jose Mourinho, earlier in the season. Jol said: "If the recent problems with Robben and Chelsea had got out of hand then we were prepared to offer a mega-amount to get him. Spurs have lots of quality. We're a financially healthy club who can maybe buy any player we want. But all we have done so far is win the Peace Cup in pre-season and hanging a photo of that among the White Hart Lane legends isn't an option."

The signs of improvement at White Hart Lane were good, but still probems remained. More than a quarter of the way into this season and Jermain Defoe had managed three goals. Then Tottenham surrendered the last unbeaten away record in the Premiership at Bolton despite their attempts to retrieve parity being denied twice by the woodwork and once by an assistant referee's flag. Bolton boss Sam Allardyce gloated after the 1-0 victory: "For us to beat a big city club who have spent millions like them is an immense move forward for this club." This was Spurs' sixth successive defeat by Wanderers. The two draws against big four clubs would count for nothing if results like this followed.

But there were also signs of fight in Jol's nascent team. Bolton basked in their lead for barely 60 seconds when Tainio – playing at the top of a narrow midfield diamond – slipped Defoe in between Jaidi and Ben Haim. The striker's finish was emphatic but the assistant referee jerked his flag up for offside, television replays suggesting the hosts had escaped and Allardyce later admitting Defoe had been definitely onside. Jol, face like thunder, made a bee-line for the official at the interval to remonstrate. "I appreciate the referee has a difficult job but it should be easier for a linesman. We did everything right and created chances. I could have lived with a draw, but not a defeat like this. I am satisfied with the boys, but we should have had a draw." Just to add to the visitors' sense of injustice, Stalteri sliced a cross on to the bar in the dying moments before Bolton's relief erupted on the final whistle. The defeat ended a run of five games unbeaten for Spurs with the Trotters moving to third in the Premiership.

Courtesy of Spurs' Head of Communiucations Donna Cullen, I took my son Simon and his girl friend Ellie to White Hart Lane as a special birthday treat for the following week's home game with West Ham. Simon enjoyed all the special treatment, his name up in lights on the scoreboard, his name in the programme and a constant stream of Tottenham legends to meet. Unfortunately there wasn't the fairytale ending on the pitch as Spurs felt the strain of sustaining their ambitions as West Ham clinched an equaliser in the third minute of stoppage-time. With the visitors' 6ft 6in goalkeeper Shaka Hislop distractingly up for a corner, Paul Konchesky delivered an in-swinger from the right and Paul Robinson, coming off his line to try to collect, found himself blocked by his centre-backs Dawson and King to allow Anton Ferdinand to head home from the six-yard line.

But this game was a moment when Martin Jol the human being began to appeal to football fans across the country. Mido, the Egyptian who scored Spurs' goal, had met with chants from the West Ham fans of "shoe bomber" and "your mum's a terrorist". Jol, interviewed on television and radio, contrasted such conduct with the "fantastic" welcome the Spurs supporters accorded the Hammers' Teddy Sheringham on his return to the ground. He didn't deride the opposing fans allowing viewers to make their own minds up. It was a clever gambit and one which ended with Jol saying: "What West Ham fans do is their responsibility." Spurs right-back Paul Stalteri, when told about the attempted provocation, agreed more blatantly: "It is a form of racism. It doesn't belong in sport."

Jol was under no illusions. He admitted it was a high-pressure role trying to bring back the glory, glory days of this sleeping giant.

"It is hard for the fans because there were times over the past decade when they expected too much of the club. But that's understandable. Before this season had even started people were saying we were going to do this or that and it's hard for the players because they want to be successful, they want to give the fans something back and then they find themselves saying: "Oh, we can reach the Champions League" and it's all over the press. But there's Chelsea and Arsenal and Manchester United and Liverpool, that's four clubs already you'd expect to finish high up. Then there are clubs like Bolton, who are very experienced and difficult to beat, or Middlesbrough.

We are trying to build something here. I understand about hope and the fans' dreams. We have some good young players, Michael Dawson, Jermain Defoe, Jermaine Jenas, but what we don't have right now is the sort of player like Arjen Robben or Ronaldo at United, the player who can make a big difference. We need that if we are to compete at the top level.

Of course there are times when it's important to entertain my lads, but I don't spend my time looking after them. Edgar Davids is 32, I can't put him on my knee and feed him milk from a bottle. We are a young team, but there are older players here as well – Davids, Naybet – and they have their part to play. Davids, for example, he has been working with Lennon and Routledge after training. He is giving them the benefit of his experience. Maybe they found it odd at first that he was giving up his time, but this is the Dutch way. In Holland it is very common for the older players to pass down their knowledge and experience to the younger ones."

Davids, according to Jol, took it upon himself to deliver a speech after each match, during which he praised or criticised his team-mates. It was a practice that had surfaced in August when Davids reacted with dismay to the idea that Spurs should be satisfied with a draw at Blackburn. Three days later Davids showed a different side of his character when he broke the silence that followed defeat against Chelsea by telling his colleagues: "there's nothing to be ashamed of". The Dutchman was becoming an influential figure in the dressing room, just as Jol had known he would. He could just prove the key signing to improving the mentality which had let Spurs down in previous seasons.

After Davids marked his first goal in English football at Wigan in a splendid 2-1 win in late November over the newly promoted side who had begun life in the Premiership with a bang, Jol refused to compare his influential midfielder with Roy Keane, as many newspapers were choosing to do, claiming his compatriot is without equal. "Davids is a different player from Roy Keane," Jol explained. "Keane's a winner, he's always playing for himself, he tries to be fit and wants to prove something to everybody, but Edgar Davids doesn't have to do that because maybe he's the biggest player in England if you think about his silverware. And he still likes to play for us because it's a young team; they listen to him and he leads by example."

Given the impressive list of Davids' previous formidable clubs – Internazionale, Barcelona, Juventus, Milan and Ajax – then Wigan might have seem a touch underwhelming, though that was not apparent when he celebrated with unrestrained joy after pummelling a low shot under Mike Pollitt with 13 minutes remaining.

Inside eight minutes Arjan de Zeeuw had misjudged Tainio's through-ball, giving Keane the chance to score which he did with aplomb. Davids rampaged forward to add a second before Lee McCulloch tapped in with two minutes remaining. Davids also picked up his seventh booking in 11 appearances: the latest for a cynical challenge on Henri Camara. "I have been given so many cards since I came here it feels like Christmas," he said, clearly adapting to the lingo.

The new year always means the FA Cup, but Tottenham's involvement ended in a shock televised defeat at Leicester. On a weekend when giants were slain across the British Isles, with Celtic losing at Clyde in the Scottish Cup, south of the border the FA Cup threw up shocks aplenty. Fulham succumbed to Leyton Orient 2-1 at home, Everton drew at Millwall and Liverpool fell two goals behind to Luton, while Burton Albion drew at home to Manchester United. At Leicester Spurs cantered into a 2-0 lead before half-time. But then the Foxes mounted an incredible fightback, one completely unexpected given the dismal season they had experienced up to that point. Elvis Hammond pulled a goal back right on half-time before Stephen Hughes and then, dramatically in the last minute, Mark de Vries, netted the winner.

Defeat meant Spurs had gone out of both domestic cup competitions to lower division opposition away from home at the first time of asking. It was not a record that stood up to any scrutiny. Still, at least there was the League to concentrate on. January 2006 proved to be a woeful month as Spurs failed to score a Premiership goal, losing twice and drawing once. It was form that was all the more costly as the other top four contenders, most notably Arsenal, were dropping points too. Most notably the Gunners suffered a 3-2 defeat at home to West Ham at half-time in which Sol Campbell walked out of the club with his nerves in shreds and mind in a whirl, considering his future in the game.

Left out of that defeat at the Walker's Stadium, Mido knew that Jol had been unhappy with him in his first few months in charge. He revealed: "Before I left at the end of last season I spoke to Martin and said: 'I know this season was disappointing'." He promised to return from Egypt in shape and lost a stone and a half over the break. "I was working every day by myself. I had a vacation for maybe four or five days and then started working again. I have a gym at home."

January also took Mido back to Egypt. His homeland hosted the African Nations Cup and he would carry the hopes of a nation. But in a sign of his commitment to Tottenham he tried to delay his departure for the tournament, which began on 20 January, to face Liverpool the previous weekend. He would then miss up to four league matches. Mido's presence meant that 18 million Egyptians watched Tottenham's televised draw against West Ham and there were estimates that 100,000 crowds would attend the country's Nations Cup games. But when a star player like that decamps for a significant period in a season, it disrupts. To distill that, Jol opened talks with Egypt officials about flying Mido home to play in Premiership games during the African Nations Cup. "It is a bit of a problem for us as we have Grzegorz Rasiak and he knows that he is a substitute for Mido," said Jol. "Mido could go there and come back for the odd game. It is possible but we have to talk about that with the Egyptian management."

Meanwhile, to show who was boss, Jol refused to rule out another move for Kuyt. Mido got the message. The problem was that his temperament swung from the utterly dedicated professional that had lost over 20 pounds over the summer to the egomaniac who, stoked up with his own pride at leading Egypt to the Nations' Cup final, then spectacularly fell out with team boss Hassan Shehata as he left the field after being substituted in the 78th minute of the semi-final victory over Senegal and found himself banned from the team which lifted the trophy amidst scenes of patriotic fervour.

After his month away in Egypt, Mido only played seven more games for Spurs that season, scoring just twice. Spurs hadn't performed wonderfully without the shy and retiring African. A goalless draw at home to ten man Villa being followed, on the night Arsenal lost to West Ham, by a 1-0 defeat at Fulham, where Spurs themselves had a man dismissed, Michael Dawson, but fell prey to a last minute goal by Carlos Bocanegra. It would be a goal with a fearful consequence come the end of the season.

FISTS, FIGHTS AND
FOURTH PLACE

"ANXIOUS?" ASKED JOL rhetorically. "I felt anxious before." So Spurs entered the final stretch having been fourth in the Premiership since December, looking over their shoulders at who else? But their old rivals Arsenal. The battle for the crucial fourth place had gone down to the wire. Could Jol finish the job and steal it away from the club who had lorded their success over Tottenham for over 15 years?

Not if they played like they did at St James' Park. Tottenham suffered their sixth away Premiership defeat of the season at Newcastle and the fixture list now showed visits to Goodison Park, Highbury and, on the final day, Upton Park. At home it was Manchester City, Manchester United and Bolton Wanderers; a hard run-in.

Newcastle were the lowest-ranked club Spurs faced in their last seven games and after four straight defeats Souness's team were fragile. Yet Tottenham failed to take advantage and Jol shouldered some responsibility. He had positioned Carrick in front of a back four that had just lost King to a twisted ankle. About 15 yards ahead of Carrick was Davids. But despite this defensive shape to the side, in the first half-hour Newcastle scored three, but it could and should have been five.

If Spurs played badly, then they also suffered from the rough side of referee Mike Dean's decicions. Jol was disappointed that Dean failed to punish clear foul by defender Craig Moore on Carrick. Had a card been forthcoming it would have been Moore's second yellow and it was deserved, especially in the context of the second half. After Jenas – mocked with the chant "3-1 to the goldfish bowl", following his terse comments on life in the north east on his first return to St James' Park – rounded Given in the 53rd minute to score, it seemed Spurs were back in contention and ready to stage a memorable fight-back. But, Jenas missed an open goal and six minutes later Keane hit the woodwork again.

Then Dawson, booked earlier for clattering into Shearer, grasped the No. 9's famous shirt as Shearer wheeled away. Unlike the Moore incident, Dean felt this was worthy of another yellow and Dawson was off; again. The chances of a Spurs revival ended there and news of Arsenal's five goals at Highbury against Aston Villa came through. "If they win all their games and play in the league as they do to beat Real Madrid and Juve, it will be difficult to be fourth," Jol said. "For us it is important we get more than 60 points and wait and see where that puts us."

Jol warned his players that they had to cut out the mistakes made in the absence of King in order to pick up the points they need to finish fourth. King was ruled out of the 3-1 defeat by Newcastle because of ankle and knee injuries, although the England international was having such a rotten time with injuries that he was once famously asked about his broken leg and wasn't able to tell a reporter which one it was. "We played without Ledley against West Brom away when Kanu scored two goals and Leicester in the FA Cup when we conceded three goals – which is very rare for us," said Jol. "The worry for me is that we concede more goals when he is not playing and that is not a good thing for a squad."

With Arsenal now just two points behind with a game in hand, on 8 April Manchester City, with Stuart Pearce in temporary charge, arrived at White Hart Lane on the back of four straight Premiership defeats. Spurs fans certainly had their reward in the lunch-time encounter. In an open game, Jol's team dominated and maintained their run of not losing consecutively in the Premiership since the previous March, when Southampton and Charlton did the trick, 42 games ago. More importantly, though, Spurs were still fourth and five points ahead of Arsenal before the Gunners' tough encounter at Old Trafford the next day.

Was Jol confident his team would finish fourth? "Yeah," he said. And what of Spurs' final five games, against Manchester United and Bolton at home and Everton, Arsenal and West Ham away? "Don't depress me. I want to go home and enjoy this with a nice glass of lager." Although Tottenham deserved the 2-1 victory over City, Jol was concerned at the fragility evident against a rather average opponent, who towards the end of the game forced Spurs to cling on. "That's inexperience," Jol said. "But if it wasn't for David James, we could've had five today, to be honest."

James made one embarrassing gaffe when an attempted dribble outside the box awarded Mido a chance from which the striker should have scored in the first half, but otherwise he was outstanding. In fact the City goalkeeper did not deserve the bad luck that presented the ball to Stalteri, who turned it in for his first Premiership goal. Trevor Sinclair was guilty of a wayward pass that resulted in Carrick's strike four minutes into the second half. The City winger gave away possession and off went Tainio. The Finn was allowed to advance and win a corner and Carrick's delivery was then returned to him from a clever chip by Tainio that the Englishman chested down before firing a volley beyond James.

At 2-0 up, Spurs should have cruised to victory. "We gave a soft goal away," Jol said of the strike by Samaras that came from a throw-in by Distin that was not dealt with. "We made it difficult, but to be honest it doesn't mean anything if we get the results. Already we have 58 points. A friend of mine from Italy came over and said: 'What a team Arsenal are.' And I told him: 'Yes and we have been ahead of them for most of the season.'"

The Gunners' 2-0 defeat at Old Trafford made the weekend perfect and a 1-0 victory a week later at 11th placed Everton merely added to the feeling that this could be Tottenham's year. Robbie Keane's penalty was his 16th goal of the season and his ninth goal in ten games. In the week leading up to that game, Jol admitted he admired Wenger for spending up to £12m on the potential of Theo Walcott from Southampton, but Sol Campbell's appearance against Portsmouth a week earlier represented the only glimpse of an Englishman in Arsenal colours for 15 matches. That he felt was shame.

Spurs' Englishmen were excellent at Everton, Jenas's energy dominating central midfield and Carrick a reassuring presence. Defoe rasped a glorious curled shot against the bar that would have doubled the margin achieved when Stubbs barged Keane from the ball inside the box.

Lennon, the youngest Premiership player of all time [16 years and 129 days at Leeds] and still just turned 19, was tricky, elusive and lightning quick. The teenager tore into the home side to leave his markers gasping. He was credited with having the greatest influence on the latter part of Spurs' season. His homesickness for Leeds, since overcome thanks to the company of young colleagues such as Huddlestone and Dawson, was but a memory as his form put him into contention for England 2006 World Cup squad. His importance to Spurs was shown by the fact that in March he had signed a contract extension to 2010. "For his age, Lennon is the best prospect in the Premiership," said Jol. "He would certainly benefit from going to Germany with England, but the World Cup's too important to gamble. He can cross, he's more and more productive and he can only get better. That's exciting."

Lennon had first caught Jol's eye during a 29-minute stint as a substitute in Tottenham's 1-0 League Cup defeat at Blundell Park in September. "Aaron came on and beat his man four times," said Jol. "To beat people, like he is doing, in Europe there's just a couple of players who can. There's maybe Joaquín from Seville, Robben is like that, Duff last season, Cristiano Ronaldo, Giggs on his day."

Jol had worked hard to enhance Lennon's crossing. But the crucial addition of goals to his game had proved difficult to find; thus far he had scored only twice in 69 senior appearances.

By now confidence was flooding throughout the club. It lead to Jol predicting that Tottenham would be contesting the Premiership title within three years. He also revelled in his five point cushion by joining in criticising the non-British nature of the Highbury team which had now reached the Champions League semi-finals by claiming that domestic football fans would welcome his side winning the league with a British backbone. "I would like to challenge for the title. It's not easy, but I think that in the next three years we could make a good challenge," Jol said. "You need consistency at the club. Our spine always remains the same with Ledley, Paul, Carrick. Robbie Keane is there for another four years and Defoe too. It is probably an advantage over a lot of other clubs having a British base. Last week there was not one single British player in the Champions League. Did you notice? That's very strange. That's why I think everybody in England should get behind us and be proud that we've got an English team. So if we could do it, I don't think it would only be a big achievement for us but for English football as well. When I was younger, Spurs was the best club in Britain. There is still the same fan base, the same sell-outs every week and the best away crowd, along with one or two other clubs."

Jol was picking up on the mood among many Premiership fans of non-top four clubs who were delighted to see a new face in with a chance of breaking the dominance. That they were doing it by playing some cracking football only added to Spurs' attraction to the neutral fan.

Former Spurs manager Keith Burkinshaw observed: "I admire what Spurs are doing now, with seven or eight English players challenging for first-team places. Martin Jol believes they could start contesting the title in three years. It will be interesting to see if that happens."

For now the question was could they hold on to fourth place?

Entering the crucial last four games Spurs had their destiny in their own hands. But the run in was tough and Jol began to show the first signs of anxiety. "We've probably got over 100 points in the last 15 months and there's huge potential. We're still not there yet. A couple of injuries and it'd be difficult because we have a couple of key players without whom we struggle, so maybe we'll have to strengthen if we want to be prepared for Europe." Indeed a major cloud loomed on the horizon, as reports held that Ledley King – substituted in the 90th minute of a 1-0 victory at Goodison

– had sustained a broken ankle. On Easter Monday, 17 April, shorn of their defensive rock, Spurs faced Manchester United at White Hart Lane. Sir Alex was determined to prolong the argument that the title was bound for the Bridge for a second season in succession for as long as possible. Rooney's two goals before half-time merely delayed the inevitable as far as the championship was concerned. United may have won ten out of their last 11 Premiership games, but Chelsea just needed a point to ensure the Premiership would be theirs. Indeed Rooney's brace mattered more to Tottenham. Jenas pulled a goal back, but try as they might, Spurs could not find a dramatic late equaliser. They were now only four points ahead having played a game more than Arsenal.

"It's a big disappointment," said Jol. "Even if we had got a point it would have felt like a nice, warm, sunny afternoon. Instead we're all disappointed. We thought this could be a really big day for us." Jol spoke at length about the number of chances that his players squandered and their spirited attempts to level the game after Jenas profited from a lucky ricochet off Rio Ferdinand to score from a corner eight minutes into the second half. But perhaps what he had said prior to the game had acted as a spur for his opponents rather than his own players. "I heard an interview with Martin Jol on the radio after Tottenham's game against Everton and he said they were getting Manchester United at a good time," said Ferguson. "I thought to myself: 'oh, really?'"

Jol's attacking, adventurous team still were not taking points off the other competitors for those vital top four spots, although they would get an early opportunity to redress that record as their next fixture, the following Saturday, was at Arsenal. The manager still maintained that there was plenty to admire about his side, even in defeat to United. "The first 20 minutes was the best we have played since I have been manager," said Jol. "We punished ourselves. I may exaggerate a bit, but I can't remember a game where we have played so well yet found ourselves two-nil down."

The home side undoubtedly missed the aerial presence of the injured Mido, although thereby hung another tale. Jol was forced to dismiss suggestions that Mido had stormed out of White Hart Lane before the game after being told he was not fit to play. "Mido came in for an early fitness test but it was just too painful for him," Jol said, referring to the striker's groin injury. "We all agreed he was not fit to play; we also thought he might have a bit of an infection, so it was sensible he returned home."

Highbury hosted the biggest north London derby in years and added to the already spicy taste of this fixture was the fact that it was the last ever derby at the famous old ground. But what was to follow could never have been predicted. One of the stormiest games in this turbulent derby's history led to mud-slinging and almost a pitchside fist fight.

An intense, competitive game burst into flames when, on 66 minutes Eboue and Silva collided in the build-up to Robbie Keane's opening goal of the game. Arsenal had two players down in the centre of the pitch, although not due to any involvement of a Tottenham player. The ball was played out to Davids on the left, who crossed for Keane to score.

As Spurs' players celebrated triumphantly on the pitch, Arsenal's took out their anger on Davids for playing on while their colleagues lay on the turf and Wenger raged at Jol on the touchline. What got Wenger's goat was the fact that not only did Tottenham's players fail to kick the ball out of play when Eboue and Silva lay injured, but that Jol claimed not to have seen the incident. An unusually ruffled Wenger had a head-to-head confrontation with Jol, then refused to shake hands with him afterwards and accused him of lying when the Spurs manager echoed what has become Wenger's trademark comment on controversy – "I didn't see it."

Wenger accused Jol of myopia, lying and "stealing the game away". Jol, television pictures seemed to show, had a point. He was more concerned with ensuring Davids did not stray offside as Spurs counter-attacked. When Wenger's accusations were put to him, the Dutchman said: "Irrespective of all the rights and wrongs, I don't think a manager should behave like that. He called me a liar and I am not a liar. I told him I didn't see it, and you can see that on television. I was telling Edgar Davids twice 'Don't be offside' and then we scored."

Keane's goal put Tottenham a goal ahead with just 24 minutes to go. Spurs had fourth place in their hands. Arsenal had a serious bee in their bonnet.

Henry, on just after the hour mark for Robin van Persie as Wenger rotated his squad in the face of a vital Champions League semi-final second leg at Villareal in midweek where the Gunners had just a single goal lead to defend, rampaged at the perceived injustice. Arsenal threw everything at the heart of Spurs' central defence. Robinson made a flying save from Reyes' volley as Tottenham clung on, but on 84 minutes Henry took a ball from Adebayor and shot past the England keeper to level matters. It could have been far worse for Spurs. Davids was sent off a minute later after clattering Fabregas and earning a second yellow from referee Steve Bennett.

What is forgotten about this game is that Wenger, under pressure to win a trophy, chose to begin the match, an incredibly important match, with Thierry Henry and Cesc Fabregas on the bench. He was protecting them for the Champions League semi-final, but was forced to fling them on in an attempt to win. That, and his behaviour when Tottenham scored the opening goal shows that Jol had his usually unrufflable adversary running scared.

Wenger, steaming at the perceived injustice, accused Davids of cheating as he strode off the pitch having earned that red card, and it was claimed that officers had to split up the pair and escort them to the changing rooms before the situation got any worse. But a spokesperson for the Met insisted that no incident occurred in the tunnel. "As is always the case, police are in the tunnel area at the end of every game. But no officer was involved or witnessed any altercation between Mr Wenger and Mr Davids," came the statement.

In heated post-match interviews, Jol hit back at the Arsenal players for making more of their injuries than necessary. "I didn't see it myself, but people told me that of the two players involved, one was standing up and then fell down again after seeing Davids going towards goal. You shouldn't act like that." He had a point.

The incident was replayed over and over again on television news and sport broadcasts, fuelling the conflagration further. The newspapers lapped it up. Here were London's oldest rivals, head to head in a battle to the death for that all important fourth Champions League spot and Arsène Wenger, the redoubtable professor was losing it. Going from 'Invincibles', as his side were declared rightly when they won the 2003/4 Premiership without losing a game, to struggling to finish fourth was clearly more than Wenger could handle. Jol, however, having kept his cool, came out of the affair with his reputation enhanced. "Don't mess with him," echoed in supporters' heads across the land. How was the situation with Wenger left? "It was just left because he left," Jol said with a wry smile.

The 1-1 draw was certainly a better result for Jol than it was for the irate Wenger. It maintained Spurs' four-point lead over Arsenal, although the Gunners still had a game in hand, but if Tottenham could beat Bolton at home and West Ham away on the final day, Jol, and not Wenger, would qualify for the Champions League – unless Arsenal won the competition.

And thereby hung yet another tale. Liverpool's incredible comeback victory over AC Milan in 2005 had lead to UEFA having to clarify the entry rules into the competition. Now it was abundantly clear that if a team won the Champions League and did not finish in a qualifying position in their national league, then their national FA would have the choice of which team to propose to the next season's competition; the Champions of Europe or the lowest-ranked qualified team. Emphatically UEFA would not allow both teams to enter, which had been the result when similar local rivalry had been tested when Everton stole fourth spot in 2004/05, but Liverpool won in Istanbul.

It was obvious that the FA would support a team which won the Champions League and so, if Arsenal beat Barcelona in Paris it would be a massive blow for Tottenham and a massive blow for their supporters.

With exclusion from the Champions League due to Arsenal victory in the final a serious possibility, Tottenham began their PR campaign to remain in the elite competition. "It's an injustice, everybody would agree," said Jol. "If you see the strength of this league, where a team that's near the bottom [Middlesbrough] can play in the UEFA Cup final. Then Liverpool came fifth in the Premiership and still won the Champions League in the same season. That is only possible in the Premiership. Maybe Arsenal will be fifth and win the Champions League, but why should that cost us our place?"

The night before Spurs' final home game of the season against Bolton, Keith Burkinshaw and his 1981 FA Cup-winning team were gathered at The Dorchester in London to celebrate the twenty-fifth anniversary of their win over Manchester City. As the luminaries descended, minds were cast back to the match that marked the beginning of a new era for Tottenham in the 1980s. After a succession of years in the wilderness, they retained the FA Cup the next year and went on to win the UEFA Cup in 1984. The old players smiled at the memories and hinted that Jol may be the man to restore pride to White Hart Lane. "We had some terrific players then," said Burkinshaw. "We entertained people and I think they're playing that way now." A little like their neighbours then? "But with a lot of English players in there, and that delights me."

The difference for Tottenham, Burkinshaw maintained, was Jol. Popular with players past and present, he has an element of the Englishman in him that endears him to the fans. "It's that he knows the history of the club," said assistant manager Chris Hughton. "He understands the football tradition."

Settling into his seat for the Bolton match, Jol surveyed the press assembled in front of him. It was an indication of how far his team had come during this season. "It's all good," he said, smoothly employing the north London vernacular. But the onus was heavily on Spurs to beat Bolton.

Spurs almost took the decision out of UEFA's hands after being completely outplayed throughout the first half of the match. Keane, the victim of an ankle injury after a strong tackle from Kevin Davies, was withdrawn at half-time, allowing Jol to shuffle his side. Tainio came infield to exert greater influence and it produced instant dividends. Within 15 minutes of the restart Spurs had their precious advantage. Lennon brought the ball infield from wide and dabbed it to Carrick, who beat two players before squaring back to Lennon on the edge of the box. The youngster advanced and fired beyond Jaaskelainen.

The post-match debate should have been about the goalscorer Lennon's compelling case for World Cup selection, but instead it was about how, for the second time in eight days, Spurs' opponents were writhing with indignation at the perceived injustice of events. It seemed a clear penalty decision when, 74 minutes in and with Bolton a goal down, Dawson brought down Giannakopoulos with an arm and leg. The Greece international had been eight yards from goal; but referee Alan Wiley put his whistle to his lips and then chose not to pursue the matter.

The result put Tottenham seven points clear of Arsenal with one game to go, although with the Gunners yet to play that weekend, they had two games in hand. To raise the pressure, Jol had another a cheeky jibe for the Arsenal manager over the lucky escape for Bolton's phantom penalty. "I haven't seen the incident yet," he said with an impish grin.

Jol had plenty of other reasons to smile. The result at Highbury already meant that his team had already qualified for Europe through league position for the first time in 23 years, but if they were now to be displaced from the top competition Arsenal had to win all three of their remaining matches, while hoping Spurs slipped up in their final game at West Ham United.

What could possibly go wrong?

THE MYSTERY LASAGNE

'Tottenham's historic rivalry with Arsenal has endured numerous twists and turns but nothing in its long turbulent history – not even when Henry Norris, the then-Arsenal chairman, got the Football League to promote Arsenal illegally to the First Division after the First World War, at the expense of Tottenham – has matched the drama that started at one o'clock yesterday morning in the Marriott Hotel at Canary Wharf. It was worthy of a Hercule Poirot mystery.'
Mihir Bose, Daily Telegraph

MARTIN JOL KEPT HIS own counsel for months about the emotional fall-out, the devastating financial loss and the enormous ramifications of the final day of the 2005/06 season when Spurs missed out on the fourth Champions League spot to their bitter rivals Arsenal because of the most bizarre circumstances in the club's history.

Peversely, on reflecton, when he finally commented on the incredible situation, Jol believed the catastrophe of being leapfrogged by his club's fiercest rivals was the best thing that could have happened. But he admitted it took its toll on his personal, as well as professional life. Spurs went down 2-1 at West Ham, while Arsenal's 4-2 win over Wigan meant the two North London teams swapped places, with the Gunners nicking the last Champions League spot by two points.

Jol confessed, in terms which every football fan could relate to: "I didn't take it too badly. I just didn't talk to people for the next three weeks. Not even my wife. I touched her, but I didn't speak to her. Even when I did touch her it was with one arm behind my back. I tried to forget it as quickly as possible – it was not easy though. I watch all the games on video, but not the one at West Ham because it was the last one of the season. There were no more team meetings planned, so it served no purpose for analysis. It is still around at the club somewhere, but I won't watch it in the future either.

But it was probably the best thing that happened to us. Everybody realises that Arsenal take us seriously now. If they told me a couple of months before that we would qualify for Europe, I would have been very happy, but on that day and in those circumstances missing out on fourth place was hard to take. Although we were disappointed, we knew we achieved something with a very young team."

But it could have been so much more. In truth Tottenham should have secured their grasp on Champions League football long before the final day of the season. Two weeks earlier, they had led 1-0 away to Arsenal when Jol substituted Aaron Lennon, who was occupying two players. It ranks among his tactical decisions that have been questioned by some fans. Arsenal drew momentum from the substitutions and equalised to stay in touch with their rivals.

Then there was the last minute defeat at Fulham. A point there with ten men could have made all the difference. But that was all water under the bridge as Tottenham's players awoke on the morning of 7 May 2006. Despite Arsenal's serene progress to the Champions League final and victories in each of their games in hand over Spurs, the scene was still set for a glorious climax to a wonderful season. The omens boded well. West Ham, with an FA Cup final to prepare for, had already declared that they would omit players, a decision which balanced Spurs' loss of several injured players. Ledley King was recuperating with a chance of making the England World Cup squad and Jol gave Robbie Keane (ankle) only a 10% chance of playing.

As is Jol's custom for London matches, the Tottenham players spent the night before the match at the Marriott, gathering around 7 o'clock in the evening. Curiously, the neighbouring Four Seasons was used by Arsenal, one of the quirks of fate which led to the supposition and claims of underhand dealings afterwards.

A buffet dinner was laid out for the Tottenham party in a specially booked room and Jol was feeling particularly happy. Many of the players who had been carrying knocks were now fit, including Keane and Carrick.

The Marriott, a five-star hotel, is proud of its cuisine. It claims to "satisfy the most discerning palates with its fresh approach" and the players made the most of the buffet, a lot of them having lasagne. Spurs often used the hotel prior to Premiership games and had suffered no previous problems.

But after a literally off-colour Spurs crashed to a 2-1 defeat at West Ham, Police were called in to investigate a mystery food poisoning outbreak that struck ten players and possibly denied the club a place in the Champions League.

The most tortuous day in Spurs' modern history began early. Jol was woken by the doctor at 5am with news of several sick players and confessed to feeling unwell himself. Jol later joked it was easier for him to reveal the names of players not affected than those who were. "I can sum up the players who were not sick. There was Paul Robinson, Stephen Kelly, Anthony Gardner and Jermain Defoe and the rest were sick. So we had to call for some reserve players."

By 11am, as news spread like wildfire that Tottenham were the victims of a poisoning, Premier League officials were called to the hotel after Tottenham officials expressed concern about their ability to fulfil the 3pm fixture. Jol explains: "We asked the Premier League to postpone the match for one day because you know how it is with food poisoning – you can feel better after six to eight hours. The only thing they said was that it was our responsibility [to decide whether to play]. We had ten players in bed. Then we asked the Premier League to postpone the kick-off for three hours until six o'clock and that wasn't possible."

Frantic negotiations took place between league officials, Tottenham's management and medical staff and the police. The latter said the kick-off could be delayed until 5pm, but no later, because of concerns about public order if fans had been drinking all day. Amid reminders that the only previous instance of a fixture not being fulfilled had led to the offending team being deducted three points, plus there was the added complication that West Ham told Premier League Chief Executive Peter Scudamore they were quite ready to postpone the game but did not want the rearranged fixture to be played before the FA Cup final on the following Saturday, Spurs were foced to make a decision. A Premier League spokesman said: "Tottenham Hotspur took the decision that a two-hour delay would have no material medical benefit for those players affected and accordingly decided to fulfil the fixture at the original 3pm kick-off time."

To add to Spurs' trauma, Scudamore was at Highbury, as a guest for the club's farewell celebrations for the old stadium, and it was from this bastion of Tottenham's enemy that he let it be known he could not postpone the match.

Then came the news that lasagne was being blamed as the most likely cause of the problem. The local environmental health department were alerted – a potentially serious embarrassment for the Marriott. There was even a police presence on the team coach to Upton Park after it was mooted that Spurs could have been victims of a deliberate poisoning to ensure Arsenal finished fourth.

The players affected were Michael Dawson, Michael Carrick, Edgar Davids, Robbie Keane, Radek Cerny, Callum Davenport, Teemu Tainio, Aaron Lennon, Lee Barnard and Tom Huddlestone. All but Huddlestone played some part in the game, though Cerny remained on the bench. "We made the decision with the whole squad to do the warm-up and everybody said they wanted to play the game," said Jol, praising his team's resilience in the face of this unexpected problem.

During the last match of the season the crowd tell the players what is happening elsewhere. Within five minutes, Upton Park was singing: "One-nil to the Arsenal". Five minutes later West Ham scored when Paul Robinson was beaten by a 25-yarder from Fletcher. Even though it swerved and bounced Robinson should have done better. Remember, he was not affected by the illness. Shortly before the interval he recovered authority and reacted wonderfully to stop a volley from Zamora.

Then the Tottenham supporters started cheering as Wigan equalised. Barely had Tottenham hailed Wigan as they led 2-1, than Upton Park erupted with "Two-two to the Arsenal". There is no love lost between fans of London clubs.

On 35 minutes the Tottenham player Upton Park hates, Jermain Defoe, scored an equaliser. Carrick was applauded as a returning old boy, while Defoe's every touch was booed and his goal was greeted with total, hateful silence. Carrick fed a pass to Defoe and his touch was as exquisite as his accuracy. The England striker slipped away from Anton Ferdinand and glided the ball into the far corner of the net. Spurs were level at Upton Park as Arsenal trailed to Wigan at Highbury.

Four minutes later Aaron Lennon, who came to life only sporadically, earned a corner that Carrick delivered and Anthony Gardner, applying almost too much power, headed over the bar. During that spell it looked, incredibly, as if Spurs could muster the energy to alter the course of the match.

The second half saw Upton Park in much finer voice as they relayed news of Henry's hat-trick in the final match at Highbury and also saw their team dominate a visibly wilting Spurs team. Carrick left on the hour. Jol made other changes, but one Spurs player refused to leave. Edgar Davids' number was held up, but he would not let the dream go.

West Ham settled the outcome with slick play after 80 minutes. Shaun Newton guided a pass to Nigel Reo-Coker and he back-heeled to Yossi Benayoun, who had temporarily gone towards the right of the area. The Israeli international slipped the ball across and past Dawson before wheeling to shoot high past Robinson at the near post. It was a cruel, cruel blow, although the ultimate outcome of the season was already known due to happenings at Highbury, where Arsenal led 4-2.

Only two late Spurs goals could save fourth place and the players were out on their feet.

When it was all over, Davids walked to the Spurs end and tossed his shirt to the crowd. When Levy visted the dressing room, he found many of the players in tears. It could not have been more dramatic, more stomach-churningly devastating.

Spurs, willing as they were, might have been beaten by a larger margin. With the score at 1-1, Teemu Tainio brought down Bobby Zamora, but Paul Robinson leapt to his right and saved Teddy Sheringham's penalty after 55 minutes. "If Tottenham hadn't been under the weather they would still have been in difficulty," said Alan Pardew with justification.

Jol, who like his assistant Chris Hughton, was affected, said: "I've never experienced anything like this in football before. I don't want to blame our defeat on the circumstances and I don't think personally that there was any foul play involved. We would like to have postponed the match for one day, but that wasn't really possible and I understand that."

Jol revealed the litany of players who had been affected and what they had gone through to try and win Spurs that vital last Champions League place. "Dawson was very sick but played 90 minutes. Carrick [substituted midway through the second half] couldn't go on. One of the problems was they couldn't take food or any fluids before the match."

As Arsenal fans celebrated, Spurs were left wondering what had caused the bug to sweep through their squad. Police were called in at 1pm after consultations between the chairman Daniel Levy, the club secretary John Alexander and club doctor Charlotte Cowie. Blood and urine samples were taken from the sick players.

Jol didn't join in with the speculation that his players had been nobbled. He said the club had a "rough idea" what had caused the poisoning, leading to suggestions that the ten players had eaten the same dish at their east London hotel.

Paul Downing, the Marriott's general manager, said: "We don't know that it's food poisoning, but we need to establish what has made some of the players unwell. We are taking part in an investigation with club management to try to find that out." It was understood that no other guests at the hotel fell ill.

Arsenal manager Arsène Wenger commiserated. "What happened to Tottenham I don't know. I feel sorry for that. We knew what happened at West Ham was out of our hands. It is cruel for Tottenham, but sport is like that."

Michael Carrick, one of the players who succumbed to what was thought to be at first a devious poisoning plot by the Gunners to undermine their rivals' chances, has long since left White Hart Lane, but the memories of that fateful day are still etched in the memory. Carrick recalls: "We all knew what we could have done and to get into the Champions League for the first time would have been an unbelievable achievement for Tottenham. I'll never forget what happened that May. I lasted an hour, but I simply couldn't play any longer than that and had to go off. In the end we lost the game and were overtaken by Arsenal. Everybody had waited so long for it. To be so close and then have it snatched away at the last minute would have been bad enough in any case, but the way it happened made it far, far worse. It was a terrible and torrid day for the club because it was such a big occasion. It was a horrible way to miss out and for me that was as bad as it could get.

When I woke up on the Sunday morning I was pretty ill. I didn't know what had happened and as the day went on it just got more and more surreal as we began to realise what had happened to us all. We didn't know if it was the food or a bug, but, of course, none of us could do anything about it. For it to happen on that day of all days was so hard to take. Any other day in the season and it wouldn't have been so bad, but there was so much money at stake for the club on that one game."

Mihir Bose, in the *Daily Telegraph* wrote: 'Tottenham's historic rivalry with Arsenal has endured numerous twists and turns but nothing in its long turbulent history – not even when Henry Norris, the then-Arsenal chairman, got the Football League to promote Arsenal illegally to the First Division after the First World War, at the expense of Tottenham – has, matched the drama that started at 1 o'clock yesterday morning in the Marriott Hotel at Canary Wharf. It was worthy of a Hercule Poirot mystery.'

Tottenham's belief that skulduggery was behind several players falling ill before their defeat at Upton Park was expelled by the FA Premier League. And then, it emerged that some players had been exposed to a virus before arriving at the team hotel. But for all the controversy and drama of what went on that fateful day in May 2006, Spurs ended the season in their highest league position since coming third in 1990, and accrued the most points in a season since 1987, when they also finished third.

"It will take a hell of an effort for any Spurs team, even us, to beat that 65 points-total," Jol said.

Initially Tottenham chairman Daniel Levy petitioned his Premier League rivals to garner support for a replay. Although Spurs sought to play down the possibility of taking legal action against the League or the hotel where the club stayed the night before the game, Levy contacted fellow chairmen to put pressure on Richard Scudamore. At this stage Spurs still suspected sabotage.

The idea of an Arsenal supporter penetrating the hotel's kitchens in an effort to derail their north London rivals in their quest for Champions League football was considered fanciful. If it proved that the players had been poisoned then the level of sophistication required to carry off such a crime would lead many to point the finger at a betting scam. The sums of money riding on the game were enormous, particularly in the Far East, and the Premier League's previous experience with floodlight tampering in 1999 showed anything is possible. On that occasion police discovered a plot by a betting syndicate run from Malaysia to tamper with Charlton's lights ahead of their Premiership game against Liverpool. They did it with the collusion of a corrupt club official. Senior sources at Spurs were keeping an open mind to the possibility that the club were victim of sabotage.

A Premier League spokesman said: "If someone has done something like that and there is hard and fast evidence, not internet chat rooms, then clearly it's something that not just ourselves but everyone in the game should be concerned about."

The fall out continued for weeks to come. The Premier League held an emergency board meeting to discuss Tottenham's request for a replay. In an unprecedented move, Levy made public a letter he had written to Premier League chairman David Richards, demanding the game was played again. Levy claimed that:

- The club's chances of winning the game and clinching fourth place in the Premiership and a Champions League place ahead of Arsenal were "significantly reduced" by the mystery illness.

- The Premier League, and in particular chief executive Richard Scudamore, put the club in an "impossible situation" and acted inconsistently and failed to obtain all the facts before ruling out a postponement of the match at Upton Park.

- The Premier League gave Arsenal a "significant advantage" in the race for fourth by refusing to postpone and Scudamore "added insult to injury" by announcing his decision on Sky TV from the pitch at Highbury.

- A majority of Premier League clubs he had contacted supported the call for a replay.

But it looked extremely unlikely that the Premier League would sanction a replay. A spokesman said: "The fixture was fulfilled and the result stands."

Inevitably Tottenham were left licking their wounds as the Premier League emphatically rejected their calls for a replay. Following a one hour meeting of the League's three-man board Scudamore issued a statement which cast serious doubt over the club's claims that Jol's squad had been decimated by a mystery illness. They would in time, be proved correct in this assertion.

Levy responded by saying the Tottenham board would consider their next move at a meeting. They were still awaiting the results of tests on the ten players they say were struck down by possible food poisoning. But even if they proved that they were the victim of sabotage or, more likely, a virus which spread among the players, the League made it clear they would not allow a replay. When those tests came back showing that a form of gastroenteritis bug, most probably already being carried by a member of the squad when the team arrived at the Marriott, was responsible for the problem, Levy's battle to win a reprieve was over.

In truth it was an inability to beat any member of the top four in the Premiership during the season, rather than what proved to be a viral infection, that cost Jol's Spurs side that fourth place finish. A recognition of that lingered in the manager's words. "I would like to have 68 points," he said, "but 65 is an unbelievable total for our team. I still believe we can do better and better."

Tottenham felt sick long after the symptoms had subsided. The memory of that afternoon's events are seared into the club, and in particular its supporters, for ever more. There is no end to the wondering over what might have happened had illness not struck.

Still, Spurs had finished fifth in the Premiership, although a place in the UEFA Cup was scant consolation for missing out on the Champions League. The defeat cost Spurs an estimated £10m cash bonanza from a spot in European football's top club competition. A very expensive Italian indeed.

BACK IN EUROPE AFTER
A GENERATION

DIMITAR BERBATOV, A MAN who had been chased by Spurs' Director of Football Damien Comolli, became Tottenham's new £10.9m signing from Bayer Leverkusen in the summer of 2006. In doing so the Bulgarian rejected an offer from Manchester United after talking to Martin Jol; and for that Jol deserved the freedom of Haringay.

The 25-year-old striker, who agreed a four-year deal, said: "I can reveal now that I had an offer from Manchester United and everyone knows what that means. But after talking to Martin I decided to choose Spurs. It was our first meeting but I realised that he's a very special man."

Berbatov was to become the new arrival to have the most impact on a Premiership club's fortunes during the 2006/07 season. Arguably only Didier Drogba at Chelsea and United's Cristiano Ronaldo contributed more to their respective causes. And it was Jol who had come up trumps with his signature.

The manager declared: "Dimitar Berbatov is a stylish player. He can score good goals and he is a player who is always looking to be on the end of attacks."

Berbatov gave Spurs fans an appetiser for the new season by hitting two superb goals as Jol's side won a friendly 2-0 at Birmingham City. His first came in the 12th minute when he controlled Hossam Ghaly's deep cross and volleyed past Maik Taylor. Two minutes later the Bulgarian struck again with a thunderous drive that went in off the bar. Not since Jürgen Klinsmann graced White Hart Lane more than a decade ago has a Tottenham player scored 20 league goals in a season. That contribution ensured the German not only won the hearts of the fans, but also left them with indelible memories. Now another imported striker appeared ready to begin a love affair with the supporters.

Given Berbatov's goalscoring record in the Bundesliga, where he managed 21 goals in 34 appearances in 2005/06 finishing second in the charts behind Miroslav Klose, Spurs' considerable investment seemed wisely spent. It was also easy to see why Jol preferred the former Bayer Leverkusen striker to Mido, whose ego had moments of rock star excess.

Berbatov's movement is more fluent than the Egyptian's and he was set to form a formidable attacking partnership with either Jermain Defoe or Robbie Keane or maybe both with Keane in a more withdrawn role, as was the case against Birmingham. It was a system that left the home side chasing shadows. "A very, very good way of playing," said home manager Steve Bruce.

Under pressure after Berbatov's acquisition, Jermain Defoe scored in the next pre-season friendly and Jol backed the striker to force his way into new coach Steve McClaren's England squad: "He had another couple of chances, but when he faces on to goal nine times out of ten it will go in the net. Jermain is a 20-goals-a-season player. He started tonight because we needed him and the first thing he did was score a goal, so what else can you ask for?"

But while Berbatov's arrival offered hope for the immediate future, there was an impending departure which threatened the solidity of Spurs' spine, such an important element in the success of the previous season. Michael Carrick wanted out. Jol tried and tried to persuade the England man to change his mind, but eventually halted his attempts to dissuade Carrick from moving to his destination of choice; Old Trafford. As Carrick had made the central midfield berth his own since being given his chance by the Dutchman after being ignored by Santini, Jol had allowed Pedro Mendes, Michael Brown and Sean Davis to leave in the January transfer window. Now light in midfield, Jol faced a difficult task to replace the young Englishman. New £8.2m arrival Didier Zokora, who had chosen Spurs above Arsenal on leaving St-Etienne, Davids and Huddlestone were strong candidates to play in the centre in Carrick's stead.

Carrick had made it clear that he wanted to move, pointing to Manchester United's participation in the Champions League and their greater proximity to his family home in Newcastle as key attractions. Once the player had made his mind up, Jol knew Spurs had lost their man. United had bid £10m for Carrick at first and initially refused to pay more than £12m, but Spurs insisted on a price of £17m which weakened United in the transfer market. Real Madrid's initial offer for van Nistelrooy was knocked back, but the striker was bound for Madrid, a move which freed up more cash for Sir Alex to splash on Carrick to meet Spurs' demands.

Ferguson's desire to bring Carrick to Old Traford seemingly at any cost didn't meet with wholesale approval. "I have not spoken to anybody who, with £18.6m, would have spent it on Carrick," said Mark Longden of the Independent Manchester United Supporters' Association.

With a return of about £15m on their £2.75m investment on Carrick, Tottenham had not done badly out of the deal. "We were in a situation where we could say 'no' – he still had two years on his contract – but he wanted to go and I respect him because he is a very nice man," Jol reflected. "He came in and said goodbye and that we will keep in touch and he loved playing for us. We bought him from West Ham and he did ever so well, so good luck to him."

Thanks to the progress under Jol, Tottenham were now beginning to play in a different league off the pitch, which would allow them to compete on a regular basis with the big four clubs on the pitch. It was imperative that the 2005/06 near miss should be shown as the beginning of a new era, rather than a flash in the pan. That was the challenge facing Martin Jol.

It all seemed to be brewing up nicely. Teemu Tainio's brace in the victory over Internazionale meant Tottenham had now won all their pre-season friendlies and the expectations intensified despite Carrick's departure.

Getting back into Europe and the desire to climb into the top four were targets the fans were setting, even if Jol was far more pragmatic. With Stalteri injured and Routledge not looking a long-term option at full-back, the manager lined up Pascal Chimbonda, who was keen on the move from Wigan after making such an inpact in the Lancashire club's first season i the Premiership. Spurs needed, though, to increase their £3.5m offer to land the Frenchman. Chairman Levy was happy to open the purse strings and the right-back was soon at the Lane. Jol also prepared a fresh offer for Middlesbrough's Stewart Downing, a young England player who fitted Spurs' buying policy perfectly. Boro confirmed: "They did make an offer. We rejected it immediately and told Tottenham that Stewart is not for sale, that we are not interested and that they should not pursue the matter any further. As a consequence, Tottenham have told us they have no further interest in Stewart." With Downing unreachable, Jol opened discussions with Chelsea for their Irish winger, Damien Duff opted, although the tricky winger would also feel the tug of the north east as he joined Newcastle United.

Why did Duff not move to Tottenham when Jol was keen and the price of £5 million well within the club's range? The stumbling block was Tottenham's wage ceiling being around £45,000 a week, while Duff was used to earning £70,000 a week at Stamford Bridge. Levy suggested that Chelsea pay the difference between Duff's salary and what he would earn at White Hart Lane. In other words Chelsea would continue paying Duff about £20,000 a week. This was similar to Levy's proposal a year earlier when, following Chelsea's poaching of football director Frank Arnesen, Levy met the West London club to discuss compensation. Part of the package demanded by Tottenham was the transfer of Scott Parker to White Hart Lane with Chelsea paying his wage bill. Chelsea refused. Parker moved to Newcastle and exactly the same scenario occured with Duff.

Jol had worked hard to assemble a squad of young players, the spine of which was English, but he would have to find another solution to the lack of width in his formation that accommodated Keane behind Berbatov and Defoe.

Just before the transfer window closed Tottenham saw off competition from several other Premiership clubs to secure the signing of left-sided player Steed Malbranque from Fulham, with Wayne Routledge moving in the opposite direction on a season-long loan. Bolton, Newcastle and West Ham were among the clubs interested in signing Malbranque, the Belgium-born Frenchman. "Steed is a skillful, versatile midfielder of real quality," said Jol. "He is a player we have always admired and we are delighted he has come to us."

There was a major downside, though; Malbranque was sidelined with a groin injury, and was unlikely to make his Tottenham debut until early November. For Jol it was a breathless close to the transfer window.

But while squad building had continued on until the end of August, the season had begun a couple of weeks earlier, and not well. Spurs lost three of the first four league games, beating only Sheffield United. The impressive array of additions mollified restless fans, unhappy at the unimpressive start to the season, which tested Jol to the limit as he fathomed out what was wrong. Take opening day for instance. Everything seemed to be headed in Spurs' direction when Kevin Kilbane was sent off for two fouls on Lee Young-Pyo. Strangely though the reduction to ten men galvanised Everton and they pushed forward with some defiance. Andy Johnson, the £8.6m man from Crystal Palace, fired the Toffees to a 2-0 victory at White Hart Lane. Jol called i: "one of those poxy little days in England", but it was not what Spurs fans expected after the previous season's tilt at a Champions League place. Little wonder Jol went out and spent some serious money.

SPURS WERE BACK in Europe for the first time in seven years after coming so close to pulling off a precious and lucrative Champions League place. Jol said: "We raised everybody's expectations last year, I know that. People have always talked about Tottenham as a big club – and we are.

We've got a million fans, we sell out every home game and there's a tradition that makes us bigger than, say, Newcastle or West Ham. But we're not a big club in terms of achievement because we haven't had sustained success for more than 20 years. Last season the four big clubs finished in the top four places and we were the best of the rest. That was good, that was ahead of schedule, but it made everybody think we were in a different position, that the next step was breaking into the Champions League places. Not yet. We're getting there, though. When I have everybody fit, then I think we will be on the verge of something which could be quite special.

Jol's first European adventure began with a 1-0 away win at Slavia Prague. A first-half goal from Jenas gave Tottenham the advantage in their first round first leg tie over a poor Slavia Prague side on the return to the European stage despite Spurs producing a performance that mirrored their inauspicious start to the Premiership. Without the services of Lennon – who needed surgery on his knee that would keep him out for six weeks – Jol's men made a relatively subdued start against inexperienced opponents, but the manager was delighted nonetheless. "It was the best result you could wish for," he said. "To win 1-0 away from home. It was a good goal – Jenas can do that, he can score goals and that is what you want in away games in Europe."

Jol hoped that progress in Europe would inspire an upturn in Premiership form. With injuries to Defoe and Berbatov among a growing list of casualties, there were problems scoring. There was no panic from Jol, despite just three goals from seven games. Talk was of a hangover form the last day failure to qualify for the Champions League and also memories of Everton's struggles the previous season, following a similarly successful previous campaign, were a reminder for Jol not to allow expectations to become unrealistic. He said: "That is a concern, but we can't be concerned about a positive thing. I can't say I would prefer to go out of Europe because I want to do well in the league. It happened to Middlesbrough last year, as well. The only thing I have to do is keep a good spirit. I don't have to do a lot. They are a good group of players and I have three skippers who are looking after them in Ledley King, Robbie Keane and Paul Robinson. They do that in the dressing room. You need a structure. I have my structure. We have two team meetings every week and I talk to the individual players on a set day each week. Sometimes you only need 30 seconds. But we have to start scoring goals because if Jermaine Jenas is your top scorer after six or seven matches, that's not what you would have wanted before the season."

In fact Robbie Keane, the man whose run of goals had so nearly fired Spurs into the Champions League at the end of the previous campaign, had yet to score.

Spurs eased through to the group stages after a 1-0 home win over Slavia clinched a 2-0 aggregate win. Keane's first goal of the season ten minutes from time won the game and settled more thanna few nerves. The draw paired Tottenham with Dimitar Berbatov's last club Bayer Leverkusen, Club Bruges, Besiktas and Dinamo Bucharest. It was a tough-looking group. Jol said: "Leverkusen are a club with a great history. They will probably be favourites to win the group. There are no weaker clubs in our group and we will not be viewed as such by the other teams. It will be an exciting journey for us."

With Premiership form picking up, after the low point of a 3-0 defeat at Anfield, thanks to a 2-1 win over Portsmouth and a 1-1 draw at Villa Park, Spurs got off to a flyer in the UEFA Cup group stages with a 2-0 away in in Besitkas. Before the game Jol acclimatised the side to the cacophony of the Turkish support by playing tapes of their crowd. Berbatov certainly responded. He had shown only glimpses of his undoubted ability since his arrival, but the Bulgarian gave a masterful display of the forward's art to propel Spurs to a much-deserved victory. There are few tougher places to visit in European football than Istanbul, yet Spurs, with their most accomplished performance of the season, overwhelmed Besiktas and could easily have scored more than the two goals which provided them with the perfect start to their campaign.

Berbatov, havng shaken off his annoying groin injury, created the opening goal for Ghaly, another player making an impact at Spurs after an injury-plagued arrival, and then scored a wonderful second as Spurs finally hit their stride after an inconsistent start to the season. Jol said: "Tonight showed the extra quality that Berbatov has. If he can make the difference, then this is what we need. Hopefully this will break the spell for us, in terms of not scoring so many goals. We were also a bit too strong to concede."

While club policy remained to recruit young homegrown talent, not one of Jol's seven summer signings was actually British. Conversely two of the eight departures were English and two hailed from the Republic of Ireland. Jol clarified the thinking. "We've bought more players from abroad because the British were too expensive. Last week we played three games in six days and Jermaine Jenas, for example, did more in the third game than he did in the first because he knows [how to handle it]. That is perhaps not the same with continental players. You play so many games here and you need players who have got a great mentality. The foreign players will get the same mentality if they see their British team-mates and that is why I prefer a British spine."

With form picking up, Jol wanted to keep the European buzz going. Spurs comfortably defeated Club Bruges, netting three goals in a game for the first time in the season, the 5-0 romp at MK Dons in the League Cup excepted. Th 3-1 win over Bruges, which saw Berbatov score twice and Keane once as Tottenham came from behind after conceding an early goal, followed two consecutive clean sheets that yielded four league points as Spurs began to climb the table from the fringes of the relagation zone, where their worrying opening spell of four points from the first six games had sent them.

Jol had already shown that he liked to rotate his squad and the sublime performance against Bruges of Berbatov, who linked effortlessly with Keane, made matters even more contentious up front. Jol admitted that, when Mido and Defoe each scored twice in the Carling Cup win over MK Dons at the end of last month, he had received several emails from supporters imploring him to stick with the winning combination. Jol shrugged: "I will play who I think is best at the time. When Defoe is scoring goals everyone says he should start. But now I have choices." Tension increaased through-out the season as each of the four strikers, Mido, Berbatov, Defoe and Keane had spells of good and indifferent form. Jol clearly favoured a com-bination which saw one of the two larger strikers alongside one of the two smaller, but the debates grew long and loud over who was the 'best' among media and supporters alike. It would not help Jol's position when things began to go wrong at the start of the following season.

Before the crucial UEFA Cup group tie against Leverkusen their former striker Berbatov admitted he regretted stifling yawns when Zinedine Zidane brought the house down at Hampden Park with a wonder goal as Real Madrid beat Bayer Leverkusen 2-1 to win the Champions League. He said: "Back then I was so young that I didn't give a ****. I was just sitting on the Bayer bench thinking 'whatever'. But as time goes by you appreciate it more – it might not ever happen again. I must learn from my mistake and try not to do that again. I had five wonderful years at Leverkusen but now they are over and I must concentrate on Tottenham."

Once again Berbatov scored the goal that confirmed Tottenham's passage to the knockout phase in a superb 1-0 win in Germany, but his goal celbration was muted in deference to his old club. Berbatov's name rang out from the Tottenham end as he left the field to a standing ovation. The

Leverkusen fans drowned out the Spurs support with their own gracious tribute. It was already his fourth goal in Europe, the winner in Spurs' third consecutive victory, and gave Tottenham the chance to top the group and thus avoid one of the Champions League departees in the draw for the knockout stages.

In the UEFA Cup finishing positions in the group are vital. Teams topping the groups will play those finishing third in another group, while the group runners-up will come up against one of the eight clubs who finish third in their Champions League groups and enter the UEFA Cup. Spurs group now could come down to a head-to-head wiith Dinamo Bucharest – if the Romanians beat Leverkusen at home, it would be the winner of the final game at the Lane which took top spot. Said a delighted Jol: "Now we want to go on and finish top of the group. The UEFA Cup has been a great experience for us and these wins are good for the confidence of the team. I'm sure White Hart Lane will be sold out – it always is – and the support of our fans will be an important factor for us again."

Jol, perhaps inadvisedly given the ultimate reaction it would engender amongst some of his board, admitted he would rather win the UEFA Cup than finish in the top four of the Premiership. Indeed Jol's outlook was at odds with the consensus within modern football – the rewards that go with the Champions League mean qualification is regarded as a glittering prize. Was this the romantic side of the Dutchman shining through – silverware over hard cash?

Jol explained: "I want to win the UEFA Cup. If you're in the Champions League you could end up with a problem, while winning the UEFA Cup would be a big success for this club. Going into a Champions League place doesn't mean anything. It would signify we are in the top four in England, but, after that, there are so many games to play until you can win something. I don't feel we're strong enough to win the Champions League yet. In the end we were just not strong enough last season, but maybe it did help the long-term development. I tell everybody that it's better to compete for Europe than to be there and get knocked out because that's a big disappointment."

Jol argued that Everton's experience in the previous 2005/06 season had underlined the risks that accompany a Premiership top-four finish. They had crashed out in the Champions League qualifying stage, then went straight out of the UEFA Cup, leaving manager David Moyes with the task of picking up the pieces of his team's shattered confidence before the end of September. He said: "Their whole campaign disintegrated. I don't feel we are strong enough to win the Champions League, but if you look at the last few years in the UEFA Cup, there are clubs from many different countries who have won it. We could be one of them."

This was a crucial statement in the long term game which was beginning to play itself out. Jol had laid his marker down. The board's ambitions did not match his own. They wanted qualification for the Champions League and thus the ability to sell the club at the highest possible price. A collisions course had been set, although it would not rise to the surface until the end of the season and that second successive fifth-placed finish that won so many plaudits from fans and press, but grumblings from the White Hart Lane boardroom.

Dinamo Bucharest provided stern opposition as they arrived at the Lane in contention for top spot in the group following a 2-1 win over Leverkusen. They were 13 points clear at the top of the Romanian Premier Division, having won 17 of 19 league games this season. A draw would have sufficed in terms of qualification for both sides, but there was little doubt as to which team was the hungrier to win the group.

Spurs started in a whirlwind. It was not long before Dinamo keeper Hayeu inexplicably bowled a clearance straight to the feet of Berbatov who lashed the ball home from 25 yards for his 10th goal of the season and his fifth in four Uefa Cup games. Defoe was thwarted by the crossbar, but soon enough the England striker spun past Cristian Pulhac, raced through the Dinamo defence and drilled home his first ever European goal.

At the interval Tottenham's two UEFA Cup winning captains, Alan Mullery from 1972 and Graham Roberts from 1984, were introduced to the crowd and within minutes of the restart the side's hopes of making it a hat-trick were further enhanced. Defoe, enjoying a licence to roam from deep, picked out Lennon on the left, who unselfishly squared for Ghaly. The Egyptian's shot was parried and Defoe was on hand to roll the rebound into the net. "The goals will give Jermain confidence," Jol licked his lips afterwards. "Like Berbatov he is a goalscorer and they are both scoring goals."

A Mendi strike in stoppage time did little to dim the euphoria engulfing White Hart Lane, and Jol played to the gallery who were hoping for Tottenham to earn European glory for the first time in 22 years. "You have to give our boys credit," said Jol. "Dinamo are a good team and we made them look very average."

Jol was delighted with Tottenham's pairing with Feyenoord in the first knock out stage as the tie would mark a managerial return to the Netherlands. Damien Comolli, said. "For Martin, it will be even more interesting, because he is going back home. That's an advantage because he knows all their players and he knows the way they play, but we will need character and quality to go through."

Jol, speaking at the draw in Nyon, said: "It is not a bad draw for us. They are probably not as good as when they played Spurs in the final of the UEFA Cup in 1984, but they are still a big club who get crowds averaging 45-50,000. They've got a young squad who have done well and beat a good Wisla Krakow side this week, but I feel if we play with confidence like we have been then we can go further. I am looking forward to going to Rotterdam."

The draw was also made for the last 16 in which, should Spurs beat Feyenoord, they would take on SC Braga of Portugal or Serie A side Parma.

But then; a major shock. Feyenoord were excluded from the competition as punishment by UEFA after crowd trouble in their group match against Nancy on 30 November. Tottenham had to wait to discover whether officials decide to give them a bye or possibly face Wisla Krakow, who finished behind Feyenoord in the group stages. A bye would mean a loss of revenue from gate receipts and television money although they would be closer to ending their eight-year wait for a trophy. It would also give Jol's men more recovery time in their busy schedule, with the club challenging in three cups and pushing for a European place in the Premiership.

Jol had been looking forward to going back to Holland, but, ideally, wanted a bye and compensation for missing out on a plum European tie. He said: "If I'm honest, I would take a bye and the reason is that we have so many matches that it could be a helping hand to leave that one out to give us some more rest. But my chairman thinks if we want to play in Europe then we should play in Europe and he is right because it's a big tie against Feyenoord. Hopefully we will get some compensation, but maybe other people will think differently. But if we have to play then we will play."

Tottenham were eventually given a bye into the last 16 after an appeal by Feyenoord to the Court of Arbitration for Sport was dismissed. CAS also upheld a fine of 100,000 Swiss francs.

The ruling gave Spurs and Jol a further advantage; a clear week to work with the players ahead of the FA Cup 5th round trip to Fulham. At this crucial stage of the season in late February, rest counted for much in Jol's book. He said: "We've played a tremendous amount of games in all competitions in the last three months so it's an advantage for us to have a little rest and spend some quality time on the training pitch."

In the event, after a four goal blitz sent Fulham carshing out of the Cup at Craven Cottage, refreshed Spurs played Portuguese side SC Braga in the Round of 16. It would be no easy task. Braga boasted a significant scalp after beating Parma 1-0 home and away. Known in Portugal as "Arsenal do Minho" in recognition of Jose Szabo, one of the club's former coaches, who returned from a match at Highbury in the 1930s and persuaded the team to ditch their green strip in favour of red-and-white stripes, the club also lies outside Portugal's traditional axis of power – encompassing Porto, Benfica and Sporting Lisbon – and Jol succinctly summed up their threat. "Braga don't concede a lot, but they don't score a lot, either."

With 14 goals in their last four matches, Tottenham did. To prevail they would probably have to become the first club this season to score in Europe at Braga's spectacular stadium, hewn out of the vulcanic rock of central northern Portugal. To make things more difficult Jenas was out with a groin injury and King suffered a further set-back to his continuing injury nightmar with bruising to the metatarsal in his right foot.

In the build up to the game Jol was provided with a great motivating force when Jose Mourinho described Tottenham as "not a great side" and predicted that their UEFA Cup dream would end in tears against Braga. Mourinho's best pal, Eladio Parames, ran the Portuguese club, while the coach was former Charlton defender Jorge Costa who had played under Mourinho at Porto. Mourinho said: "Tottenham are a good team but not a great team. Braga have to get a good result at home and they can do that by being well organised."

For his part, the Impish One was hoping to sneak into White Hart Lane for the second leg. Mourinho said: "When Portugal played Brazil at the Emirates, I was there in a corner, hidden. If it's possible, I'll be at White Hart Lane."

But Spurs were up to the task. Braga had cancelled out Keane's opener and Malbranque's goal with strikes from Paulo Jorge and Ze Carlos to set Spurs' hearts a flutter when all had seemed to be going so well with a two-goal lead, but Keane struck late to grab victory at Estadio Municipal de Braga. Said Jol: "It was disappointing that we were at 2-2, but every break we had was dangerous and Robbie made the difference. It would have been a good result to draw, but it would have been an injustice having seen the match. There was only one winner and it was Spurs."

Before the return leg Spurs suffered a new blow when Gardner broke his left leg in a freak injury in the FA Cup quarter-final draw at Stamford Bridge. It left Jol to shuffle their defence for the second leg against Braga.

Jol said: "It's bad news, a big blow, as Anthony will be out for six weeks. He did it within seconds of coming on against Chelsea. He jumped and landed on a heel. It was a strange injury to pick up. Didier Zokora can also play at centre-back and, at a push, so could Tom Huddlestone."

He then reiterated his belief that his squad, stretched to breaking point, would mean he preferred the hunt for silverware over that fourth Champions League place which was now in Spurs' sights. The board, no doubt, took note. Jol said: "It is not an ideal situation and it means we can't afford to prioritise the competitions. It's not realistic to say that we can win both the UEFA Cup and the FA Cup because it has never been done before. But that is what we want."

Berbatov's remarkable run of form continued as he helped ease Tottenham into the quarter-final with a 3-2 win over Braga at the Lane, clinching a 6-4 aggregate victory. The Portuguese side levelled on aggregate with the opener before Berbatov notched his 18th and 19th goals of the season before the break, both goals of the highest quality. The striker had been playing with a nagging groin problem and there were suggestions Jol wanted to rest him in Spurs' hectic schedule, but he showed no signs of fatigue or suggestions he was struggling as his classy finishes and approach play sent Braga packing. Andrade's powerful free-kick in the second half gave the Portuguese side hope of forcing extra-time, but Berbatov then set up Malbranque to seal the win and maintain Tottenham's 100% record in the competition.

Jol tipped Berbatov to go onto greater goalscoring feats now he was finding his bearings at the club. "In Germany he scored 18 goals after Christmas. When you're as good as him, next year he will score 25 goals probably."

With his growing reputation inevitably came interest from major clubs across the continent in the Bulgarian striker. Reports in a national newspaper held that, despite Berbatov having another four years on his contract, he was demanding Spurs offered improved terms and a further two years exrtension. A new deal could be worth around £50,000 a week. Spurs fans were fearful of a repeat of when the club's ambition was questioned after the sale of Carrick to Manchester United and morale at the Lane could also be affected if the striker didn't commit himself fully and openly.

Berbatov, though, was irritated by any suggestion that he was making demands. "My contract is long enough. I was really surprised and disappointed to read that I was seeking more money in the newspaper and I want to say that it is not true. I don't think about these things, I concentrate on my career, my football and my goals. I am very happy here and it is not correct to put things like that in the newspapers."

Then Tottenham's luck ran out. They were drawn against holders Sevilla in the quarter-finals. Sevilla were challenging for the title in La Liga, and had former Spurs striker Fredi Kanoute in their ranks. There was some better news; should Spurs come through this exacting test, they took on either Leverkusen – who had knocked Blackburn out of the competition, but who Tottenham had already beaten in this season's group stage – or Rangers' conquerors Osasuna in the semi-finals.

Spurs' 100 per cent record in Europe faced its stiffest test yet. The Andalusians, level on points with Barcelona at the top of La Liga, had thrashed Middlesbrough 4-0 in last season's UEFA Cup final and had beaten Barca 3-0 in the UEFA Super Cup. Kanoute had scored 21 goals in two seasons at White Hart Lane before joining Seville in 2005. Manuel Vizcaino, a Seville official, began the war of words by saying: "I am convinced that Tottenham's officials were making glum faces at the draw, even though they are one of the best teams."

Jol countered: "You have got to beat the best to get to the final and there is no such thing as an easy draw at this stage."

And from there the problems mounted. The build up to the first leg in Seville was surrounded by problems off the field with threats of strike action as more than 120 stewards were due to organise a mass walk-out to coincide with the match. Security workers for private security firm Prosegur wanted a sacked colleague reinstated and their action meant about 6,000 travelling Spurs fans could make the trip unaccompanied. Then Sevilla applied to UEFA to move the tie after local authorities in the Spanish city admitted they were concerned at the prospect of thousands of rival fans meeting in the middle of their annual Easter processions when locals and tourists pack the streets to see religious processions. The 5 April match fell on Maundy Thursday, a day when locals and tourists pack the streets in the staunchly Catholic area to see the religious processions. Hundreds of extra officers were drafted in.

By now the stakes were high as defeat in the FA Cup quarter-final replay meant that the UEFA Cup had become Tottenham's one remaining chance of much sought after silverware.

Jol could not resist a playful dig at Kanoute: "He gets all the crosses – I would score seven or eight goals over here with all the tap-ins – and he was a terrific player at Spurs, especially at home. In the last eight or nine years he has not been a prolific goalscorer [but] he has scored 19 goals in the Spanish league which is fantastic – maybe the service is better." The implication clearly being that maybe the defences were weaker. Kanoute had already scored 22 goals in all competitions in the 2006/07 season after managing only 21 in 73 games during his two years at Tottenham.

The tie, of course, also marked the first meeting of Tottenham Hotspur FC and Sevilla coach Juande Ramos, the man who would eventually, with a little help from the Spurs board, destabilise and then succeed Jol at the Lane. Ramos had largely built his team around the Mali international striker, with an instruction to his full-backs to overlap the midfielders and get plenty of balls into the penalty area. He said: "We watched him [Kanoute] play with Spurs, we saw the characteristics that would allow him to become a great footballer in Spain and we have developed those."

Certainly the Sevilla coach had the respect of Jol. "I feel that Sevilla is probably as good as or better than Arsenal and they are as good as Chelsea. Football-wise they are stronger than Barcelona; they are the most talented team in the UEFA Cup," he said.

Those defeats in the quarter-finals of the FA Cup to Chelsea and the semi-finals of the Carling Cup to Arsenal, were being used by Jol to provide the Spurs players with extra motivation. The manager was looking to Lennon and Berbatov to produce: "Lennon is one of those young talents that is going like a rocket – he is getting better every week. He has got to learn one or two things, like to go on the outside like [Cristiano] Ronaldo. But Lennon played in the hole against Chelsea and he was second to none. You need top players with top talent to be a good side and I think we have got one or two."

But Spurs' run of eight consecutive UEFA Cup victories, a record for a British club, came to an end at the Ramon Sanchez Pizjuan stadium as the reigning champions edged an exciting contest 2-1. The game couldn't have got off to a better start for Tottenham. Keane conjured an opening goal after less than 90 seconds, but Sevilla hit back through a controversially-awarded penalty from Kanoute and a header from Kerzhakov.

But the game was overshadowed by an incident involving riot police and travelling English fans, just 24 hours after Italian riot police had clashed with Manchester United supporters during a Champions League match in Rome. On this occasion, however, there apeared to be no blame attached to Spurs fans in the slightest as the attack was, regrettably, unprovoked. Police, clearly ready for action, had already made their presence known an hour before the match, using batons to disperse a group of Spurs fans who had congregated near the hotel where the Sevilla team were located. A couple of cups of liquid were thrown from the area where the Spurs fans were standing and, as the visiting supporters moved closer to the Sevilla team bus, the riot police intervened.

The first 30 minutes of the match itself passed with little incident in the stands, but then police entered the section of the stadium where the Spurs fans were located. The confrontation continued for around five minutes until Sevilla netted their second goal in the 36th minute. Trouble flared again during the half-time interval, with seats again being thrown as the riot police moved in, before things calmed down after their departure at the start of the second half.

Spurs went in at half-time 2-1 down and Jol's men were quickly back out on the pitch after the break, eager to start the second half as well as they did the first. With questions remaining over his use of substitutes in the defeats by Chelsea and Arsenal, when Spurs had lost winning positions, Jol made his first substitution with ten minutes remaining, sending on Malbranque for Lennon, and soon after that replaced Tainio with Ghaly. Malbranque was quickly in the action with a shot that went wide, but Spurs were unable to make the breakthrough as Sevilla held on to earn a narrow advantage.

Keane labelled Sevilla's equalising penalty "a disgrace". The spot-kick award changed the game after Keane's well-worked second minute goal had given Tottenham the advantage. The award was certainly extremely harsh. Robinson was judged to have fouled Adriano in the area even though he clearly touched the ball first with his hands and Keane said: "The penalty – I have to choose my words carefully – I thought it was a disgrace."

Robinson was similarly angered by the penalty. The England keeper said: "I clearly got two hands on the ball. The referee said I got the ball and then the man. Well, surely that is a fair challenge? At that stage in the game it's hard for us. For them to get back into the game like that was disappointing." Jol did not mince his words either. "Everybody could see it was not a penalty. He got two hands on the ball so we are very disappointed," he said.

Jol believed his side could have prevented Kerzakhov's winning goal, but aside from that felt they did well to limit the attacking threat of the Spanish outfit. "We probably could have done better with their second goal. I felt we took control (with Keane's goal), and then after the penalty they took over, but they never created a lot. We created three or four chances in the second half. Robinson barely had a save to make, so we are a bit disappointed, well not a bit, a lot, with the decision, but those things happen."

Equally unequivocal was Jol's defence of the Spurs fans, one a disabled fan in a wheelchair, who were battered by riot police inside Seville's stadium. He said: "What happened in the crowd was a concern and must be looked into. You have to make your own judgments when things like this happen but you must remember it is not always one-way traffic if you know what I mean." Seven Spurs fans were taken to hospital and six were arrested when violence boiled over behind keeper Paul Robinson's goal after half an hour. Spurs supporters claimed trouble kicked off when they were stopped from going to the toilets by police, who then waded in with batons. It was a sorry incident.

Among those held was a 31-year-old computer programmer, Paul Inskip, who was struck while trying to take a photograph of the Tottenham team bus as it derparted the stadium. "He was a real fan with his brother and two other friends," said Jol. "This guy wanted to take a picture and they didn't even warn him – he lost three or four teeth."

Robinson had got off the team bus and helped the injured Tottenham supporter into the dressing room. "He [the fan] said: 'I don't know if I have to cry or laugh'," said Jol. "He was in the dressing room, he felt happy but he had a lot of pain as well. His teeth were on the ground but he was still smiling. We left and then they arrested him. The only thing I regret is that we didn't take him on the coach.

The police were very different from other police forces I have seen in Europe. Can you remember English fans going to a foreign country, having no clashes with fans and then still getting bashed? That is what we have to expect now and in the future if you are English. That is why we have to stand up for ourselves."

In the cold light of day, Jol called on English football to make a concerted stand against the over-zealous policing that marred matches across Europe. He believed that his club's fans were attacked indiscriminately by Spanish police and issued a statement praising Spurs' travelling support. In his programme notes for the return leg Jol said: "You, our fans, have been fantastic ambassadors for the club all across Europe this season and it has made a real difference to have you there, in real numbers, and at home, raising us when we need it most. Be in no doubt that when we step out there tonight we shall do so determined to get the result for us all."

With Spurs desperate to salvage something from a seaosn of promise in the cups, Jol gambled with King's comeback with Tainio as an emergency left back. "Normally I wouldn't have included Ledley in the squad, I would have waited, but he said he is ready to go," explained Jol. King had last played against Aston Villa on Boxing Day, but fractured a bone in his left foot and then suffered severe bruising to his right when attempting a come-back. He had not been truly injury free for over a year, having missed out on England's 2006 World Cup squad due to injury. The return of the skipper would be a huge boost.

After returning 600 of their ticket allocation, Sevilla had 1,200 fans inside White Hart Lane to watch as once again Spurs' luck was out when Steed Malbranque's comic-book own goal began the match in atrocious fashion and Tottenham went hurtling out of Europe in eight minutes of madness. Malbranque, stationed at the far post at a Sevilla corner, turned Christian Poulsen's off-target header into the Spurs net with a ghastly miskick after just three minutes and former White Hart Lane striker Fredi Kanoute added a second for Seville soon after amidst more sloppy defending.

Jol's team were two down (and three goals behind on aggregate and having conceded two at home, but scored just one away), so early that it shocked the Lane faithful, but two goals in the second half from substitute Defoe, with his first touch, and from Lennon, gave them hope,. Ultimately, though, Tottenham ran out of time in their search for two more, drawing 2-2 on the night and losing 4-3 on aggreggate.

Jol said: "If you play a European tie at home and concede a goal like we did from a corner so early on it's a real blow. We were in shock when we conceded a second one from a throw-in and realised we needed to score four goals. It was a very bad start, but we tend to give away cheap goals. You can't legislate for things like that, but it happened today and it didn't help because we could have gone on to the semi-finals of the UEFA Cup."

Defeat by Sevilla left Tottenham chasing a place in the same competition via the Premiership. "We are out of all the cups but for me it was a good year," said Jol once again failing to deliver the rhetoric that the board wanted to hear. "The only thing now is to pick ourselves up and finish well in the league. It will not be easy, but we'll be OK and, hopefully, we can finish in the top six."

Ultimately it was Jol's misfortune that he came up against Arsenal, Chelsea and Seville – whom the Dutchman rates as the "best footballing side in Spain" and were Europe's team of the year. But the board demanded both ambition and results and to ensure that progress could truly be said to have been made they wanted that fourth-placed finish. Jol's Spurs were now out of all the cups without even a final to show for their efforts and the rumblings were growing.

There was bound to be some unease among some senior figures at the club that Jol failed to negotiate his way through any of those ties. Losing to Arsenal after being two goals to the good, in particular, still rankled.

FIGHTING BACK

AT FOUR O'CLOCK on Sunday 5 November 2006, live on Sky, against Chelsea, Spurs hoped to prove that they had truly turned around a miserable start to the Premiership season.

A return of four points and two goals from their opening six Premiership games for a team that had ambitions of playing in the Champions League was not how Tottenham fans would have expected to begin the season. The pressure was mounting on what felt like an hourly basis. Jol would have to earn his money – and quickly.

To do so, he calmly kept faith with the squad he had assembled, which certainly on paper looked brim full of goals. "The fact that Jermaine Jenas is top scorer with two says it all," he told me wistfully. "Yet I remain confident in the potential of Keane, Defoe, Mido and, when fit, Dimitar Berbatov to score in every game. True, we have not been helped by injuries, but we have the squad to cope."

Spurs had suffered a glut of injuries, missing up to eight first-team players on occaions, but to pull through such mini-crises is surely the sign that a club is strong enough to compete at the highest level. As yet Spurs were not showing that strength in depth, but Jol was not yet ready to panic. "We are creating chances, as we've done against Manchester United and Liverpool on their own grounds. That's hard enough," he said. "So when there's even a sniff of a chance you have to be sharp enough to seize the moment and score. Scoring goals is the one area of the game we have not exactly shone at so far this season." It certainly seemed that Spurs were already heavily missing the departed Michael Carrick.

Jol was unequivocal about what the England midfielder's loss meant to his side: "I said all along that we would miss him. When people said he wouldn't have much influence at Old Trafford I said he would and he is helping them win the championship, making them tick in midfield."

Inside the club morale was fine and Jol was still very much in control of the dressing room. Spurs' poor start had seen them occupy the fourth bottom position in the Premiership before defeating high-flying Portsmouth in early autumn in a game overshadowed by a blatant piece of cheating. Didier Zokora dived after no contact whatsoever from the aghast Pedro Mendes. To mkae matters worse, when a penalty was awarded, the Ivory Coast international celebrated with immodest passion. Tottenham duly won the game thanks to that goal which established a 2-0 lead, but there were bound to be recriminations afterwards. Spurs' former icon Glenn Hoddle, to whom the victory should have been pleasurable, commentating in the Sky TV suite, called Zokora: "a despicable cheat". Portsmouth manager Harry Redknapp, who himself initially believed a foul had been committed and sympathised with referee Chris Foy, who as a referee is still denied recourse to video evidence during a game, muttered: "He [Foy] feels embarrassed. He's a good referee. I've been to see him and he said: 'Harry, I've made a big mistake.' He would have loved a bit of help. Now the whole country is saying: 'What a mess he's made of that'."

But what tack would Martin Jol take in the uproar? The Spurs manager was left to champion Zokora. "He told me he was off balance and I thought he was. You could see he was anticipating Mendes coming in. I don't think it was a blatant dive." Most of the country disagreed, although, after years of seeing clubs such as Manchester United and Liverpool hog the seemingly biased penalty decisions, to have one go the way of the poopular Dutchman helped quell some of the opprobrium. Relief over the penalty, which Defoe converted, was universal among Spurs fans. Their club had not won in the Premiership since August 22. Perhaps Jol's luck had turned.

But despite that ublic defence of his midfielder, after the mid-October international break for internationals, Jol told Zokora that he would not stand for any more diving antics. Publicly Jol is the kind of manager who will always defend his players, much like Sir Alex Ferguson, but the former St-Etienne player was certain to come under the spotlight from opposing fans when he lined up against Aston Villa just as much as Paul Robinson, returning from England duty having been the victim of a freak own goal by Gary Neville in a humiliating 2-0 defeat in Croatia which damaged England's qualification chances for Euro 2008.

Jol said: "I know fans in England hate it. I'm sure everyone does it when they are young, but in Latin America and some other countries it's part of the result. More and more players are doing it. But if it is a real habit – if it is part of your play – then you must get rid of it. I told him [Zokora] he's a midfield player and it is better to stay out of the box. But then we will probably not get penalties any more! He will be watched now by referees but that is something he has to get on with. That's English football."

As for helping Robinson to get over the clanger in Croatia when Gary

Neville's tame backpass flicked up off a divot and bounced over his foot as he attempted to kick out, Jol said: "The only thing I could say to Paul was that all the big players, like Ray Clemence and Tim Flowers, had things like that happen to them during their careers. I even think this was different because you can't say he made a big mistake. Paul is a strong character, but football is full of contradictions. He was fantastic for England in the second half and I was proud of him because he made some good saves. He has always been very good if he has made a mistake. He had kept nine clean sheets for England in 11 games and would have broken a record for not conceding against Croatia which would have been nice for him."

An unbeaten run and significant progress in Europe meant Jol and his team were full of beans as they prepared for a dish best served cold against Chelsea at White Hart Lane. Revenge.

Tottenham had not beaten Chelsea in the league in 32 attempts. In fact they had won just one game in 37 in all competitions. That had been the hugely satisfying 5-1 victory in the League Cup semi-final second leg which had brought a 6-3 aggregate win in January 2002 to send Spurs through to the Millennium Stadium, where they suffered a 2-1 defeat by Blackburn Rovers. That was hardly a record which suggested that Jol's side could defeat the double Premiership Champions. And yet that was what they did. After falling behind to a rare Claude Makelele strike, Michael Dawson quickly equalised. Game on. An end to end thriller was won when Aaron Lennon neatly tucked away a goal from 15 yards out following a left wing cross. Spurs weathered a strong resurgence from Chelsea to hold their lead nd spark wild celebrations at lifting the hoodoo at the final whistle. What impressed observers and fans alike was the manner in which Spurs took on Chelsea in a blood and thunder battle which showed off Premiership football to its most entertaining best.

The delirium amongst Spurs supporters was matched by general delight among football fans of any hue except the Blue of Chelsea. For two years Jose Mourinho's men had waltzed away with the title backed by the oil squillions of Roman Abramovich which brought results, if not style, to Stamford Bridge. Now, not only did Chelsea have serious competition in the shape of resurgent Manchester United, they were being out-footballed by a number of clubs on a regular basis. Injuries would cost Chelsea the title in the end, with the likes of Petr Cech, John Terry and Frank Lampard out for lengthy periods. Perhaps it wasn't only Spurs who had a squad that could be called into question through injuries to key men.

The Autumn of 2007 had its moments as Jol was called on to calm down the ire over a 41st minute clach between West Ham's new Argentinean signing Javier Mascherano, and Jermain Defoe. The pair were involved in a scuffle which then escalated into a scrum involving all 22 players. Mascherano had fouled Defoe, but the Spurs striker, once again roundly booed from all quarters by the West Ham faithful, gathered in the corner of White Hart Lane, retaliated. Players from both sides then became involved before referee Steve Bennett restored order and booked both Defoe and Mascherano.

Jol came up with one of his legendary quips as he played down suggestions that Defoe had bitten Mascherano as several morning newspapers seemed to show in damning pictures. Jol, somehow keeping a straight face, claimed it was nothing more than 'playing nibbling' on Defoe's behalf and insisted his actions would have left no marks on the Argentinian. Jol said: "He was nibbling his arm – there will be no mark. Ask Mascherano if he has got a mark. It is part of the game. They kicked him three times from behind in ten minutes and he wanted to show his frustration in a nice, comical way." The comedy in Jol's comments made headline news, and was not lost on football supporters in general.

The victory over Chelsea was a wonderful way for Jol to celebrate his second anniversary in charge at the Lane. The result meant Spurs had picked up eight points in five unbeaten games. The charge up the table was well and truly on. Jol had arrested the early season slide, but with Spurs resurgent, and challenging for honours on four fronts for the remainder of the season, leading to rising expectations amongst fans and the board – and with expectancy almost demanding a similar level of success to the previous season – Jol's managerial skills would be tested to the limit.

THE HAIRDRYER AND THE CHOCOLATE SOLDIERS

"Tottenham have got the resources and the history that suggests there shouldn't be a gap that is there at the moment and I think the ambitions of Martin Jol are beyond that. He's got ambitions to make them better and you can't just do it in one year. You need four or five years really to implement the vision of the club and the development of the team."
Sir Alex Ferguson

After all the glory and the praise at beating Chelsea at long last, Spurs headed off to Reading, full of renewed confidence and expectation – at least that's how the theory went. Would it be a touch of after the Lord Mayor_s Show or would it be their chance to push up to seventh place in the Premiership?

In the build up, Jol claimed his squad was now strong enough to cope with a string of injuries. Aside from Dawson, Jol had rested all his first-team players for the midweek Carling Cup win over Port Vale, but Chimbonda would not return after picking up medial ligament damage. Mido had a cyst on his knee, while injuries to Davenport and Gardner meant King and Dawson were the only out-and-out centre-backs available. Zokora had only recently returned from a bout of malaria and had impressed in the win over Chelsea, with Spurs fans hailing the Ivory Coast midfielder at the final whistle. A top-four finish was now back on the agenda.

But defeat at 'little' Reading ignited a spate of unwelcome headlines… "Gutless" screamed the front page of the *Sun's* pull out on the Monday morning. *The Mirror* ridiculed the team using their chocolate away strip to inspire the headline "Chocolate Soldiers" on the front page of their pull out. *The Independent* was a touch more circumspect but nonetheless hard hitting. "Angry Jol questions Spurs' appetite for battle".

There was another headline which caused some ire over that result, although this time on the Reading side of the fence. Royals keeper Marcus Hahnemann revealed the Berkshire side were furious over comments made by Jol after Spurs had been beaten 3-1. Hahnemann said: "Most teams don't look at league positions, particularly the Tottenham manager, who thinks we are crap. He said: 'If we lose to a team like Reading then we are in serious trouble.' Well, they must be in serious trouble." In fact only Arsenal and Chelsea had won at the Madjski Stadium since the beginning of 2005/06, so Spurs would have been very wrong to take Reading lightly. Hahnemann, the USA international goalkeeper who shoots guns in his spare time, continued: "Obviously that sort of stuff motivates you. It's a nice little poster on our training-ground wall and we've got it in the locker room now as well. We are one of the promoted teams and we haven't brought in a load of players, so people don't understand why we are winning games or how we are even staying in the league. But we will keep surprising people."

The result meant Reading stood above Tottenham in the league. Jol's side had yet to win on their travels in the league, and after the 3-1 defeat he had shut the dressing room door and given his men the Sir Alex 'Hairdryer' treatment. He emerged to mutter tersely: "A win here would probably have taken us seventh in the league and we threw it away. We did OK in the first part of the match, we did everything we had to do. We attacked them in the spaces with the midfield players, we had a couple of chances and a penalty kick. So that was good. But after that a couple of a players did the wrong things. Maybe we should play all our games at White Hart Lane."

Jol knew Spurs' away form could cost them a place in Europe: "Our away form could be the difference. If we struggle to get away points we will not be up there. Normally we talk about things and go through videos on a Sunday or Monday. This week was different because of the international games and I had to wait. Now we've talked about what happened at Reading and what we could do better. We need to be tougher and more pro-fessional than we were at Reading. It's not only about mentality it's about physical toughness. Players have to take responsibility. We don't buy Vinnie Jones-style players. We have football players, but if they want to prove they can be tough and physical as well, I don't have a problem with that. I saw Ryan Giggs do a left-back job against Blackburn for example. Even the top players need a physical side to them."

That challenge to match his own fierce, passionate determination to succeed was laid down to his players as Jol was voted the 'manager you'd least like to pick a fight with'. He'd been awareded that accolade after snarling and pointing an accusing finger at referee Phil Dowd following Ghaly's late dismissal for an elbow on Gray in Spurs' 1-1 draw at Blackburn. Jol said: "I felt the ref reacted to the crowd and I told him he was totally wrong. He seemed a bit emotional and he said to me 'you can go off as well then'. That's the first one [sending off] of my career as a coach and I hope he will think again. Was I abusive towards him? Well, afterwards maybe! It was a difficult game for us. They were full of energy and tried to break us."

The situation descended into farce after it emerged that Jol had not actually been dismissed, despite believing he had been shown a red card when he protested at Dowd's decision to send off Ghaly in injury-time. When Dowd learned that Jol had spoken about being sent off he contacted Keith Hackett, head of the Professional Game Match Officials Board, and asked him to clarify the situation through the Premier League. "I think there was a misunderstanding in that Phil Dowd said: 'Can you stand back' and 'Can you stand away,'" said a Premier League spokesman. "He [Jol] wasn't technically sent off." Jol clearly thought otherwise.

Rovers' Turkish international Tugay, who had scored a wonderful long-range goal to give Blackburn the lead, had been sent off earlier in an incident which led to Defoe's spot-kick equaliser. Tugay brought down Ghaly, who was clean through on goal, and had to go. It was a solid point, but Jol confessed that, despite losing only once in 11 games, to Reading, it was a frustrating time failing to win away form home. "When we beat Chelsea it was heaven and if we had beaten Reading we'd have been sixth in the table. Jermian Defoe missed a chance to make it 2-2 at Reading and then they went and scored. That's why its is heaven and hell for me."

In fact Spurs had yet to even score away from home in the league from open play. Of their three goals thus far, two had been penalties and the other an own goal.

It was a different kettle of fish at White Hart Lane. Two goals in 89 scintillating seconds inspired Tottenham to victory over battling Wigan. Jol's side had trailed to Camara's 24th-minute opener, but fought back in stunning style just prior to the interval through Defoe, his 50th in the Premiership, and Berbatov. Lennon then completed the scoring in the last seconds of stoppage time to condemn Wigan to their first defeat in six games and help Spurs leapfrog them and move up to 10th place in the table. Jol, who was now regularly being criticised in the press and amongst certain sectors of fans for selecting Mido ahead of Defoe, recalled the young Englishman to partner the Bulgarian and the pair were unstoppable. Jol's famed sense of humour came out to play again when quizzed about his relationship with Defoe which he claimed was excellent:."I wouldn't swap him for Miss World, but he would probably swap me for her," Jol quipped.

But Spurs still chased a first away win in the league as they travelled the short distance to The Emirates. After the previous season's antics in that showdown which had almost descended into a fistfight, Jol planned to extend his hand to Wenger before the lunch-time kick-off. He said: "There are no hard feelings at all for what happened last season and afterwards I could appreciate what he was on about. To be honest I had forgotten what happened between us, but I won't have a problem shaking hands with Arsene on Saturday. It's an emotional game for the players, referees, and the managers."

The North London derby was played to a backdrop of a sweep of the Emirates stadium for the radioactive isotope polonium 210, which had recently killed Russian dissident Alexander Litvinenko. In fact, a few days after the game traces were found, although the Health Protection Agency announced that the radiation – which was discovered at "barely detectable" levels – posed no risk to public health.

It was found after Andrei Lugovoi, who now lay in hospital in Moscow, attended the Champions League match between Arsenal and CSKA Moscow. The game kicked off hours after Lugovoi had met Mr Litvinenko on 1 November – the day the former KGB agent believed he was poisoned.

The match turned very sour for Jol and Spurs. Arsenal convincingly won the first north London derby at the Emirates 3-0, even without injured skipper Thierry Henry. Most disturbing was the complete surrender of Jol's side. The manager held his hands up: "We can't complain about the result," he said. In truth the key decisions went Arsenal's way. It was a marginal offside call for the first goal after 20 minutes, Chimbonda connected with the ball first in the tackle that lead to number two via the penalty spot just before half-time and Robin van Persie appeared to handle before winning the second penalty in the second half that completed the scoreline. Jol was quizzed in the post-match press conference about those decisions: "We are all disappointed and all very quiet because we wanted to do something here, the first derby of the season and first at the new stadium. I won't be silly and talk about the decisions because I want to focus on our performance. If we'd created five or six chances you could have said that the penalties cost us, but we gave them too much of the ball. Normally they create a lot of chances but they didn't this time."

Once again Jol's honesty struck a chord with his own and other fans, but it was clear he was becoming more concerned about his team's lack of bite away from the friendly environs of the Lane where results such as the victory over Chelsea could be achieved.

Jol was furious after the derby drubbing and called a first-team meeting on the following day, but was stunned when some of his players answered back. According to a back page tabloid story: "Jol ripped into his Spurs players with a dressing down which 'tore paint off the walls' after their lacklustre display. But he had angered some of his players with his team selection – and they told him he should shoulder some of the blame as they felt they didn't do too much wrong." Was Jol losing the dressing room?

Jol had sprung a surprise by picking Teemu Tainio to mark Fabregas, even though the Finnish midfielder had only started one game in nearly three months. Defoe's omission again left his future in doubt as Jol dropped him despite his stunning goal in the previous game. Thedecisions looked questionable in retrospect. The question was, how would they all react to this humbling setback?

In the cold light of day Jol was honest enough to admit that his team had not progressed as desired. "I feel we have taken a step back and are not as strong as last season, even though we have more talent. We have to grow up and be stronger and more physical and fight harder for the ball. We have to get tougher up front. We have players who are talented and get lots of praise – Berbatov, Benoit, guys who have done well in Europe – but they have to do well in these sort of games too."

Prior to the home ganme against Middlesbrough Jol took the unusual step of strongly criticising his players in his programme notes, condemning their lack of 'commitment', 'steel' and 'determination' in the defeat at Arsenal. But, he claimed, he was delighted by their reaction in training. And indeed no questions could be asked about Tottenham's spirit when they responded to Middlesbrough's 80th-minute equaliser by snatching the victory they deserved. Jol was entitled to feel especially pleased that Keane got Tottenham's winner with almost his first touch after being introduced from the bench, though the Irishman soon departed with a knee injury. Spurs' failure to kill the game after Berbatov's exquisite opener allowed Boro back in. Then, in the closing minutes, Zokora and Boateng were sent off after a set-to by the touchline after a late Lennon tackle on Boatengin retaltion to the robust Boro midfielder's tackle on the Spurs winger sparked a melée which attracted every player but Robinson.

Jol defended Zokora's actions. "My players will never start a fight. They are disciplined. Zokora wanted to prevent a fight. Believe me, you can see it on TV." But you got the feeling that he was secretly pleased with the reaction his players had shown in standing up for themselves physically and also coming back to win the game after such a late equaliser.

Jol received a double injury blow as Jenas had aggravated an ankle problem on his return from injury in the north London derby, while

Keane faced a six-week lay-off damaging knee ligaments minutes after scoring the winner against Middlesbrough. But it didn't stop the scintillating home form continuing as Berbatov scored the first and last goals as Tottenham opened the floodgates to thrash relegation-threatened Charlton 5-1. Tainio, Malbranque and Defoe also scored for Spurs, who extended their run of wins at home to nine and revived hopes of challenging for a Champions League place. Defoe's goal was particularly sweet as he was jeered by away fans throughout for his move from Charlton to West Ham as a teenager.

Spurs had now lost only twice in 17 matches, with Jol saying: "I feel we are more consistent than people give us credit for. I think every other team besides the top two would be satisfied with those results. Last year, we were the best of the rest. At Spurs, the expectancy levels are always high because our home record is very good."

Jol was full of praise for one of his many young Englishmen, as he decalred that he thought Huddlestone could be the new Carrick. Jol said: "He's a bit like Carrick, but a bit younger. That is what we want – someone has left and then someone else is standing up ready to take his place. Tom is outstanding in nine out of every 10 games. On the ball he is probably one of the best in the Premiership in his position. But if you want to be a top player, you have to develop all parts of your game and he's doing that now. It's so rare that you have such a big player who is so comfortable on the ball and yet so mobile. I think he can play in any game because in Europe he plays well and in the league he plays well."

In Jol's landmark 100th game in charge of Tottenham, Huddlestone scored his first Premiership goal as Spurs survived a spirited second-half fightback to finally claim their first away league victory of the season by beating Manchester City 2-1. Huddlestone crashed home a 25th-minute half-volley to add to Davenport's early opener and make a mockery of City's proud unbeaten home record. The victory showed that Jol was getting through to his team and, while many managers moan about the hectic schedule over Christmas and the New Year, Jol was now looking forward to it. "There is a good feeling among the players at the moment," he said. "They are fit enough and the squad is big enough to play a lot of games. That is our strength. All the other teams who are big or who are at the top, they all have big squads. I feel we have done well this season as we're still in all the competitions. We're still in the Uefa Cup and Carling Cup and are seventh in the league."

But over Christmas Spurs' weak underbelly showed again as resurgent Newcastle staged a first-half blitz to win 3-1. Dyer set the tone with a superb third-minute opener in front of a crowd of 52,079 – the biggest of the season at St James' Park. Jol was dealt a blow after the warm-up when he was forced to withdraw Defoe, who injured himself in the warm up, and name midfielder Danny Murphy in his place. The former Liverpool man was to make his mark, but his 15th-minute strike, which was deflected past Given, proved little more than consolation.

Jol was frustrated: "We were 2-0 down after seven minutes and that is exactly what you do not want. All credit to them because they played in a very aggressive manner. They were clinical in the centre of the park. We were not clinical enough."

Once again White Hart Lane proved a haven as, on Boxing Day, Defoe scored twice to defeat Aston Villa 2-1, Dimitar Berbatov creating both goals. But it was a different story four days later when Liverpool visited. Luis Garcia scored on the stroke of half-time to give Rafa Benitez's men a 1-0 victory and bring Tottenham's run of 12 consecutive home successes to a halt. Spurs were undone in first-half stoppage time as Liverpool took advantage of poor defending. Zokora gave the ball away to Kuyt, who played in Gerrard, who sliced his shot, but Garcia nipped in to steer the ball past Robinson to secure only the Reds' second triumph at White Hart Lane in the ten years. It was a scrappy strike to win a scrappy match.

Despite that setback Jol insisted: "2006 is the best year Tottenham have had [in the recent past]. We qualified for Europe through the league for the first time in 25 or 26 years and have won six matches in the UEFA Cup. We took a big step forward when we beat Chelsea and I would have loved to win against Liverpool because then we would have been level on points with them. Now we're ending the year on a bit of a negative because we gave away a soft goal and the reality is we have to cut out these mistakes. We're less creative without players like Lennon, Keane and Berbatov and there's a big difference when we have everyone on board. This was our eighth game in 25 days so it's not easy for regulars like Zokora and Huddlestone to come up with the goods in every match."

Jol's men made it consecutive losses at home as Newcastle completed a fine comeback to win a thrilling clash 3-2. Spurs could barely believe that they had lost the game after leading twice, nor that Nicky Butt won the match with just his fourth goal for the Magpies after Martins' stunning strike just a minute earlier had brought them back into the match at 2-2. Jol observed: "We played marvellous football at 1-0, then they scored from a free-kick and that didn't help. Even at 2-1 we should have scored. Overall this afternoon we are very unfortunate not to get more out of this game. But all credit to Newcastle – if you score three goals at White Hart Lane you have done something well."

This patch of indifferent form continued as Pascal Chimbonda scored a late leveller to earn Tottenham a point after Montella's penalty looked to have earned 10-man Fulham victory at Craven Cottage. Fulham had Helguson dismissed in the second half, but almost snatched victory when Dawson conceded a penalty for handball and Montella broke the deadlock with eight minutes left. But the lead did not last long as Chimbonda finished at the far post. Malbranque was making his first appearance back at Craven Cottage since being sold five months earlier, with the home fans never wasting an opportunity taunt the Frenchman. He was booked late in the first half and also drew the lunge from Helguson which earned the Iceland striker his first yellow card. Fulham skipper Michael Brown, who had signed from Spurs a year ago, was also guilty of a couple of naughty challenges. A draw in a feisty derby was hardly the end of the world, but this was not the for of a club that was destined to win silverware of any kind – and Jol knew it.

He said: "I'm disappointed. At home we create sometimes 20 chances, we are not as good away. I always say you have to be ambitious to score in the first 15 minutes. There was no danger. We brought Lennon on and he was dangerous a couple of times with our width. We also had two strikers high up the pitch."

But it wasn't just on the field of play that Jol had problems. He was also riled by Defoe delivering a wild haymaker to the dug-out wall when he made way for Keane. Jol said: "Jermain was our best man last week but didn't look that dangerous here. I have Robbie on the bench, who is a quality player. We'll do what we have to do. The team is the most important thing. It's about team spirit. They can be disappointed and not show it – that is always what we like. But they are human beings. Robbie did it against Birmingham last season, so it can happen – once." The message was clear to the England striker – I'm in charge.

With the January transfer window well and truly open, Tottenham signed centre-half Ricardo Rocha from Benfica. The 28-year-old defender bolstered Spurs' defence following recent injuries and departures. He had been at Benfica for more than four years after signing in 2002 from Braga. Damien Comolli observed: "Ricardo is an accomplished defender who gives us further options in defence as he can play both in the centre and on the right. He brings considerable experience to Tottenham having played at the highest level in European competition and is also a current Portuguese international. Ricardo has shown a great desire to come to White Hart Lane and will no doubt prove to be a valuable addition to the squad at this important time."

Spurs were also linked with Southampton's highly-rated Welsh left-back Gareth Bale, with Saints having already turned down an £8m bid from Manchester United for the talented 17-year-old. Jol was confident of landing Bale before the transfer window shut, but in the event, with Southampton in the hunt for a play-off spot for a place back in the Premiership, he would not arrive until the summer. Jol was also keen on Watford forward Ashley Young, but the speeedster's price kept going up until he moved for £9.65m to Aston Villa. The 21-year-old had rejected a move to West Ham as he preferred Spurs, but Tottenham would not match the asking price that Villa happily shelled out.

Jol's quest for a left-winger led him to consider a £7m bid for Irishman Damien Duff, struggling to make an impact at new club Newcastle, having seemingly abandoned hope – for the moment at least – of luring Stewart Downing from Middlesbrough. But United manager Glenn Roeder declared he would not contemplate any such offer.

With results not going his way and things not falling for him in the transfer window, Jol was building up a head of steam that needed to be released. Perhaps it should not have been surprising then that the bullish manager and tigerish Edgar Davids had to be pulled apart following a training ground bust-up. The combustible Davids then emptied his locker at the Spurs Lodge training ground, said his goodbyes to members of the backroom staff, and stormed out claiming he was leaving for good. The row was witnessed by players, who saw the pair go nose-to-nose before being pulled apart by coaches Chris Hughton and Clive Allen.

Just over a year earlier Davids had fought with Robbie Keane before again storming away from the club's base in Chigwell, Essex, before being accepted back into the fold. There was only ever one winner on this occasion, however; the manager. The 33-year-old Davids, who had not started a Premiership match since 19 November, and had a history of flare-ups throughout his career, did not return the next day and he agitated for a move back home to his first club Ajax before the window closed.

Jol confirmed that Davids' final weeks at the club were disruptive as he expressed his frustration at being left out in favour of the 19-year-old Huddlestone. "I've had many arguments with him," Jol revealed. "He asks if he is playing and I tell him no. Edgar is a legend and Tom is only 19, so it is a difficult situation. Ajax have said they have an agreement with him, so the only thing is for us to agree a deal with Ajax. It will go through before the deadline."

Punch ups aside, injuries continued to be a disruption. Ledley King was the biggest worry. "The previous scan showed he had a bruised foot," Jol explained, "but there is still bruising and that is a bit strange because normally it would be over after two weeks. He trained last week and did everything and then came back to the medical room and said there was still pain. We can't push him, he can't push himself. If we push him, maybe it could break and then we get another problem."

In the event King was ruled out for up to eight weeks following a further setback with his foot injury. King's importance to Spurs' solidity in defence and as captain had been exemplified throughout his stop-start season. The team had not won since his last game before this latest injury, at home to Villa and now he would be missing again just as the cup competitions, Spurs' serious chance of silverware, began to get serious.

In early February Michael Carrick returned to White Hart Lane for the first time with his new club Manchester United with Jol being brutally honest about what his young midfield star's de[arture had cost the club. Jol reckoned Carrick's departure had the same effect on Spurs as skipper John Terry's injury absence had on Chelsea. Jol elaborated,: "Chelsea have invested hundreds of millions on players, but have a problem when Terry isn't there. They may have bought Khalid Boulahrouz, Mikel John Obi, Salomon Kalou and Andriy Shevchenko, but that doesn't solve the problem. They are all good players but don't have the qualities of Terry. He never wants to lose and he is so important to them. We've realised we miss Michael Carrick. His biggest quality was to move play from defence to attack and win the ball. Because of him, other players played better. Tom Huddlestone has that quality, but he has just turned 20 and he still has to make the next stage in his development."

Indeed while Wayne Rooney and Cristiano Ronaldo had taken the plaudits for United's sustained title challenge with their goalscoring heroics, Sir Alex Ferguson identified Carrick as the linchpin of United's season.

Little went in Jol's favour during the game as Ronaldo set United up for a comprehensive victory, which kept them six points ahead of Chelsea, by winning a controversial penalty. Opinion was divided on whether the Portuguese trickster was touched by Malbranque in the area, although TV evidence seemed to indicate he wasn't. Ronaldo took the 44th-minute kick himself and drilled it into the opposite side of Robinson's goal to where he had smacked his decisive penalty in the shootout for Portugal that sent England crashing out of the World Cup. But there was controversy as Spurs fans watched replays of the penalty incident on the big screen during half-time. They clearly felt Ronaldo had pulled a fast one. The home crowd booed Ronaldo incessantly until he was subbed with 20 minutes remaining. By then United were 3-0 up.

It really wasn't Spurs' night. When sub Keane's shot was blocked by Edwin Van der Sar, Keane kept going and caught the Dutch keeper on the nose with his knee. Van der Sar was flat out for a good couple of minutes, blood pouring dramatically from a broken nose. He was carried off and, as United had used their three subs, it was down to an outfield player to take over in goal. Rio Ferdinand put on the shirt at first but John O'Shea took it off him on skipper Gary Neville's orders. Immediately, he had to punch away a Huddlestone free-kick before a poor back-pass by Ferdinand left Keane one-on-one with his Republic of Ireland team-mate. O'Shea stood up to the Spurs striker and, as Keane tried to go round him, stuck out a foot to win it. "Ireland's, Ireland's Number One" and "Are You Watching, Robinson?" chanted the amused United fans.

Jol, pride worn thin at the 4-0 loss, described the defeat as "a bad day at the office". The truth was it was another bad day at the office. As for Jol's opposing manager, Sir Alex, on his way to a record ninth league title in England, well, the maestro thought Jol was doing a fine job but needed more time to build the kind of dynasty he himself had managed at Old Trafford in his 20-year spell in charge. Ferguson said: "Tottenham have got the resources and the history that suggests there shouldn't be a gap that is there at the moment and I think the ambitions of Martin Jol are beyond that. He's got ambitions to make them better but you can't just do it in one year. You need four or five years really to implement the vision of the club and the development of the team."

Defeat left Spurs in 11th place, 13 points away from the Champions League places and 13 points ahead of West Ham in the drop zone. And there would be further slippage into mid-table obscurity after relegation-threatened Sheffield United came from behind to secure victory thanks to skipper Phil Jagielka's thunderous penalty. The 2-1 loss was Spurs' seventh on the road in the league this season, they had won just onceand they had not won at all in the six Premier League games since Boxing Day. The Champions League looked a long way off. "We haven't had the best of spells," muttered Jol darkly. But could he turn things around once again?

THE GLORY GAME

'It's the same as if you said to my Missus that I was gay. It's nonsense.
Nobody, nobody can change my mind or tell me what to do.'
Martin Jol (on rumours he was told to pick Berbatov):

MARTIN JOL WAS DETERMINED to restore Tottenham Hotspur's great FA Cup tradition by winning the most famous club trophy in the world for a ninth time. The romantic in him loved the duelling nature of cup football and he knew his team was ideally suited to the task of reaching a major final.

Jol recalled playing for Holland schoolboys at the home of the Cup final, Wembley, and declared he would love to walk out at the famous stadium, albeit in its newly revamped form complete with dominating arch over the north London sky, for this year's showcase. He said: "Wembley has a great tradition and is a fantastic place. I played there when I was 14 against England. In Holland that would have attracted four or five thousand people, but there were 80,000 there. That was why I was sad when the stadium was knocked down. I won't tell you what the score was that day, all I will say is the English players were much bigger than us!"

The previous season's embarrassing 3-2 FA Cup exit to Leicester at the first hurdle had shown the potential for slip-ups and, with Spurs drawn away at Championship club Cardiff in their threatening Ninian Park stadium, which had witnessed the exit of Premiership side Leeds United from the competition five years earlier, Jol wasn't pulling any punches in terms of letting his players know what he expected of them as they entered the cauldron of Cardiff. Jol said: "Last year there was something missing. It's coming from my heart. It's the best competition in Europe. I won the Dutch Cup – 50,000 there, unbelievable – but I would swap it for the FA Cup. We were in shock. Players tell each other, we don't want that feeling [again]. The FA Cup is special for us and all of our players want to win it because of its profile here. Everything at our stadium is linked with the past. That includes the FA Cup, the UEFA Cup and the Double – everything. But it can go both ways. I remember being in the dressing room after the game last year at Leicester and it was a shock."

A hard-fought tie ended in a goalless draw and, back at the Lane, Spurs disposed of the Welshmen clinically 4-1 the day after the manager celebrated his 51st birthday. In the fourth round of the Cup Spurs drew Southend, the Championship strugglers who they had defeated in the Carling Cup quarter-final the previous month.

With Tottenham fighting on four cup fronts, their next assignment was the task of disposing of Arsenal in the Carling Cup semi-final over two legs. The Gunners had been undergoing something of a rejuvenation after a poor start to life in their new home, the Emirates Stadium, where they had developed the unwanted habit of conceding the first goal, but also the happier talent for not losing a game. In what again would come to be seen as an admission of weakness by those elements on the Tottenham board which had their question marks about Jol's desire and ambition, the Dutchman admitted his side could not compete with their local rivals. Jol said: "You can lose against Arsenal even if you are playing their so-called second string side. They simply bring in Cesc Fabregas, Gael Clichy, Julio Baptista then there's Theo Walcott, Johan Djourou. Everyone knows they scored six against Liverpool so you can go on about a kids' team, but they have played with lesser teams than that and won in the Carling Cup. I feel their reserve team are as strong as any Premiership side outside of the top four. Baptista last year was worth £24m and he is playing for that team. We haven't seen much of him but then he scored four goals at Anfield. This is definitely not just a kids' team."

Paradoxically, the pragmatic Dutchman was categorical in valuing the development of a young squad above the collection of silverware, but almost in the same breath he indicated that a trophy represented the club's biggest ambition. "We are developing but some people do not see that as an achievement. The league is probably the most important but if you can assure me I'll end up with a trophy, I would go for it."

Jol also sensed the excitement of a semi-final would bring something fresh out of his team. One of them, Aaron Lennon, was certainly after some silverware. He said: "A lot of the lads are desperate to win something this season. With the squad we've got, you have to think we're more than capable of winning a trophy this year. Whether it be the UEFA Cup, the FA Cup or the Carling Cup, that's our target. But we also want to finish in the top four and qualify for the Champions League, especially after missing out on it last season."

Much as with Chelsea Spurs had prevailed over Wenger's side only once in 23 attempts, seven years ago, yet in the first leg of the semi-final towards the end of January a 2-0 lead at the interval promised so much. Arsenal were in peril, but realism also helped the Gunners who tempered their dependence on the kids in this tournament by bringing on Eboué and Hleb, with the latter applying some expertise and guile as Arsenal clambered back into the tie. Baptista scored twice to enable his team to draw 2-2. "Two-up and you fucked it up," sang the relieved Gooners.

Baptista had not got off to the best of starts, his own-goal putting Spurs 2-0 up, and his overall display was not that impressive, but his second-half goals gave Arsenal the initiative for the second leg.

Jol was entitled to curse the loss of Berbatov with a groin strain so soon after he had put his team in front during a blistering start. The Bulgarian orchestrated the attack, bringing out the best in Defoe, and Tottenham were never so cogent without him. With 12 minutes gone, Chimbonda passed to Defoe and an unmarked Berbatov headed in his cross. The Bulgarian was at the hub of move after superb Tottenham move. After five minutes, he had stepped inside Touré to brush the post with his shot and soon after the opener a measured pass saw Defoe's first shot parried by Almunia and the next blocked by Senderos as Spurs threatened to overwhelm Arsenal.

Without Berbatov, the shape of Spurs team altered with the arrival of Keane, and it was never quite the same even when Huddlestone struck a dipping free-kick from the left after 21 minutes, Dawson cleverly stepped over the ball at the near post and Baptista's boot sent the ball into the net for an own-goal.

But half-time crystallised Arsenal thoughts and the dynamic Eboué and the skilful Hleb transformed the night. Eboué passed to Baptista, who eluded Dawson to score with a low drive. The equaliser completed the Brazilian's rehabilitation from own goal misery as he easily converted Hoyte's low cross after Fabregas picked out the right-back.

Not surprisingly the Arsenal manager's post-match demeanour contrasted markedly with that of Jol: "Very disappointed, but we have ourselves to blame," said the Dutchman. "If you give away the initiative you will concede goals and that's what we did second half."

Jol's wounds were open: "That felt worse than a defeat. We went from football heaven to football hell," he winced. "The worst part is the second half stays with you, especially when e-mails come in complaining."

And yet, despite the disappointment of losing that two-goal lead, Spurs were still involved in all three cup competitions and Keane was unfazed by the challenge of ending Arsenal's unbeaten record at the Emirates. Away goals count after extra-time, so Spurs had to beat their rivals for the first time since 1999, or draw 3-3 or better, if they were to reach the final against Chelsea. Keane said: "We are all really looking forward to it and Arsenal have to get beaten some time at home, why not on Wednesday? If anyone thinks this tie is over for one second they have another thing coming. People will probably say that they have the advantage but ask anyone in our dressing room and they are really up for this game and raring to go."

Spurs were still without King as the captain continued to struggle back from a bruised foot, and now they had to do without the superlative Berbatov, whose departure had changed the face of that first leg so dramatically, and the misfortune continued as Tottenham lost winger Lennon through illness just before the kick-off. Lennon pulled out so late that Spurs had only four subs instead of five as Young-Pyo Lee's name was missed off the team sheet.

Spurs sub Mido's leveller forced extra-time after Adebayor put Gunners ahead. But Spurs' luck ran out once again as Jeremie Aliadiere grabbed Arsenal's second and Tomas Rosicky's shot was turned in inadvertently by Chimbonda when it struck the full-back after rebounding off the post. That goal killed of Spurs' chances of reaching the final at the Millennium Stadium, although Jol wasn't complaining about the misfortune his side had suffered. He said: "It wasn't through bad luck that we lost the match. Aaron could have given us the spark we needed, but he reported sick after dinner. Even though he recovered slightly when I named him on the bench, he said he could not even sit there. When we equalised I felt Arsenal were a bit worried. But we just could not get another breakthrough."

Jol couldn't help but look back at the first leg as he reflected on the failure to make the final. Jol pointed out: "It was 3-3 on aggregate [over 108 minutes] and that's not bad, the problem was that we gave away a 2-0 lead in the first leg at home. That is what we've got to learn. If you are playing two legs, in hindsight perhaps you should protect that lead. In two legs, 2-2 at home is not a good result."

Afterwards Jol faced the fiercest criticism he has endured since his appointment, much of it focussing on his substitutions. What nobody gave him credit for was the introduction of Mido, ten minutes from time, which saw the striker net the equaliser within five minutes of coming on.

"In Holland we call it scoreboard journalism," said Jol. "For example, you look at the scoreboard, compete for 80 minutes at 1-0 down, you create five chances and then there are two breaks and they beat you 3-0. Bloody hell, they say, 3-0. That's scoreboard journalism."

But the failure to secure victory after leading the tie 2-0 brought a change in perception over the manager's abilities. For the first time Jol came under increasing attack from disgruntled fans phoning radio phone-ins with calls for his head. "I haven't listened to any phone-ins recently," he said. "Ninety per cent of fans won't slag me off because they love me too much – and that is a burden. I have to do well. I feel that we are closer than ever. It is just a few little pieces, but you need your best players available. I have no fear, no fear of anything. I don't want sad supporters, I want happy people around me. I want compliments because that is what I am used to. It is an addiction. I am a football man. When I was nine years-old I scored 13 goals in a match and everybody was giving me compliments. That is an addiction, you want to do well in your profession. That is what I want to do."

Jol felt the shift in Spurs fans' perception of him. "The thing I hate is when the supporters are unhappy with us, that is the only pressure I've got," he said. "It's maybe a bit more, but not less, than, say, Stuart Pearce [at Manchester City] got, Aston Villa, Newcastle, who are similar teams to us. But it's more pressure because it's Spurs and we want to do well. It's a big compliment because these clubs are not under pressure and we are because everybody expects more of us. That is the only thing. I hate to not fulfil their [the fans'] hope and expectation."

He then went on to ask the simple question: "Do you know why I am under pressure? Because I want to do well. The fans have sung my name for the last two and a half years. That is probably the first time in the history of Spurs. So I want to do well. I want to give them what they want."

With things going awry, did he fear the sack? "There is no fear, no fear," he insisted. "My fear is that I have got a little one, she is four next week, my fear is that something happens to her.

I would love to be here in a couple of years' time and do a Ferguson or a Wenger because I feel we are capable of doing that. We have got young players, we have got experienced players. Not as good as I would like to have, not like an Arsenal or a Liverpool, but I feel it is only a matter of time. But fear? No."

Robbie Keane, who had been the stand-in captain in the continued absence of club skipper Ledley King, offered a rallying call to his under-fire manager: "I have been through times like this before when you just can't get that win, but we know it will not last with the players we have. We've too many good players to just sit back and accept it. We've got winners in our squad and we know a win is just around the corner and once we get that we will be back on song again. It is about sticking together, working hard for each other and bouncing back. I've got no doubt in my mind that we will be back."

Back in the FA Cup, Spurs defeated Southend comfortably 3-1. Having eased through two ties with lower division clubs, Spurs drew Fulham at Craven Cottage in the fifth round. There was one worrying statistic. This being late February, Tottenham had not beaten a Premiership side in any competition since Boxing Day. Not only that, Fulham had not lost at Craven Cottage in eight matches. Spurs needed to start to make things happen and they had been given the added and unexpected boost of having a break from European competition because of Feyenoord's removal from the UEFA Cup. Refreshed and with their manager's words ringing in their ears, Jol's team ripped Chris Coleman's men to shreds to advance to the quarter-finals. Two wonder goals from Keane plus a brilliant Berbatov double after he came off the bench secured a 4-0 win and put Spurs back on track thanks to their first win at Craven Cottage for nearly five years.

After his side cruised through Jol came out fighting: "People have been complaining, but this shows we are going in the right direction. They had a similar year in 1991 under Terry Venables. They only had three wins in the last 25 games, but they won the FA Cup. If we can do that, it would be a dream. As I found out with the Carling Cup, even when you go out in the semi-finals it is considered a disappointment. That's why it is important for us to do something special this season."

But the same Terry Venables would prove to be the man who undid Spurs' season as he drew the No. 8 ball to pair two of his old clubs – Spurs and cup favourites Chelsea at Stamford Bridge. This was going to be make or break time. Did Tottenham have what it takes to win at Chelsea for the first time since 1990, or was that famous victory at White Hart Lane earlier in the season a flash in the pan?

As yet speculation was not circulating that Jol would be shown the door if his side failed to win a trophy or qualify for the Champions League, but Jol was candid about what he felt his legacy would be if he did leave. "I'm 100 per cent certain that if I left the club, people will say in five years' time: 'He did well, he did well'. I feel that with the things we had, with the tools we had, we could have done a bit better in the League. But I still feel, at the end of the day, next season, if I don't have a cup that I will not be 100 per cent satisfied."

There had been disquiet, sure, following the defeat in the Carling Cup semi-final by Arsenal, but no-one was seriously questioning his future. Not yet. The challenge continued at Stamford Bridge, although Jol was more than aware of the scale of the task ahead of his charges. Chelsea held a three year unbeaten run at the Bridge in domestic football. "Chelsea, at home, is probably the most difficult draw you could imagine. When we were looking at the draw we were not pleased, I can tell you. Nobody was. It was quiet. We waited for the draw and there was not even a sound. We would have played against other teams at home, even Chelsea at our home."

And yet Tottenham, with Berbatov back from injury, began this tie in a whirlwind once again. The Bulgarian gave Jol's side the perfect side with a fifth-minute strike only for Lampard to equalise 17 minutes later. An own goal from Essien and third from Ghaly in the 36th minute put the north Londoners in control at the break. Yet Spurs could not hold on, once again, and strikes from Lampard (71) and substitute Kalou (85) spared Chelsea's blushes. Even then Spurs could have won it two minutes from time when Defoe burst clear of the Chelsea defence, but the England striker smashed his effort against the bar to leave a stirring cup-tie all square

Jol put the late collapse down to tired legs and the fact Chelsea had two more days rest than his side after midweek European football. His critics once again focussed on his substitutions, although Jol mounted a strong defence to the changes he had made.

Jol said: "Even when they played with three strikers, we left it because I thought we needed a fourth goal. It almost came off because Lennon had a one-on-one with the keeper. Their second goal was a bit of a soft one, but we tend to concede those sort of goals. We have to get that out of our system. Jose didn't want a replay and neither did I. I went for the victory, but we had some tired legs at the end as well, We played on Thursday, they played on Tuesday, otherwise I am confident we would have beaten them. We cannot sit down and blame ourselves because we have another game on Wednesday and we have to pick ourselves up. It is a great compliment to us that we are disappointed after a draw at Stamford Bridge. We have played 17 cup games this season and over 90 minutes we have not lost at all. The pleasing thing is we have scored 20 goals in six matches. There are a lot of positives after a disappointing spell two or three weeks ago."

But it was not to be. Stunning strikes from Shevchenko and Wright-Phillips kept the Blues' quadruple dreams alive by sending Tottenham spinning out of the FA Cup with a 2-1 defeat in the replay. Keane pulled a goal back with a 79th minute penalty, but he could not take his record of scoring in every round of this season's FA Cup into the last four. Tottenham were ultimately undone by goals of genuine quality, Shevchenko's quite clearly his finest since arriving for his troubled spell in London. Then came Wright-Phillips' classy volley. Tottenham could not mount their own two-goal comeback as both Arsenal and Chelsea had managed to do.

Paul Robinson was devastated at the defeat which left Tottenham with only the UEFA Cup to play for in terms of silverware: "It was quiet in the changing room, everyone was bitterly disappointed. We all felt we were on top and didn't get what we deserved. Look at the bigger picture though. We reached the semi-finals of the Carling Cup and the quarter-finals of the FA Cup and we've been beaten by Arsenal and Chelsea. We're still in the quarter-finals of the UEFA Cup and we've put ourselves back in a great position in the league. There is so much still to play for."

And yet the pressure was beginning to build. Despite three good cup runs at home and only bowing out of Europe to the eventual Champions, results were just too inconsistent for the board to feel confident that Jol had the ability to take Spurs forward that one, massive step that everyone at White Hart Lane craved. The tension had begun to slowly build and there were several small, but significant, stories which when taken on an individual basis amounted to nothing, but as a whole showed that all was not rosy in the Tottenham camp.

To start with Jol was forced to hit back at claims he was ordered by the board to play Berbatov in the first match against Chelsea after *The Independent* ran an article to that effect. He dismissed suggestions that he wanted to rest the Bulgarian because he was struggling with a groin injury, but was overruled by the White Hart Lane board.

Jol was having none of it, though, issuing a rebuff in typical style: "It's the same as if you said to my Missus that I was gay. It's nonsense. Nobody, nobody can change my mind or tell me what to do." Berbatov – who had been troubled by a groin problem and missed several matches recently – scored the opening goal at Stamford Bridge and tormented the champions' defence. He then tired and was replaced by Mido midway through the second period. Jol added: "The only person who might be able to change my mind is my assistant Chris Hughton. If you play five or six matches you have to have a rest. But Berbatov is flying. He is one of our best players. At half-time I asked him if he could play 10 minutes of the second half and he played 20. If someone died on the pitch you would have to take him off and yet still there would be people who think you should not do it."

Jol was by now forced to remark upon the strength of his relationship with his board, and in particular chairman Daniel Levy: "I love the board and they love me. We are good and getting on well and it's a bit annoying for them because when things like this happen they start asking who it is that said that. I could get angry as well, but I am very independent and very strong indeed."

In the two key matches in which the striker was withdrawn – the Carling Cup semi-final first leg against Arsenal and the original cup clash against Chelsea – Spurs surrendered the lead he had secured. Jol reiterated he was influenced by no-one else. "I can swear for the second time it did not happen," he insisted. "I am the one who decides who plays along with Chris and Clive Allen. Everyone else can talk about football with me – even the chairman who knows nothing about football – but after the match."

Jol went on to declare how he believed that Berbatov's value had soared to £40m by comparing him to Dutch legend Johan Cruyff. The Bulgarian's 19-goal haul and impressive all-round play had, not surprisingly, attracted attention from the big guns of England and Europe. Jol said: "In this market he would be £30-40m. But even if somebody offered that we would never sell him. He reminds me a bit of Johan Cruyff when he started. He's a link-up player, he's a finisher, he's good in the air, he's a target-man, but he can move as well.

I don't think there's another No.9 who moves that well into the space. Sometimes he looks a bit like a ballerina, but he keeps the ball. Normally you would say, how many technical players are there up front? And he is really technical. You can't compare Berbatov with anybody else, because he can play on the left flank, on the right flank, in the middle. He can set up attacks, he can come behind, he is complete."

Jol's buy of the season had turned down Manchester United and others to go to White Hart Lane and Jol added: "I knew him for five years and I thought we had a big chance at one stage, 80 per cent, of getting him. Then other clubs came in at the final stages and I thought: "There we go again". And then he came here one week. He watched the match and it was strange, he said: 'I want to come to Spurs'."

But the future of his star striker – only at the club for eight months – had by now become one of the pressure points on Jol. The Bulgarian's demeanour was never outwardly effusive. Indeed Jol himself told me that he thinks he looks like 'a depressive', but that is the outward appearance of Dimitar Berbatov. Inside his head lurks the incisive mind of a top international footballer. Despite persistent stories of interest from Manchester United, Berbatov's agent, Emil Dantchev, insisted the striker would stay at Spurs for the 2007/08 season despite attracting the attention of numerous sides. Manchester United, the club he originally rejected in favour of Spurs, and Liverpool were glancing an envious eye over the striker. Dantchev said: "When a player has a good season it is normal that there is interest, but he has a good contract, so it is not something to discuss and he will be at least next season at Tottenham, too."

But all these issues were calling Jol's ability and thus future as manager of Spurs into question and he was called to rebuff the criticism, particularly of his substitutions against Chelsea which supporters and media alke felt had cost Tottenham victory in the first game. He argued: "Before Chelsea we had a difficult series of games, but we went on great run. If we hadn't there would have been some fans wanting me out of a job, but I believe nobody else could have done better. I get letters from fans who call me all sorts of things, and one week later say they love me. That's football, but the most important thing for me is that I get 100 per cent out of my players and that we perform and get the results, then I am the happiest man in the world. It's about my club, football and my job. It's a pain in the neck when people don't analyse. People wondered why we went on such a great run of form. It's because I had a settled team for the first time in weeks. Players like Jermaine Jenas came back from injury and Didier Zokora is playing better. They questioned why I took Dimitar Berbatov and Aaron Lennon off in the first game against Chelsea, but Dimitar had a groin injury and Aaron was tired after playing in the UEFA Cup just three days before. Losing to Chelsea was our first defeat over 90 minutes in 19 cup games this season. It shows we are getting there."

Keane and his team-mates were totally deflated. Keane said: "All the lads are devastated. We got back into the game but the second goal killed us off. The good thing about football is that there is always another game – and ours is a massive one in a few days time [versus Arsenal]. Once we get back into training, the lads will start looking forward to it and focus our minds on that. We are gutted for the supporters who were tremendous. I wish we could have sent them home happier. I have to give credit to the lads though, we worked our socks off. But it wasn't to be. We gave it everything but it just wasn't good enough."

Would that turn out to be Jol's epitaph?

THE GOING GETS TOUGH

WITH NO SILVERWARE to show for a season of such expectation and struggling to make the all-important fourth place, which Jol had publicly stated as less important to him than bringing a trophy to White Hart Lane, the Dutchman was left in his most vulnerable position since taking over the reigns at Spurs over two years earlier.

From the turn of the year the media had been buzzing with speculation about the future of Tottenham Hotspur, and thus their. *The Times'* version was that Spurs vice-chairman Paul Kemsley, the man who acted as one of Alan Sugar's feared panel of interrogators on his TV show *The Apprentice*, was interested in putting together a takeover together with Mike Ashley, the billionaire who owns Sports World, the UK's largest sports retailer. *The People* took it a stage further by suggesting that would mean the axe for manager Jol and sporting director Damien Comolli with Kemsley's big mate Harry Redknapp taking over. Kemsley denied the speculation on the club's website. As it turned out it would be Alan Sugar who sold his stake in the club to Daniel Levy's ENIC International for £25 million in June 2007. But only after, during the season, the takeover rumours had sent shares soaring by 60 per cent in the previous four months.

The Ashley rumour did not transpire. A committed Spurs fan, Ashley eventually bought Newcastle United where he would make a statement about his commitment to bringing success to a club even more starved than Spurs by taking to wearing the famous black-and-white striped shirt in the directors' box at games and sitting with the Toon fans when Newcastle travelled away.

Still Jol was in his most vulnerable position since taking over as manager. Only somehow scraping into the fabled fourth place could rescue the season and leave Jol's reputation undamaged. A 4-3 Premier League victory at Upton Park in early March gave fans hope. The win was only Spurs' third away victory of the season and it brought a smile back to Jol's lips, although it would soon be wiped away by defeats in both Europe and the FA Cup. But whatever the scenario within the club, importantly, Jol very clearly had the backing of the fans. Having booed their team off at half-time against

Sevilla when they were two goals down on th night and three on aggregate, they did not direct any criticism at the manager. 'Martin Jol's blue and white army' was a chant constantly heard.

Defeat to Chelsea, in a Premier League game played just 39 hours after the first leg loss in Seville, had left Spurs seventh in the Premier League, seven points behind Arsenal in the fight for fourth place, with just a month of the season remaining. A 3-3 draw at Wigan, battling against relegation, didn't close the gap, but the opportunity to make inroads into Arsenal's lead came in the next game, the visit of the Gunners to White Hart Lane.

Prior to the match, Jol reminded everyone that his brief on taking the job was that the club had to compete regularly in European competition after a five-year absence. The Dutchman therefore argued that he had succeeded, as Tottenham had an excellent chance of qualifying for the Uefa Cup once again. "When I came, the only goal was to compete for European football," Jol said. "I feel that we are almost at the same level as Arsenal, we could have done a bit better in the league. It would be a disappointment if we couldn't be in the top six or seven this season."

But the goalposts had shifted. Finishing in the top seven and qualifying for Europe was no longer good enough. Coupled with all the disappointments of the season, a failure to beat deadly rivals Arsenal under Jol, or indeed under any manager since George Graham in November 1999, grated as much as anything. Here was an opportunity to redress at least that and leave Spurs' fans with something tangible to celebrate.

In the event, Spurs took the lead, but were delighted to score a last minute equaliser through Jermaine Jenas to 2-2 draw. After Keane opened the scoring, his 19th of the season and fifth in the last five games, Toure and Adebayor finished off set-pieces in the second half – both delivered by Fabregas, a young man establishing himself as one of the world's best midfielders – to establish a lead before they were denied maximum points. With seconds remaining Jenas picked the ball up 30 yards out and drilled into the bottom corner with a fierce shot. Cue wild celebrations, but only of face being saved against the old enemy.

The failure to beat Arsenal meant that all hopes of pipping them to fourth place had evaporated and even victory over Middlesbrough as Jol celebrated his 100th Premiership game in charge wasn't enough to stop the Gunners sealing Tottenham's fate. Arsenal's win over Fulham meant Spurs could now no longer qualify for the Champions League. The question now was, could eighth-placed Tottenham grab one of the three automatic UEFA Cup spots ahead of Blackburn, Portsmouth, Bolton and Everton?

Tottenham captain Ledley King came to the defence of his manager by insisting the 2006/07 campaign represented an improvement on the previous campaign. "It's been tough this season," King reflected. "We lost Michael Carrick at the beginning and he was a big player for us. We brought in new faces and it probably took a little bit of time for them to gel, but there have been times when we showed we can be a very good side. Last season we were just pipped for fourth. This time we're not going to quite finish that high, but we've done a lot better in the cups. It's been a better season, in fact, but again we want to improve next season. That means breaking into the top four."

After all the high pressure games, the end of the season had the kind of pressure no manager wants, having to avoid defeat to clinch the most basic of targets. At least Tottenham were able to do that, thanks to a draw and a win in their last two games of the season.

Blackburn's hopes of a direct route into the UEFA Cup were ended by Defoe's equaliser in the 1-1 result at a soggy White Hart Lane. Mark Hughes' side, who were reduced to ten men following Jason Roberts' late dismissal, needed a win to stay in the hunt for a top-seven finish. The away side were on course for victory when McCarthy opened the scoring, but Berbatov then played his part in Defoe's equaliser, with a magical turn and shot the keeper could only parry. Spurs now needed just a point against Manchester City in their final game of a long, hard season to play in the UEFA Cup again.

Against Rovers, though, there were more signs of dissent amidst the camp. When Jol brought on Keane in the 59th minute to replace Hossam Ghaly, the Egyptian threw his shirt to the floor in front of his manager. A flagrant display of anger, which left the supporters in attendance with a dfecision to make. Who would they back? The manager or the player?

'You're not fit to wear the shirt,' was the Spurs fans' assessment of Ghaly's actions, firmly backing the manager's decision.

Despite fielding three strikers with 60 goals between them, Spurs were inches from going 2-0 down when Samba's header from Pedersen's free-kick glanced off the bar to safety. And it proved a telling moment as Tottenhamm levelled with 23 minutes left – with all three forwards having a hand in the goal. Keane fed Berbatov, who spun on the edge of the area and fired in a shot which Friedel could only parry and Defoe tapped in. Spurs almost snatched it, Keane hitting the post in stoppage-time.

Ghaly faced internal disciplinary action. "You can't do that, so we will deal with that," said Jol. "We always deal with that sort of thing, we will deal with it internally." And the manager couldn't resist making a point. "I make the decisions. I was right in hindsight because we played better and equalised."

Tottenham booked their place in the UEFA Cup and finished fifth for the second year running after Keane and Berbatov fired them to a 2-1 victory over Manchester City at White Hart Lane. No mystery illness ravaging the squad and there was no final-day disappointment, but City gave Spurs the jitters as Robinson produced two saves of the highest quality to keep Spurs ahead. He could do nothing to prevent Mpenza pulling a goal back before the break, but, coupled with Everton's result at Chelsea, Spurs' win meant they had finished as 'best of the rest' for the second season running. That meant that Jol's side had earned back-to-back European campaigns for the first time in more than 20 years. Hadn't Jol over-achieved again?

The manager was bullish about his ability to help the club try again next season to dance at 'four weddings'. In a reference to the different fronts – League, Carling Cup, FA Cup and UEFA Cup – on which the north Londoners punched their weight in 2006/07, the Dutchman maintained his men had been outstanding. Jol said: "Maybe we cannot dance at four weddings, as they say in Holland. But you could say, with all the cup runs and finishing fifth, it has been our best season in 20 years. After 59 games, we finished the best of the rest again. Fifth place means the world to us."

But could he take them beyond, into the promised land of the Champions League? That was where his ambition lay as he added: "Everybody was worried about us finishing in Europe but I wasn't. We have a talented team and everybody showed once again what we can do. But we want more."

And yet, and yet. Unlike the previous summer, when finishing fifth led to so much optimism and positivity, it didn't feel such a big deal. Expectations had risen so high, and Spurs had come so close to bridging the gap in the League, in domestic cups and in Europe, that many believed that the club needed to deliver something tangible.

In an attempt to break through the glass ceiling, Tottenham would prove to be the Premiership's big spender again over the summer of 2007 after lining up a £20m treble swoop. Spurs agreed a £7.5m deal for Auxerre defender Younes Kaboul, 21, who will join at the end of the season. Jol also landed Southampton's teenage Welsh international left-back Gareth Bale in a £9m swoop and blew the incredible sum of £16.5m on Darren Bent from Charlton. In addition, Hertha Berlin midfielder Kevin-Prince Boateng, 20, arrived for £3.5m, and toyed with a bid for Toulouse's Swedish forward Johan Elmander. Targets also included West Ham's unsettled England Under-21 midfielder Nigel Reo-Coker. Equally Spurs clung onto their best talent, having learnt the harsh lesson of Michael Carrick's departure just 12 months earlier which had cost the club so much strength and stability in the middle of the pitch, and were adamant they would not sell star striker Berbatov despite continuing interest from Chelsea and Manchester United.

Jol must have watched with regret as Carrick scored twice for Manchester United in the Champions League quarter-final romp over Roma. Despite potentially yielding more than £18m – undeniably good business despite Carrick's strong season – the north-easterner's passing and solidity in midfield had not been adequately replaced. In hindsight the timing of the deal, close to the end of August, had also vastly hindered Jol's preparations. He had built his team around Carrick and then lost that important cog to a major competitor.

In the end almost £41 million was spent preparing for 2007/08, but was it on players that the manager wanted? There were still rumours about an ongoing disagreement over transfer policy. Although he never said so publicly, Jol always declared in private that it was not he who was responsible for such transfer policy. He may have a voice, but he did not make final decisions. That was the structure in place at the club. It was said Sporting Director Comolli wanted to sign the Celta Vigo winger Nene, but Jol argued he was simply too small. Jol knew he needed to improve Spurs' left flank and top of his wish-list was Arjen Robben, available after his well-publicised spat with manager Jose Mourinho at Stamford Bridge. It was surmised, rightly as it turned out, that Robben would prefer a move to Spain should he leave Chelsea and the Dutch flyer eventually joined Real Madrid for an undisclosed fee in August 2007.

So Jol still sought pace and power to develop his squad for the challenge of the 2007/08 season, which he strongly felt could offer Tottenham Champions League football if all went well for them. Jol singled out Sevilla's left-winger Adriano for praise and the Brazilian certainly had the pace and strength to succeed in the Premiership, but he was not pursued by the club. England Under-21 left-back Leighton Baines of Wigan, was coveted as a player who could bolster a defence that, Jol admitted, undermined ambitions: "If you concede more than 40 goals like we did you can't be in the top four," he said.

To balance the books, Mido, who was so close to leaving for Manchester City in January, departed for Middlesbrough for £6m, a £1.5m profit. There was also, surely, only so long that Defoe, given his desire for first-team football and his England ambitions, would want to remain so emphatically behind Robbie Keane in Jol's plans. A problem for the England striker, though, was that Spurs placed a tag of £15m which proved prohibitive to brokering a move.

But there was to be, emphatically, no danger of losing the talismanic Berbatov. The Bulgarian declared he was happy to stay at Spurs and with his manager, saying: "I am really happy that I made the choice to come here to Tottenham to work with the manager Martin Jol – he is a great man. I have said it many times, when you play good, when you score goals, especially here in England, everyone is watching you. Manchester, Chelsea they take an interest, but I'm settled at Tottenham."

The Spurs chairman also moved to silence rumours that Berbatov would be sold. In his programme notes for the final game of the 2006/07 against Manchester City, Daniel Levy said: "In case anyone is under the impression that we are a selling club, I should like to once again stress the policy and position of this club. We are building for the future – we are NOT a selling club. There is a world of difference between a player who has a short period left on his contract and could look to leave on a free transfer, and a player with a long contract. If, as we do, you have players on long contracts and the finances of the club are strong, you have no need to sell.

I am happy for anyone to judge this club by who we sell and who we don't. Our ability to attract and retain top-class players is key to our ambition to compete at the highest level – regularly in Europe and with our sights set on Champions League qualification."

In his review of the season Levy added: "We saw major changes to the squad at the beginning of the season. It's easy to forget that we saw no fewer than ten players join the team. We have seen that squad settle, develop and produce results. Now we need to consolidate and look for that next step up."

But would Martin Jol be given the chance to blend the exciting youth and considerable experience into a more consistent side capable of putting together extended unbeaten runs and challenging for trophies?

THE FUTURE IS BRIGHT?

TWO SUCCESSIVE FIFTH PLACE finishes suggested that the Cockerel might be finally crowing again. All highly commendable, and the Premier League could do with a shake up at the elitist end. Otherwise it gets all too predictable. However, if Spurs did break into the cartel of the Top Four, then it begged the very serious question, who would drop out? The consequences for the fall from grace for any of the big clubs would be immense. We were all about to witness what would happen at Stamford Bridge if standards weren't met. Out with Jose Mourinho.

There would soon also be talk of what would happen at Anfield if the Reds failed to qualify for the latter stages of the 2007/08 Champions League. Off with Rafa's head. What would happen at The Emirates over the continuing power struggle over ownership? Would Wenger would see out his final season of his contract and walk away, magnanimously suggesting it was time for someone else? And at Old Trafford? The Glazers might grant Sir Alex a place on the board for his services to the club, but there would be a strong case for finding a new broom. And the candidates are multiplying; Mark Hughes and Roy Keane would be genuine possibilities without reverting to a foreign coach.

So the consequences would be just incredible for any one of those top four to lose out on a Champions League place. But for the first time for some time, it was worth pondering the ramifications for a club such as Tottenham breaking the monopoly.

Jol took it further. He believed it was possible to mount a serious title challenge within the next two seasons. But to achieve his ambitions Jol knew that his rising young stars had to perform to their maximum and become utterly ruthless in big matches. He observed: "My hopes for next season are to compete for Europe again. Liverpool, Chelsea, Man United and Arsenal have got probably got more resources than us, but it's not only about money. We've got younger players, hopefully we've got the vision and we want to compete for prizes in the Cups. We want to be in Europe and we want to do well there, but we have to be in the top six to be in Europe. And hopefully, if we can get players like Dimitar Berbatov, if we can have the likes of Tom Huddlestone, Aaron Lennon, Michael Dawson develop into star players, we can go even further. My dream is to compete for the title in the next two to three years."

During the writing of this book, Leeds United Chairman Ken Bates made a startling confession to me about football managers – and he's had a few – Martin Jol is the one he admires the most. Yes, the Tottenham manager. Not Sir Alex Ferguson. Not Jose Mourinho. Not Rafael Benitez.

Over a convivial dinner at Langan's Brasserie, with former Spurs and Arsenal manager George Graham, just two tables along, Bates suddenly volunteered this precious piece of information.

"Do you know?" he enquired, "who is the manager I admire the most?"

It was a question out of the blue, and after a few seconds' thought, I threw a few of the obvious contenders at him. I even suggested it probably wasn't Kevin Blackwell.

"It's Martin Jol," said Bates.

Naturally I wanted to know why. I pressed him.

"He goes about his job quietly, and he has quietly built a very good young team, without too much fuss. He has assembled a talented squad of players who will mature and the prospects are good at Tottenham with Jol in charge. What I really like about him is that he never boasts, never complains and just gets on with his job, a real professional in an age where there are too many egotistical showmen."

When I told Ken that I was writing a book about Jol. He commented, "There you go then. That should make you a line or two!" Bates didn't want to go on record, but his assessment of Jol's worth is also based on the fact that clubs such as Manchester United, and his old club Chelsea, in particular, have so much financial muscle in the transfer market.

When I caught up with Spurs legend Ossie Ardiles, he was in the company of his former Argentina and Spurs team-mate Ricky Villa as guest of E.on for a party to celebrate the return of the FA Cup Final back to Wembley. At the cocktail party at the Cannon Street Roof Gardens the night before the final, Ossie and Ricky discussed the merits of Jol. Ossie felt that Jol was a good manager, but he said: "There have been too many wasted years at Tottenham. Everyone is still waiting for something special to happen. It is too big a club not to be winning trophies and playing good football, especially exciting football, which is what the fans want to see. I think Jol is a good manager and the right man for Tottenham, but he still has to prove it for me. I wait to be convinced."

Ricky was sceptical about Spurs breaking into the top four, as he explained: "They do not have enough top quality players, the best players, Berbatov is an exception and if they were to sell him than all would be lost, it would be a waste of time."

Former Spurs hardman Graham Roberts agreed. Roberts said: "If Spurs ever sell him, the chairman should be shot! You never sell your best players and he's the best they've got."

Jol proved up to the task of retaining his best players, which meant he had convinced them that he and Spurs could match the ambitions of those top four giants and build a squad around the core which could finally tip them into the arena of finals, and silverware. Robbie Keane signed a new five-year contract, which committed him to the club until 2012. Keane commented: "I have felt really settled and am happy at Spurs and that is probably one of the reasons I have played the best football of my career here. It is an exciting time to be at the club and I am looking forward to even better seasons ahead." Chairman Daniel Levy said: "Robbie has been an influential part of our club for five years and this further commitment, on the part of both him and the club, is a recognition of that. He is an individual who is loyal and professional and we are delighted he will be with us long term.

The key to retaining top players is to agree long-term contracts. We have now done so with several of our existing squad, extending the contracts of Aaron Lennon, Michael Dawson and Tom Huddlestone, as well as having contracted newer players on long contracts, such as Dimitar Berbatov and Didier Zokora."

THAT TOTTENHAM HAD COME so far playing entertaining, if sometimes frustrating, football showed how Jol had galvanised a club which had languished in the doldrums, failing to live up to the promise shown by players and managers over 15 years of Premier League football. The Sky era has not been kind to Tottenham in terms of silverware, but perhaps Jol's long term plan to build for success could come to fruition. Perhaps they could break the monopoly. As any football fan will know, no matter where they finish, Martin Jol's side would always provide them with fun, entertainment and plenty of controversial talking points and the man himself would always give great value for money due ot his honesty and sense of humour. It seems incredible to think that the end of the 2006/07 season was still less than three short years since his appointment. Certainly Martin Jol seemed here to stay.

The man himself was pleased with his side's progress: "I'm glad people have more faith in us now. There's been many years of underachieving and a great deal of disappointment in this club. Tottenham's hard to explain why. I love Spurs so much and they've always been synonymous with style. It's hard to know why they failed. I know that when we get this club right the sky is the limit. It has the history, though you have to go back to the '60s when winning in Europe and the double, so there hasn't been success for a number of generations.

Spurs are a rich club with potential to go forward. When Man Utd had Ferguson it took him four years even though he had the resources. It took him time. We have a saying in Holland: 'If you listen to me'. It means that if you do it my way I will give you what you want and it will be done. That probably sums up my style of football management more than anything else. It's what I've been telling them everywhere I go: 'you have to listen to me and I will give you what you want'. It happened at my home town club who were like a conference club like Stevenage and we won the national championship.

It is amazing what can happen at Tottenham. They can sell out the stadium all the time despite underachieving. You don't see that everywhere with 36,000 gates even at Carling Cup, not like Fulham who had 11,000 at a Carling cup tie. Why? People have hope and it's up to me to give them more than hope. I took over in November, so I didn't have the benefit of pre-season or doing it my way from the start yet we were one match away from playing European football. If we'd got a result away to Middlesbrough it would have been Spurs in Europe, I'm sure, but it was hard taking over so late.

We are now building a good squad of players, but what this club needs is one more ingredient; a Dave Mackay, a leader at the back or in midfield. That's one more step this club needs to take.

Berbatov is a foreigner, a forward and he's quiet. In the past this club have had leaders and when I talk to Hughton, who has been here a long time, a player like Paul Miller, who wasn't a star, was one of the dressing room leaders. If Ledley King is not there we don't have a leader and he has suffered a lot of injuries. Ledley is the most talented central defender in English football, that's how highly I rate him. He's quick and can jump. When he is not there we really miss him. But we have players who could become our Dave Mackay. Huddlestone is one of them. He has the best passing range at our club. We have to teach him to become like Dave Mackay. Then we can succeed."

With everything going for them, and progress being made, the future, for both Martin Jol and Tottenham Hotspur looked bright.

AND THEN CAME THE destabilisation and the chop. The love affair was over. In the harsh world of football at the very highest level, where high finance, egos and the quest for glory collide, Jol had, ultimately, come up short at White Hart Lane. Where he would emerge next was, as yet, unclear, although a lof of smart money went on him taking the prize job in Dutch domestic football, Ajax, whose coach, Ten Cate, had recently joined Chelsea as number two to the newly-installed Avram Grant. Or would it be the post at PSV Eindhoven where Ronald Koeman had just resigned to join Valencia.

Jol himself told me that he was not truly interested in either post. He wanted to stay in England, remain in the Premiership and crack that top four.

Certainly, as that incredible display of loyalty from Tottenham's fans showed as Jol sat stony-faced on the bench at White Hart Lane and watched his charges fall to one, final, painful defeat, this was a man whose love affair with the game, and his fans, from all over the world, would surely soon be rekindled.

STATISTICS

Full name   **Maarten Cornelius Jol**
Date of birth   **16 January 1956**
Place of birth   **Scheveningen, Den Haag, Netherlands**
Playing position **Midfielder**

Playing Career

Years	Club	App	Goals
1973–1978	ADO Den Haag	132	9
1978–1979	Bayern Munich	9	0
1979–1982	FC Twente	71	9
1982–1984	West Bromwich Albion	63	4
1984–1985	Coventry City	15	0
1985–1989	ADO Den Haag	135	6
Total		**425**	**28**

National team

1980–81   Netherlands 3 (0)
Plus 10 schoolboy caps, 20 'B' caps, 12 Under-21 caps and 12 Under-23 caps

Managerial Career

1991–95	ADO Den Haag (amateurs)
1995–96	Scheveningen (amateurs)
1996–98	Roda JC Kerkrade
1998–2004	RKC Waalwijk
2004–2007	Tottenham Hotspur

Jol's record at Tottenham: a cut above his predecessors

Martin Jol at Spurs

Season	P	W	D	L	Pts/game	W%	Pos
2004/05	26	11	6	9	1.41	42%	9th
2005/06	38	18	11	9	1.71	47%	5th
2006/07	38	17	9	12	1.58	45%	5th
2007/08	10	1	4	5	0.70	10%	?
Total	112	47	30	35	1.53	42%	

Spurs managers in Premier League

Martin Jol

P	W	D	L	Pts	Pts/game	Win%
112	47	30	35	171	1.53	42%

Doug Livermore/ Ray Clemence

P	W	D	L	Pts	Pts/game	Win%
42	16	11	15	59	1.40	38%

David Pleat
(three spells)

P	W	D	L	Pts	Pts/game	Win%
38	14	7	17	49	1.29	37%

Gerry Francis

P	W	D	L	Pts	Pts/game	Win%
119	43	36	40	165	1.39	36%

Glenn Hoddle

P	W	D	L	Pts	Pts/game	Win%
89	32	18	39	114	1.28	36%

George Graham

P	W	D	L	Pts	Pts/game	Win%
98	33	29	36	128	1.31	34%

Christian Gross

P	W	D	L	Pts	Pts/game	Win%
27	9	7	11	34	1.26	33%

Osvaldo Ardiles

P	W	D	L	Pts	Pts/game	Win%
54	16	14	24	62	1.15	30%

Jacques Santini

P	W	D	L	Pts	Pts/game	Win%
11	3	4	4	13	1.18	27%

Doug Livermore/Ray Clemence

P	W	D	L	Pts	Pts/game	Win%
42	16	11	15	59	1.40	38%

Osvaldo Ardiles

P	W	D	L	Pts	Pts/game	Win%
54	16	14	24	62	1.15	30%

Steve Perryman (caretaker)

P	W	D	L	Pts	Pts/game	Win%
1	0	0	1	0	0.00	0%

Gerry Francis

P	W	D	L	Pts	Pts/game	Win%
119	43	36	40	165	1.39	36%

Chris Hughton (caretaker)

P	W	D	L	Pts	Pts/game	Win%
4	1	2	1	5	1.25	25%